HIGH ON THE
OKAW'S WESTERN BANK

HIGH ON THE OKAW'S WESTERN BANK

Vandalia, Illinois
1819–39

)1992

PAUL E. STROBLE, JR.

UNIVERSITY OF ILLINOIS PRESS
Urbana and Chicago

An earlier version of chapter 2 was published as "Ferdinand Ernst and the German Colony at Vandalia," in the summer of 1987 *Illinois Historical Journal* and is used here with permission of the Illinois Historic Preservation Agency, Springfield.

This book is printed on acid-free paper.

Library of Congress Cataloging-in-Publication Data

Stroble, Paul E., 1957–
    High on the Okaw's western bank : Vandalia, Illinois, 1819–39 /
Paul E. Stroble, Jr.
        p.   cm.
    Includes bibliographical references and index.
    ISBN 0-252-01892 (cl)
    1. Vandalia (Ill.)—History.   2. Illinois—Capital and capitol.
I. Title.
F549.V2S77   1992
977.3'797—dc20
                                            91-27048
                                            CIP

Contents

Chronology   vii

Preface   ix

Acknowledgments   xi

Introduction: Vandalia's Capital Period   1

1. To Reeve's Bluff   7

2. Ferdinand Ernst and the German Colony   22

3. By Their Strong Arms   29

4. High on the Okaw's Western Bank   47

5. "Boosting" the State Capital   63

6. On the Track at Vandalia   70

7. Discord and Concord   91

8. Like Oxford or Cambridge   106

9. The End of the Era   123

Notes   133

Index   171

Chronology

1818   Capital at Kaskaskia
        Convention drafts and adopts state constitution, providing for new
            state capital
        First General Assembly (Oct. 5–13, 1818; Jan. 4–March 31, 1819)
        Shadrach Bond elected governor
        Illinois statehood, Dec. 3

1819   Congress approves land grant for Vandalia
        Panic of 1819
        General Assembly appoints commissioners; they locate Vandalia site
        Vandalia surveyed; the town thereby becomes capital
        Vandalia lots sold
        First businesses
        Frederick Hollman, friend of Ferdinand Ernst, constructs buildings
            for German colony

1820   First capitol building constructed
        Second General Assembly (Dec. 4, 1820–Feb. 15, 1821)
        James Monroe reelected U.S. president
        Ferdinand Ernst arrives with about 100 German colonists (December)

1821   General Assembly creates first state bank
        Vandalia city government established
        Fayette County created and county government established

1822   Death of Ferdinand Ernst and break-up of colony
        Edward Coles elected governor
        Third General Assembly (Dec. 2, 1822–Feb. 18, 1823)

1823   General Assembly adopts constitutional convention referendum
        Year of violence: two mobs, manslaughter, suicide, mysterious confla-
            gration of the capitol building

1824	Vandalians construct the second capitol
	Convention referendum defeated
	John Quincy Adams elected U.S. president
	Fourth General Assembly (Nov. 15, 1824–Jan. 18, 1825; Jan. 2–28, 1826)
1826	Ninian Edwards elected governor
	Fifth General Assembly (Dec. 1, 1828–Feb. 19, 1829)
1827	James Hall moves to Vandalia and begins writing career at the capital (until 1833)
	First state historical society founded at Vandalia
	Cultural, religious, and educational activity
1828	Hall publishes *Letters from the West* in London
	Andrew Jackson elected U.S. president
	Sixth General Assembly (Dec. 1, 1828–Jan. 23, 1829)
	Survey of the National Road concludes at Vandalia
1829	Hall publishes *Western Souvenir*
1830	John Reynolds elected governor
	Hall publishes *Illinois Monthly Magazine* at Vandalia (through 1832)
	Seventh General Assembly (Dec. 6, 1830–Feb. 16, 1831)
1832	Black Hawk War involves Fayette County men
	Andrew Jackson reelected U.S. president
	Eighth General Assembly (Dec. 3, 1832–March 2, 1833)
	Hall publishes *Legends of the West*
1833	General Assembly passes referendum for permanent state capital
	Renewed growth of Vandalia businesses (through the decade)
1834	Alton voted Illinois capital; results inconclusive
	Vandalian William L. D. Ewing, governor for fifteen days
	Joseph Duncan elected governor
	Ninth General Assembly (Dec. 1, 1834–Feb. 13, 1835; Dec. 7, 1835–Jan. 18, 1836)
1835	General Assembly initiates legislation for a second state bank
1836	Vandalians construct the third capitol building
	Martin Van Buren elected U.S. president
	Tenth General Assembly (Dec. 5, 1836–March 6, 1837; July 10–22, 1837)
1837	General Assembly authorizes internal improvements program
	Panic of 1837
	General Assembly votes Springfield as permanent capital
1838	Thomas Carlin elected governor
	Eleventh General Assembly (Dec. 3, 1838–March 4, 1839 at Vandalia; Dec. 9, 1839–Feb. 3, 1840 at Springfield)
	Probable decline of Vandalia businesses
1839	Springfield becomes capital, July 4, 1839

Preface

AFTER CONDUCTING genealogical research in Fayette County, I undertook this book with little motive besides learning more about the town where my ancestors settled and where I, at the time, still lived. I soon discovered, however, that no single history of Vandalia's capital period had been written—even though other towns associated with Lincoln had earned book-length examination and even though Vandalia had had fine local historians.

Several years have passed since that innocent beginning, and the work passed from a young man's genealogical pastime to the full-scale research project of a parish pastor. I have tried to do three things in this book, listed here in order of importance. First, I have told the story of the state capital's civic existence from 1819 to 1839, with the modest intent of meeting that long-standing need for a general history of the second capital of Illinois. Vandalia's importance for Illinois history lies chiefly in its role as host of the state government; yet its civic and cultural history, apart from politics and legislation, also provide an important legacy. Second, I have placed Vandalia in context with the modern debate concerning the social structure and community development of frontier towns. This debate is important for Vandalia because questions arose while the town was yet capital, Why did a town with great and unusual advantages not thrive, and why did it not retain its prestige? In addition to the methodological problems involved in any examination of a midwestern community's pre-1850 history, the primary sources for the Vandalia capital period are comparatively poor but are sufficient to allow hypotheses about early Vandalia, its civic characteristics, and cultural homogeneity. Future research carrying Vandalia's history into the postbellum era may shed additional light upon local demographic and economic aspects. Third, I have considered what the capital era meant in Vandalia's and Fayette County's local memory. As with many towns, Vandalia's pioneer era—which Vandalia's capital period is—became transformed in the remembrance and recording. How does Vandalia, as a town with a particularly noteworthy pioneer era, look back upon its unique beginnings? Rather than being a detriment, the fact that Vandalia is both my native and ancestral town has given me an advantage in considering this third aspect.

With these three goals in mind, I hope this text will provide new insights into "Lincoln's Vandalia" and community-building in the early West. Chapter 1 examines Vandalia's establishment as Illinois' capital. Chapter 2 tells the story of Vandalia's German colony. Continuing the context of pioneer settlement, chapter 3 examines the social, regional, and cultural situation of Vandalia's first citizens.

Vandalia's "downtown" and local economy are the concerns of chapter 4, followed by an examination of local boosterism in chapter 5. The politics of Vandalia's ten general assemblies overarches the town's civic existence; the next chapter follows state political development. Chapters 7 and 8 examine local improvements and community conflict and the character of Vandalia's cultural life. Finally, the relocation of the seat of government, local decline, and Vandalia's later revitalization conclude this study.

Acknowledgments

THIS BOOK WAS researched and written over several years and amid two post-bachelor degrees in theology. During the summers from 1976 to 1979 I conducted the research, chiefly at Vandalia and Springfield. From 1983 to 1985, following master's studies at Yale Divinity School, I wrote most of the first version. At the time, I served three small United Methodist churches in Pope County, Illinois and wrote late at night while listening to Copland's "Appalachian Spring." I revised the manuscript from 1987 to 1989, while pursuing University of Virginia doctoral studies, pastoring a church, and teaching. Although this manner of book writing is hardly ideal, it does teach perseverance as well as the value of friends, colleagues, and family.

Financial help came from the National Endowment for the Humanities, which provided me a Youth Grant in 1979, and the Friends of the Old Capitol, whose gift assisted greatly with the manuscript's preparation. In 1977, 1978, and 1979, I worked as researcher for the Illinois Department of Conservation and accessed Fayette County courthouse records for resource material for the interpreters at the Vandalia Statehouse State Historic Site. Although the IDOC did not thereby fund this book, I was able to locate capital-era documents for later consultation; I have also credited others' earlier IDOC research on the statehouse in this book's seventh chapter. Responsibility for interpretations is, of course, mine alone.

My appreciation is extended to the staffs of the Illinois State Historical Library, particularly Janice Petterchak and Cheryl Schnirring for their time and expertise; the Illinois State Archives at Springfield; the

Illinois Historical Survey at Urbana; the Fayette County Circuit Clerk's and County Clerk's offices and the Fayette County state's attorney's office; the Chicago Historical Society; the Iowa Historical Society; the Historic Vandalia Museum; the Bond County Historical Society; the Abraham Lincoln Bookstore, Chicago; the Vandalia United Methodist and Presbyterian churches; the Glendale United Methodist Parish, Pope County, Illinois, and Trinity Heights United Methodist Church, Flagstaff, Arizona. I have appreciated the active interest in this project taken by Kathryn Tedrick Brooks, Martha Jane Downey, and Judy Baumann, past and present site superintendents at the Vandalia Statehouse.

Previous generations of local historians deserve thanks from anyone interested in Vandalia history. The compilers of the 1878 *History of Fayette County* preserved many stories and information before the elders of that generation died. Robert W. Ross (1844–1921) performed a similar and similarly laudable task some years later. Joseph C. Burtschi (1874–1962) compiled his documentary history from material buried away in archives and obscure locations. Mary Burtschi also preserved important oral traditions in her books and was the first local historian (as student of John T. Flanagan) to research James Hall's importance for Vandalia history. Mary and her sister Josephine also helped me in innumerable ways, answering many questions, over the years. Their Little Brick House museum and the Vandalia Historical Society also deserve grateful mention in this context. The Fayette County Genealogical Society's ongoing project, the *Fayette Facts* quarterly, must also be praised as a substantial source for genealogical and documentary information about Vandalia and the county. The late Harry Truitt, a happy partisan of Vandalia's legacy, took an interest in my project and obtained for me a long-out-of-print copy of Joseph Burtschi's documentary history.

My thanks also are extended to Rodney O. Davis for allowing me to consult his unpublished dissertation on Jacksonian democracy in Illinois and for reading chapter 6. John Hallwas provided insightful and indispensible comments for the last revision. At the beginning of this project, Karen S. Lankeshofer and my cousin Elfriede Crawford generously translated a number of German sources pertaining to Ferdinand Ernst. Mary Ellen McElligott, editor of the *Illinois Historical Journal*, also provided valuable assistance when the Ernst chapter was first published. I am indebted to Don Harrison Doyle for his shared insights on frontier communities, as well as to Donald C. Jordahl, G. Loran Lewis, and Daniel D. Jensen who supervised my honor's thesis at Greenville College in 1978, an early version of chapter 6. The Reverend Kurt Jensen, Jesse Graf Jensen, Florence van Antwerp, Elona Kindschi, and

Norma Bauer—descendents of capital-era figures—were all helpful as I sought individual characterizations and local undiscovered sources. My deep appreciation also goes to Richard Wentworth, Karen Hewitt, and Mary Giles at the University of Illinois Press, whose counsel and patience improved this book beyond my own expectations for it.

I am grateful to all the friends who followed the course of this project with interest and who were glad to hear my slow progress on the manuscript was progress nevertheless. One Vandalia friend, the Reverend Arthur Cullen Bryant, had a lively interest in Vandalia's history; he and I often conversed both about local history and the ministry. Here, I express my gratitude for the memory of him and his wife, Marian.

Finally, I am thankful for my family. My parents, Paul and Mildred Stroble, made it possible for me to have the support, the encouragement, the time, and the books needed for this project to begin and to continue. My wife Beth, devoted educator and fellow historian, is a helpful critic, outstanding teacher, and rare friend. She critiqued the manuscript during our first years of marriage. Our daughter Emily Elizabeth arrived at the very end of this process. May she someday discover in this book not only the heritage of Illinois, but also some of her own.

Introduction:
Vandalia's Capital Period

VANDALIA, the capital of the state, and the seat of justice for
Fayette County, . . . is situated on the west bank of the Kaskaskia river, about 82 miles northeast from St. Louis, 138
north of the junction of the Mississippi and Ohio rivers, and
781 from Washington City. The site is high, undulating, and
was originally a timbered tract.

—*Illinois in 1837*

I N 1819, Vandalia was founded specifically to be the seat of government for the new state of Illinois, but the same constitutional clause
that authorized the town limited its term as capital to twenty years.
During those two decades, Vandalia became a paradoxical community.
As capital, it was the cultural and political center of the state. Politicians,
college-trained professionals, jurists, writers, and public officials lived
in or regularly visited Vandalia. Fervent political controversy animated
the small village. But Vandalia's cultural atmosphere did not preclude
a frontier rawness shared by all new frontier towns. The state capital
remained a typical, rather torpid, and sometimes violent village. In kind
with other towns' citizens, Vandalians preached local benefits and wel-
comed opportunities for local survival, renewal, and growth.

Because ten general assemblies (the second through the first session
of the eleventh) and the supreme and federal courts convened there,
state and local history coalesced at Vandalia to a remarkable degree.
Vandalia became the stage upon which Illinois politics transformed from
territorial factionalism to party regularity in the late 1830s. Prominent
local businessmen became active in the political arena; jurists and politicians staying in town listened closely to local talk about political

issues; Vandalia newspapers become indispensible commentaries on national and state politics. Politics vitalized Vandalia, too; the local economy thrived when court- and government-related nonresidents flocked to town, then it stagnated once governmental and court sessions adjourned.

Vandalia had a greater cultural identity than most frontier villages. Ferdinand Ernst, a wealthy young German immigrant, introduced the town's pioneers to the music of Haydn, Beethoven, and Mozart. Ernst's selection of Vandalia, in fact, as the location for his colony of immigrants was motivated by the presence of the state government and the corresponding benefits of culture, education, and social progress. Certainly the learned men in town who attended to political and legal tasks there enhanced the capital's intellectual life. One legislator's wife wrote of "the intellectual feasts I enjoyed at Vandalia" as she recalled the lectures, speakers, and legislative and judicial debates available to public attendance. Some visitors were learned men accomplished in the state government and legal procedure; others were young men taking political apprenticeship for future distinction. Lincoln and Douglas are the best known of these many young men.

Vandalia itself became hometown for talented individuals. For instance, in an age when western education was still fairly rudimentary several local people were college-trained. Vandalia had a resident artist, and although self-taught painters were common on the frontier, James W. Berry was the only one formally recognized by the Illinois government for his talents. Perhaps recalling his gifts of portraits (probably of Governors Shadrach Bond and Edward Coles) to the 1824 legislature, for which he was then formally commended, the 1838–39 legislature commissioned him to paint full-length portraits of Washington and Lafayette for the new statehouse in Springfield. The two excellent portraits still hang in the Old State Capitol in Springfield. Other people in Vandalia had talents in the field of authorship. A Fayette County politician and tavern keeper wrote the first history of the Black Hawk War, still a classic, and a teacher at the local high school was author of several published stories and monographs. James Hall, a minor but underestimated figure in American letters, was the first author to capture the lore of the early West. He wrote his best fiction while living in Vandalia, stories that made him a contemporary in the craft with Nathaniel Hawthorne and Washington Irving. In Vandalia he edited the first periodical in Illinois and one of the first in the West. During his six years in Vandalia, Hall also personally founded or was the inspiration behind the founding of the first state historical society, lyceums, benevolent organizations, the first high school in Vandalia, and an interdenominational house for public worship. When seven men from Yale Theological Seminary (the "Yale Band") came to Illinois in 1829 to promote education and religion in the West, they made Hall's Vandalia home their base and drew upon his enthusiasm and vision for the founding of Illinois College in Jacksonville.

Although Vandalia was the cultural and political center of Illinois for twenty years, it also had many prosaic aspects. Most citizens were settlers concerned primarily with making a living on the frontier, rather than with the cultural advancement of their community. With its frame business places and frame or log residences, Vandalia probably looked the same as any frontier village. Local businessmen and professionals offered a wide variety of goods and services, but when legislators, politicians, attorneys, lobbyists, idlers, and office-seekers from every Illinois county descended for the biennial general assemblies and semiannual court sessions, Vandalia's services proved insufficient for the demand. Although some visitors praised local culture, others complained that the town was an unattractive capital, that the public offices were ramshackle, that lodging and services were inadequate, that the town was too drunken and violent. Even James Hall's educational endeavors and writing efforts met with popular indifference. After citizens drained the insect breeding ponds around the town, Vandalia was comparatively healthy; even the dreadful 1833 cholera epidemic missed it. Still, the tag of unhealthiness (a reputation all frontier communities feared because it potentially meant decreased settlement) became unfairly attached to the state capital.

Vandalia's local industry was not protected from economic vicissitudes simply because the town was seat of government. The Panic of 1819 and, more importantly, the disastrous 1821 state bank, hurt Vandalia's economy during the important first few years of its development. Because the surrounding Fayette County area had not been settled extensively by 1819 (and therefore the prairie lands had not previously been cultivated), area farms required several years to become productive. This fact too, according to a contemporary report, damaged local economy (and the capital's reputation) during those crucial, initial years.

Government lackadaisicalness contributed to the overall problem. Despite the Panic of 1819, Vandalia lots nevertheless comprised the best-selling property in Illinois. Thus, although Vandalia's predetermined two decades tended to give the town an unfavorable reputation from the beginning, the new state capital certainly had initial advantages and opportunities unrivaled by any other new and struggling Illinois town. The state government did not exploit those opportunities, however. Governor Bond's ringing 1820 challenge to the legislature for attractive public buildings, a governor's mansion, and a college at Vandalia was ignored by that and subsequent general assemblies. Vandalia was, after all, designated as capital for only twenty years.

Even Vandalia's status as capital brought about difficulties for local boosters. The discord of state politics interfered with the town's need for a good community reputation. As *Washington* is spoken, in anger or praise, to stand for the federal government, for Illinoisans the word *Vandalia* stood for the state government. Hooper Warren, an Edwardsville editor, even called an especially shocking sequence of legislative intrigue "Vandalism." But a struggling town such as Vandalia could ill-afford to have public opinion confuse the state government's performance (and legislators' intemperance) with the town itself. "Left to themselves," wrote Tocqueville, "the institutions of a local community can hardly struggle against a strong and enterprising government; they cannot defend themselves with success unless they have reached full development and have come to form part of national ideas and habits."[1] Although this quotation is cited somewhat out of context, it points to the fact that many of Vandalia's economic and social difficulties stemmed from its newness in the face of governmental and popular pressure.

Did Vandalians sufficiently boost their town so that economic and social difficulties could be surmounted? Modern studies of frontier communities speak of boosterism, the need of frontier people to extoll the benefits of their community and to exploit opportunities in order for that community to thrive. Evidence indicates that little or no coherent local policy or program evolved for advancing the town. Yet a considerable town spirit existed in Vandalia, resulting in frequent public forums and measures for community improvement. The quick erection of two statehouses—cooperative tasks similar to the barnraisings of rural areas—are outstanding examples, among several others, of community cooperation and civic spirit involving not only civic leaders but also county laborers and farmers. So although Vandalia never met contemporary expectations and never entirely overcame certain local problems, the capital's leaders were certainly civically active in efforts beyond their immediate business interests.

Finally Vandalia's lack of success as capital must be attributed to the direction of state settlement, a fact that would have hampered any efforts at boosterism. In 1819, the population of Illinois was concentrated almost entirely in the state's southern third. Indiana's population followed a similar pattern. When that state's legislature resolved to move the seat of government from southerly Corydon, the site chosen for the new capital of Indianapolis was the center of the state, an unsettled area. When the 1818 Illinois constitutional convention provided for the relocation of the capital from southerly Kaskaskia, however, the site chosen was not a central location but a spot at the northern edge of settlement—still in the lower third of Illinois. Within six years, a Vandalia editor noted the large numbers of settlers bypassing Southern Illinois for the fertile central and northern counties. Before the 1820s ended, Vandalia was in an area of comparably slow growth. Its capital-era population never surpassed a peak of eight hundred or nine hundred around 1830, compared to such younger Central Illinois communities as Springfield and Jacksonville, which in 1830 had 1,600 and 2,000 persons. Likewise, the Vandalia land office showed the lowest rate of sales in Illinois during the boom years of the mid-1830s. These factors in turn contributed to Vandalia's reputation for mediocrity.

One travel author in the 1830s was perplexed that "a town like Vandalia with all the natural and artificial advantages it possesses . . . in the heart of a healthy and fertile region, should have flourished no more than seems to have been the case."[2] A Galena, Illinois, editor summed up the thoughts of many in a remark telling in its unenthusiasm: "Vandalia is a pleasant place enough; but there are other pleasant places nearer the geographic centre of the State."[3] The same travel writer—copying the eloquent, hopeful words of James Hall—reached the same conclusion.

The growth of Vandalia, though tardy, can perhaps be deemed so only in comparison with the more rapid advancement of neighboring towns; for a few years after it was laid off it was unsurpassed in improvement by any other. We are told that the first legislators who assembled in session at this place sought their way through the neighboring prairies as the mariner steers over the trackless ocean, by his knowledge of the cardinal points. Judges and lawyers came pouring in from opposite directions, as wandering tribes assemble to council; and many were the tales of adventure and mishap related at their meeting. Some had been lost in the prairies; some had slept in the woods; some had been almost chilled to death, plunging in creeks and rivers. A rich growth of majestic oaks then covered the site of the future metropolis; tangle thickets almost impervious to human foot surrounded it, and all was wilderness on every side. Wonderful accounts of the country to the north; of rich lands and pure streams, and prairies more beautiful than any yet discovered, soon began to come in by the hunters. But over that country the Indian yet roved, and the adventurous pioneer neither owned the soil he cultivated, nor had the power to retain its possession from the savage. Only eight years after this, and a change, as if by magic, had come over the little village of Vandalia; and not only so, but over the whole state, which was now discovered to be a region more extensive and more fertile than the "sacred island of Britain." The region previously the frontier formed the heart of the fairest region of the state, and a dozen new counties were formed within its extent. Mail-routes and post roads diverging in all directions from the capitol had been established, and canals and railways had been projected. Eight years more, and the whole "Northern frontier" is the seat of power and population, and here is removed the seat of government, because the older settlements have not kept pace in advancement.[4]

Whether or not Vandalia's term as capital could legally be extended beyond twenty years, given the wording of the constitutional clause, became a moot question. By the 1830s, legislation was initiated to move the seat of government to another community. That community, as of July 4, 1839, was Springfield, in the heart of the rich and beautiful Sangamon River Valley.

1

To Reeve's Bluff

SOUTHERN ILLINOIS is a lovely region. Small, winding rivers like the Kaskaskia (the "Okaw"), the Embarras, Big Muddy, the Little Wabash, the Saline, Little Muddy, Skillet Fork, and others flow through this area. The Mississippi, Wabash, and Ohio surround the whole. Hills and ridges break up the landscape; the nearly unrelenting flatness of Central Illinois is absent here. Nevertheless, for early settlers, the great prairies distinguished this terrain. The largest, the Grand Prairie, extended deeply into Southern Illinois through the Fayette County area where Vandalia is located, then up into the Edenic northern regions. This great tract consisted of many smaller tracts, set off from one another by sections of hilly, wooded lands and by timbered lands along the banks of rivers and streams. During the early nineteenth century, travelers stood in awe of these prairies. More than one likened these beautiful sections to a sea; the flowering, green prairie flora waved in the wind like an ocean and beat against the "coastal" timbered boundaries.[1] Other people likened Illinois to the Promised Land. "Like Lot," wrote James Hall, settlers " 'lifted up their eyes, and beheld all the plain of the Jordan, that it was well watered every where;' fertile, 'even as the Garden of Eden,' and abounding in the choicest gifts of nature."[2]

Vandalia sits at the northernmost, informal boundary of Southern Illinois. Today that boundary is U.S. 40 (the old National Road) and Interstate 70; in 1819 it was the vanguard of white settlement. Thomas Ford writes, "the settled part of the State extended [in 1818] a little north of Edwardsville and Alton; south, along the Mississippi to the mouth of the Ohio; east, in the direction of Carlysle to the Wabash;

and down the Wabash and the Ohio, to the mouth of the last-named river. But there was yet a very large unsettled wilderness tract of country, within these boundaries, lying between the Kaskaskia river and the Wabash; and between the Kaskaskia and the Ohio, of three days' journey across it."[3] Before the Indians ceded their lands to the federal government, few white people journeyed north of the present town of Vandalia (i.e., above the imaginary line, of which Ford writes, from the Wabash through Carlyle), and very few white people lived there. Of towns and villages in Illinois Territory, the capital, Kaskaskia, had nearly a thousand citizens by 1818. The old French metropolis was by some accounts growing. Yet some travelers perceived an air of departed greatness to Kaskaskia, applying to the capital the dreaded adjective "inconsiderable." Shawneetown, across the territory, entrusted its local economy to the nearby saline industry and to emigrants who entered Illinois across the Ohio River through Shawneetown. Shawneetown and Kaskaskia contained comparable populations. Other towns such as Edwardsville, Cahokia, Palestine, and Alton varied in size, while still others—particularly county seats like Carmi, Golconda, and Vienna—were tiny hamlets.

Between 1809 (the first year of the Illinois Territory) and 1818 when the state entered the union, white population in Illinois grew sporadically. Government land was not available for purchase until 1814, although settlers who arrived during or before 1814 later received preemption rights upon their improved tracts. The new territory was not yet improved for great migration. Major highways, such as the road from Vincennes to St. Louis, joined a crude system of local roads, foot paths, and horse trails. Farmers found it difficult to market their corn, wheat, rye, and oats over these indifferent roads. This primitiveness at first discouraged emigration into Illinois. Currency, too, was scarce; doctors, entrepreneurs, and professionals were rare; towns lay far apart; even mail service was undeveloped in some areas. Conversely, increased settlement tended to solve such problems.

Immigration increased with the end of the war with Britain in 1815, with better, congressionally set terms for purchasing land, and with more readily available western currency. Land sales in Illinois rose from about 47,000 acres in 1816 to nearly 250,000 acres in 1817.[4] After 1816, federal land officers in Kaskaskia, Shawneetown, and Edwardsville experienced a flood of requests that is reflected by their harried complaints. "The Business in our offices since we commenced," wrote the Kaskaskia officers, "has become so arduous & multiplied that we could do little more than make the Entries of Lands applied for and Journalize the Accompts. . . . Perhaps in a week we shall have Applications to the

Amount of 100,000 acres." Not only had the Shawneetown office recorded more than two hundred thousand acres sold in that land district from January through September 1818, but people were also building houses and farms upon government land they never purchased: "There are nearly a thousand improved places in this district that are not Located," wrote the head of that office, "And if the Government does not adopt some energetic Measures to nip this Conduct in the bud—it will retard the sale of all those places." Timothy Flint reminisced about the late 1810s, "[Land claims] were like the weather in other countries, standing and perpetual topics of conversation."[5] The press for land is also reflected in increased population. When the movement to secure statehood commenced in the spring of 1818, census-takers counted fewer than thirty-five thousand people in the territory. Double-counting and optimistic approximations brought the figure over the congressional requisite of forty thousand. Two years after Illinois entered the union, the white population had climbed to 55,211 settlers.

Vandalia directly owes its existence to this late-1810s enthusiasm for land and to popular speculative means of exploiting the demand. Along fertile bottomlands or atop a rolling river bluff, a speculator might purchase sections of 320 or 640 acres from the government for $2 an acre, then call the acreage a "town" and sell lots in the future metropolis at high prices. Even if the town was little more than a ferry booth on a river, or a cabin, or only a gradiose name on a map, a speculator could portray in newspaper advertisements the beauty and future of a town if such confident imagery could attract buyers of lots.

Perhaps the most ingenious way that certain speculators attracted buyers was to claim that the "permanent seat of government for this state" would be located at a site.[6] Vandalia's existence resulted from this particular ploy. Settlers and politicians alike joined in the call; as early as January 1817, a travel author noted that persons living in the area of the present Fayette County (then Bond County) expressed confidence that the state capital would soon be located in that area.[7] Bond County, at the northern edge of white settlement, became the focus of such calls. The territorial congressman Nathaniel Pope and his political associate John Messinger founded a "town" at Pope's Bluff in Bond County in 1818, in order to gain profits from a possible removal of the state capital to that place. Ripley, also in Bond County, was advertised as having "central and eligible situation in the territory [which] gives rise to a strong presumption that it will at no distant period become the seat of government." Promoters of others towns also used this tactic. Some histories state that settler Charles Reavis, whose high and rolling bluff was about six miles from his cabin, appeared before influential statesman during 1818 and 1819 and claimed that "Pope's Bluff, er Carlyle neither, [isn't] a primin' ter [my] bluff."[8]

"It was premature and unnecessary," wrote the outspoken historian John F. Snyder, "and was concocted and consummated by a lot of speculators who expected to reap large profits in building up the new capital at Reeves' Bluff." This is true, and Kaskaskia was an adequate seat of government at the time. However other states besides Illinois relocated their capital cities two or three times, with similar motives. This particular expression of land enthusiasm arose suddenly. The last territorial legislature, in its December 1817 petition to Congress for an act enabling the organization of a state government, could have also made the customary request for four sections of land for a capital city. The legislature, however, made no such request, implying that relocation of the capital from Kaskaskia had not become an issue, although by the summer of 1818 speculators made it so.[9]

Before a final admission of Illinois into the union could be approved, a state constitution had to be drafted by an elected convention. During the summer, citizens elected thirty-three representatives to perform the task.[10] In less than a month the men drafted a constitution that remained law for thirty years. A few weeks after the convention had assembled in Kaskaskia, "sundry propositions in writing, offering donations to the state of land, &c. from the proprietors of Pope's Bluff, Hill's Ferry, and Covington" were submitted. The offers were presented to the convention by a five-member committee on Tuesday, August 18.

The convention faced three choices on the issue of relocation, which, along with the question of slavery, was one of the most controversial and time-consuming issues the delegates faced. The men could simply ignore the issue, because choosing a capital lay outside their responsibilities. Due to underlying political loyalties, such an option could not be taken. For instance, Leonard White of Gallatin County, a member of a state political faction that included Nathaniel Pope, made the motion to accept Pope's Bluff's claim. The delegates had a second option: to choose a town—including Kaskaskia itself—and make their choice constitutional law. A third option was to authorize the first state general assembly to make a selection. The convention chose this last option.

On Thursday August 20 the delegates adopted Joseph Kitchell's resolution "that it is expedient at this time to remove the seat of government from the town of Kaskaskia." Then Seth Gard of Edwards County moved that five appointed commissioners should view the three petitioned sites and report to the next general assembly. For a while the issue stalled among vying communities' claims. Later Gard offered a resolution for the capital to remain at Kaskaskia until the general assembly could petition Congress for preemption rights on four sections of land along the Kaskaskia River, on or near the Third Principal Meridian. Five commissioners, according to the resolution, would choose the sections. If Congress granted preemption rights on the sections, the commissioners should survey the state's permanent seat of government. Gard's resolution passed the first reading 18 to 13 and was amended slightly on the third reading. Delegates still expressed dissatisfaction, however, until Elias Kent Kane moved to strike the word "permanent" from the resolution and insert instead, "for the term of twenty years." With that qualification, the resolution passed and became constitutional law.

By stipulating that the new capital would be located in an unsettled area rather than at an existing town site, the convention delegates deprived speculators any gain from land sales at the capital city. For years thereafter the state government itself hoped for great returns on Vandalia town lots. Kane's motion to limit the new capital's term may have been aimed at thwarting the speculative hopes of the opposing political faction—the balloting on Gard's resolution is partisan along factional lines—but the motion was fateful for Vandalia's success.[11]

The First General Assembly, in October 1818, followed the authorization of the convention and submitted a petition to Congress, asking them

> to grant and give gratuitously to this state the said four sections. . . . The said General Assembly do further present; that all the Land near the Above four Sections of Land belong to the United States, And that by establishing a seat of government on the Land so granted it would enhance the Value of this Adjoining unsold Lands of the United States—that the United States would not be injured by such donation; but should the congress of the United States be of a contrary Opinion from the General Assembly of this state, in making the Above donation: the said General Assembly do petition the congress of the United States, to give to this state the preemption in the purchase of two dollars per Acre of the said four sections of Land.[12]

The petition reached the House of Representatives in Washington, D.C. on December 7, four days after Illinois formally entered the union, and passed Congress soon after. But opponents of the plan still advertised certain town sites as "the future seat of government," and some people directly petitioned Congress. One remonstrance from Alton citizens contained apt and reverberating criticisms. The people of Illinois could not vote on the issue, the authors pointed out. Furthermore

> the proposed seat of government is not a central situation. Neither is it in the centre of the population, nor is there any possibility that it ever

will be so. Situated on the Kaskaskia river, far above the head of navigation, in a part of the country, which, as we are credibly informed, is naturally unhealthy, the only inducements which people can have to settle in such a town must be derived from a *biennial session* of a General Assembly composed of *forty-two* members! Is it possible, we ask, that the legislature can be accommodated at such a place, and under such circumstances, without putting the state to such an expense which will greatly outweigh all the profits to be derived from a beggarly speculation in village lots?

The authors complained that should the new capital prove unacceptable, no change could be made for twenty years without the great inconvenience of a constitutional amendment. "By rejecting the said petition, your honorable body will leave in the hands of the people of this state a power of which they never ought to be divested—that of locating their seat of government where it shall be most convenient to them, and of removing it, when the public interests shall require its removal."[13]

Illinois Senator Jesse B. Thomas introduced the bill for the land grant in Congress on February 25, 1819. Soon the bill passed both houses of Congress and was signed by President James Monroe on March 3. News of the grant, however, did not reach Illinois until the last week of March, and the state house of representatives refused to consider relocation legislation until news arrived from Washington. Meanwhile, the state senate asked citizens to submit proposals for land for a seat of government, if that land was suitable for a town and located north of Carlyle. Once news of the land grant reached Kaskaskia, the house and senate both passed relocation legislation and on March 30 elected five legislators to act as commissioners.[14] Those commissioners were Thomas Cox, a tall, striking, and dark-complected delegate from Union County, Samuel Whiteside of Madison County (and the namesake of another Illinois county), Levi Compton and Guy Smith, both of Edwards County, and William Alexander of Monroe County.

Presumably because he was newly married, Smith did not join the expedition.[15] During early June, the other four men rode eighty miles through fly-infested prairies and mosquito-filled timber to select a satisfactory town site. They arrived first at the cabin of Charles Reavis. Reavis was a muscular, forty-five-year-old veteran of "the late war" and a native of North Carolina. His cabin stood beside the Kaskaskia River's edge near the longitudinal Third Principal Meridian.[16] Within a short time Reavis and the officials rode north into the woods around the Okaw's bank. (The Kaskaskia's nickname, now spelled *Okaw*, in early days was rendered *Oca, Occoa, Ocar, Ocaw*, and other variations, probably originated from the French, who abbreviated such Indian words.)

Reavis, a skilled hunter, knew those woods well; he may have known the most fortuitous trail to his place. Six or seven miles up the river, on the site called "Reeve's Bluff,"[17] Cox and his friends found what they sought. Years later it was related that one of the group killed a deer for supper. While the meat cooked on a fire, the men suddenly felt captivated by the setting. Upon inspection, they discovered that the uneven bluff had good springs and streams, sufficient trees for use in building, natural drainage, and sufficient game for food until a town's businesses could be established. Later, good well water was discovered on the bluff. To the southwest and the north were some of the highest hills in the region; to the north and east were wide tracts of the Grand Prairie and patches of good timber. The men resolved that the new state capitol should stand where the deer had died. "No other situation," read the official version, "was to be found possessing the same advantages and which immediately came under the spirit of the law under which we acted."[18]

William Berry, the young editor of the Kaskaskia newspaper, the *Illinois Intelligencer*, had in the May 12 issue urged the commissioners to make a judicious selection of the new seat of government. Somehow word of the selection was carried back to Kaskaskia. In the June 16 issue Berry announced that the town site was chosen and its name was "Vandalia." The name's origin will probably never be known. Promoters of a proposed fourteenth American colony coined the name during the 1760s; the colony would have honored England's queen, who claimed descent from fifth-century Vandalia tribes. Traditions explaining why this pleasant-sounding but (in James Hall's words) "rather heathenish" name came to designate the Illinois capital seem apocryphal. According to one story, attributed ninety years later to surveyor William Greenup, workers on the bluff discussed possible town names. One man suggested "Van" (or "Vanguard") to denote the progress of human endeavor taking place at a state capital. Someone else suggested "Dalia" because of the several dales among the area's hills. Greenup resolved the issue by combining the two suggestions into "Vandalia."[19] Other explanations are: that the name commemorated a French hunter who once roamed the area, that the name derived from a spot on the Kaskaskia known to French and British fur traders, and that it commemorated a mythical Indian tribe that roamed the region along with another tribe called the Goths. "Whether these rival had fought like the two Kilkenny cats, who devoured each other until nothing was left of either *but the tips of the tails*, the learned gentleman did not state. . . . This story has probably more wit than truth in it." The truth seems to be lost; as early as James

Hall's account in 1820, there was confusion over how the name came about.[20]

The four commissioners knew Greenup, former secretary of both the constitutional convention and the state senate, and the men hired him as chief Vandalia surveyor. The thirty-four-year-old, chain-smoking, good-natured Maryland native, who made Vandalia his lifelong home, agreeably rode to Reeve's Bluff that summer.[21] With him was Beal Greenup, also from Kaskaskia but of unknown relationship. At Vandalia, the Madison County tavern keeper John McCullom joined the survey team. Sometime in that year John and his wife Sarah had a baby— the first in what is now Fayette County, although the histories disagree if the child was a boy or a girl—and named the baby Vandalia McCullom.[22] Other men employed by the commissioners partially cleared the landscape. By early July the surveyors completed a town plat, the first announcement of a September auction appeared in the Kaskaskia and Edwardsville papers, and the bare outline of a village took shape. Men staked out blocks of 320 square feet with eight 80-by-152 lots and eighty-foot city streets. One block, the public square, was set four hundred feet from the Kaskaskia River. Streets running north and south were designated First through Eighth streets. West-east streets honored such contemporary statesmen as Ninian Edwards, Albert Gallatin, Arthur St. Clair, Richard M. Johnson, and John Randolph.[23]

Federal land officials still had not completely surveyed the Vandalia area, then part of the Shawneetown land district. However, a few settlers already lived in the vicinity. In January 1817 a travel author reported that the area's settlers were hospitable, moral, and religious, if not especially polished. Bond County's seat, Perryville, and town sites Independence and Pope's Bluff lay down the Kaskaskia from Reeve's Bluff. The large Beck family had lived on government land several miles north of Reeve's Bluff since 1815 and 1816. A number of families emigrated to the area between 1816 and 1819, and many more came to the Vandalia town site in the summer of 1819 to scout for lots to purchase at the coming auction.[24]

The first advertisement for the sale of Vandalia lots appeared in Illinois newspapers in June. During the first week of September crowds began to assemble on Reeve's Bluff, waiting for the land auction to begin on the sixth. People quickly filled Charles Reavis's newly erected hotel at Fifth and Johnson streets, but many people slept in lean-tos, shacks, or on the ground. No log or frame houses yet stood. [25] Some persons at the auction were speculators. Some were notable figures in the state, like Governor Shadrach Bond, justice of the state supreme court John Reynolds, Theophilus W. Smith, Elias Kent Kane, and Adolphus F. Hubbard. Elijah Berry, the state auditor, and Robert McLaughlin, the state treasurer, also strolled around the bluff. Other people included Ferdinand Ernst, William Greenup, Frederick Hollman, Robert Blackwell, and John A. Wakefield.[26] Of these men, McLaughlin, Greenup, Berry, and Blackwell became lifelong Vandalians. McLaughlin was forty in 1819, a jowly man with long dark hair. At Vandalia he was a grocer and well-to-do businessman and was frequently involved in state politics; he ran for governor in 1834, the only Vandalian to do so until 1912. County historians recalled that McLaughlin's business and political successes were due to the perception and advice of his wife, Isabella.[27] Berry and his wife Mildred settled permanently in Vandalia in 1819 or 1820, as did Berry's brother William, the editor. Blackwell, who survived two wives and was survived by his third, was a well-known newspaperman and hotel operator. He lived in Vandalia for forty-six years until his death.[28] Wakefield became an active Fayette County politician during the 1820s and 1830s; not a town resident, he lived six miles east of town (chapter 8).

Ernst, too, lived in Vandalia until his death, but his life was much shorter than the other men's. A wealthy German farmer and magistrate who hoped to bring a colony of emigrants to Vandalia (chapter 2), Ernst appreciated Reeve's Bluff and jotted into his diary: "Ihre lage ist vortrefflich gewahlt . . . mit herrlichem Bauholz und guten quellwasser, so wie mit einer Umgebung des herrlichsten landes, reichlich versehen." [The site is well chosen . . . and richly provided with wood for building and with good spring water, as well as with a vicinage of excellent land.][29]

When the auction began early on September 6, buyers at first failed to respond enthusiastically, but as prices decreased, sales picked up. The voice of the crier was followed by loud responses, outbursts from the crowds, long silences, or cries of joy or disappointment as people gained or lost hoped-for tracts. The drama continued the next morning. Ernst himself purchased four lots. Deeply moved by the American experience displayed before him, and filled with his own hopes and dreams for his family and fellow Germans, he wrote:

> Wie schwer war es damals, durch den dicken Wald zu dringen, welcher den ganzen Umfang der Stadt inne hat. . . . Aber wie wird es in 10 oder in 20 Jahren sich verändert haben! Dann werden alle diese gewaltigen Waldmassen verschwunden sein, und eine blühende Stadt mit herrlichen Gebäuden wird an ihrer Stelle stehen. Ein freies Volk wird dann durch seine Vertreter von hier aus sich selbst regieren, und über sein Wohl und seine Freiheit wachen.
>
> [How difficult it was at that time to penetrate the dense forest which embraces the entire circuit of the future city. . . . But how it will have

changed in 10 or 20 years! All these huge forests will have then disappeared, and a flourishing city with fine buildings will stand in their place. A free people will then from this place rule itself through its representatives and watch over their freedom and well-being.][30]

The average price of a single lot was around $230. The cheapest went for $35—still more than seventeen times the price of an acre of public land—and the most expensive, at Third and Gallatin across from the public square, went to Sam McClintoc for $780. Only one man paid cash; all other buyers enjoyed liberal credit terms. The state government retained many lots for later sale.[31] Ernst left for Germany shortly after the sale, leaving Frederick Hollman as his agent.

During the autumn following the auction, the leaves on Reeve's Bluff changed color and Vandalia took shape. What became Gallatin, Main, Fourth, and Fifth streets appeared on the bluff as muddy paths and wagon ruts. The chimneys of new houses and a few businesses sent wood smoke into the chilly air. One preoccupied settler among many, Frederick Hollman dutifully set about his work of preparing quarters for the colonists that Ernst was bringing from Germany.[32] After "an old squatter" built him a cabin, Hollman traveled to St. Louis where, speaking French, he was able to negotiate for materials like cloth, sugar, coffee, tobacco, and utensils to sell, as well as food, a pine table, chairs, and furniture for his own house.

> [In the fall of 1819] I engaged an expert chopper to fell suitable timber for me to build more log houses and also as could be sawed into lumber for frame houses. I had no difficulty in finding men who desired employment and there was an abundance of the very best of timber. However as there were no pine trees in the vicinity, I in company with an expert woodsmen by the name of Ravis went into the woods and selected the finest walnut trees from which to saw boards. We selected about forty and blazed them, which mark was sufficient to secure them as my property until they were cut down. We also marked in the same manner such other trees as I deemed necessary for my future operations. . . . [33]

By the end of the year, a few markets and hotels operated in the dark shade of the bluff. Hollman operated a store "which I had opened for the accommodation of the workmen," but it "soon proved to be too small. I was forced to replenish quite often, and also to increase the quantities of my purchases. I, however, limited my purchases to such articles as were strictly necessary. A flourishing mill was operating in the vicinity which afforded a supply of breadstuff; game of all kinds, consisting of bear, elk, deer, wild turkeys, wild geese, wild ducks and fish were to be found in astonishing quantities. Beef, pork, and flour were quite cheap, all things considered." William Kinney and his nine-teen-year-old assistant Charles Prentice were in town at the time of the auction, and soon they had a grocery of their own operating for the benefits of settlers.[34]

Anticipating the needs of the immigrants with whom Ernst would return, Hollman obtained the help of a local woman, later his mother-in-law, to sew quilts, sheets, and bedding. He hired a Mr. Woods to construct a 24 by 36 two-story log hotel on Main and Third streets. A new mill twenty miles away provided clean walnut planks for many buildings, and Hollman obtained several settlers eager for employment, including two British brothers, to chop wood and saw flooring, siding, scantling, and sheeting. Hollman's brick-producing kiln was ready by summer.[35]

On September 6, 1819, Bond County officials meeting at Perryville authorized that a road be laid out "from Perryville to John Smith's, thence straight to the lower end of the prairie, between the old road and Robert Daniels', thence west of Hickman's taking the side of the ridge to Vandalia." Two days later the officials authorized a road from Pope's Bluff to the eastern county line, where it was supposed to meet the Carlyle Road. The men also authorized a road, constructed in June 1820, east of the Kaskaskia opposite Main Street in Vandalia, to end at the county line in the direction of Vincennes. The eastern mail route was soon redirected toward Vandalia.[36]

William Greenup's Kaskaskia office accepted bids for construction of a temporary state building. Edmund Tunstall of Carmi was the low bidder, and he arrived at Vandalia with twelve workers in the spring of 1820 to begin work. The statehouse was finished a few months later. Situated on the corner of Fifth and Johnson streets, the statehouse was, in the words of one legislator, "primitive and plain as a Quaker meeting house."[37] The fault was not Tunstall's but the designer's. It was a frame two-story structure, 40 by 30 feet at the foundation, with a thirty-foot-square lower room for the house of representatives and a 25 by 30 senate chamber. Two 10 by 15 committee and council rooms were added to the second floor. A ten-foot passage downstairs connected to the stairway. Two brick or stone chimneys were in the design; Tunstall did not finish the south one and thereby forfeited $40 of his $4,732 commission. Standing among other frame and wood-planked structures, the state capitol appeared nondescript. A thoughtful person would have recognized it as a fire hazard, and it did, in fact, burn in 1823.[38]

By the fall of 1820, Vandalia had emerged as a small but active village. Five or six boardinghouses stood along Main and Gallatin streets, including Daniel Bathrick's Sign of the Bell tavern and McCullom's hotel, stables, and tavern. Twenty-nine-year-old Sidney Breese, Secretary of State Kane's office staff of one and later a distinguished Illinois judge, hacked a path through the woods to Vandalia in 1820 with the state archives in one ox cart. William Berry suspended publication of his *Illinois Intelligencer* in Kaskaskia in October. Before he lost too much subscription income he hauled the bulky iron printing press, reams of paper, type, and many bottles of ink by wagon to Vandalia.[39]

The 1820 federal census listed about 525 people, including eleven slaves, in "Vandalia township"; only thirteen of the eighty-eight "heads of families" had been counted in 1818.[40] Hollman concluded his labors, including the construction of three log houses and a large frame house, and took the time to consider his efforts. He later wrote:

> About the time that winter set in the state officers and their families arrived in Vandalia. . . . The members of the legislators arrived from day to day and to their surprise found good and ample accommodations. There had been a general understanding among them that they would meet at Vandalia and then adjourn to some other place on account of a want of suitable accommodations. After finding what had been done in anticipation of their arrival they had no excuse for doing as they intended. I took twelve members of the legislature as steady boarders and four clerks who slept in the State House.

But he had heard nothing from Ernst since spring. Hollman had a difficult fifteen months in Vandalia. He had learned a little English in his free moments, but most of his time had been spent preparing quarters for the Germans. He wrote in his autobiography that "it will be seen from what I have here set forth that the young dutchman in the wilds of Illinois had enough on his shoulders to crush him."[41]

The Second General Assembly convened in December 1820 and adjourned the following February. According to Hollman, legislators expressed surprise and satisfaction with Vandalia's accommodations. William Berry, however, overheard complaints; he editorially asked state officials to remember Vandalia's better aspects. Vandalia had five or six boardinghouses to accommodate forty-two legislators and a host of state executive and judicial officers, employees of the legislature and judiciary, and many spectators, lobbyists, and office-seekers. As Hollman recalled, some clerks for the senate or house slept in the statehouse. The governor moved in with his relatives the McLaughlins, and up to four legislators shared a single room in some hotels. Complaints about accommodations and availability of necessities were inevitable.[42]

Governor Shadrach Bond opened the legislative session with an address. Bond was a dark, impressive man who had achieved sufficient political honor during the territorial period that his bid to be the state's first governor was unopposed.[43] A large portion of his address was devoted to Vandalia. Sympathetic with the village's newness, Bond said,

> I have the pleasure to address you at a place, which in a short period of time has converted from a wilderness into a village, suited to your accommodation. The influence of public treasures over individual industry and enterprise is here presented to the view of an assembly convened for the purpose of providing for the general welfare. . . . Permit me to recommend a liberal course of conduct towards improvement of this village. It may be termed the offspring of the State, and the state is responsible for its advancement. A just extension of public patronage toward it, will embrace the erection therein of Public Offices, a building for use of the Supreme and Federal courts, and a State Prison. When it shall be thought advisable to lay the foundation of a Seminary of Learning, I know of no situation more commanding than the vicinity of the Seat of Government. Here a student by an occasional visit to the houses of the General Assembly and the Courts of Justice, will find the best specimens of oratory the state can produce; imbibe the principles of legal science and political knowledge; and by an intercourse with good society his habits of life will be christened and his manners improved.[44]

Bond shared Ernst's vision for the capital as a place of exemplary culture, learning, and facility. The governor urged liberal spending for good public buildings and college professors in Vandalia. The opportunities Bond discussed, however, were not taken by this and future general assemblies; apparently the legislators were unwilling to invest the state's funds in a temporary capital. Instead, the legislature passed routine legislation to organize the local and county governments.

First, the legislature formally organized Fayette County on February 14, 1821. The name reflects a contemporary practice of naming counties and cities after Revolutionary War heroes like Washington or Lafayette. Originally the county was wider than its present boundaries, and it extended indefinitely northward. Vandalia became county seat; the village of Greenville became the new county seat of Bond County because Perryville now rested within the borders of Fayette.[45] In accordance with the state constitution and state statutes, Fayette County was administered by a county court of commissioners: the first court consisted of Paul Beck, John A. Wakefield, and William Johnson. The trio licensed several taverns, ordered construction of a brick and timber jail north of the public square on Fourth and Madison, and declared what property— town lots, carriages, distilleries, horses, and cattle three years and older— was taxable. The men named Ferdinand Ernst supervisor of the construction of the new road to Vincennes. The court also authorized roads to Greenville and to Sangamon County. Other village and county officials were elected or appointed at about the same time.[46]

One day following passage of the Fayette County bill, the legislature approved the bill organizing the Vandalia board of trustees. The first trustees were James M. Duncan, Ferdinand Ernst, Robert K. Mc-Laughlin, William L. D. Ewing, Thomas Cox, and three others. The new act authorized the trustees to supervise local activities and to prevent the waste of timber within the city limits and the cutting of timber on state-owned lots. The legislature donated fifty town lots for the trustees to sell, the funds from which to be used for a new river bridge and an eastern road to the hills. New city ordinances included one that fined people who cut trees and within forty-eight hours burned the tops, an ordinance establishing a 2 percent land tax, and another prohibiting gunfire and general disorderly conduct within the city limits. The board also called out all adult males in November 1822 for the annual street cleaning weekend, a service for which the reluctant workers were paid 50 cents a day. Periodically thereafter, the board would set a similar weekend so downtown Vandalia would be kept clean.[47]

Two months before Vandalia and Fayette County government were organized, Ernst and his colony finally arrived at their new home. The large group had made their laborious way from Baltimore since October. They arrived, therefore, at Vandalia on the far side of the Kaskaskia River. Once at the river bank, perhaps assisted by a professional ferryman, the entourage forded the cold, swiftly flowing river. As the wagons and horses proceeded the last few hundred yards up the dirt road, the emigrants who owned instruments struck up (probably out-of-tune) renditions of "Yankee Doodle" and "Hail Columbia."

In the dining rooms of McCullom's, Cox's, Hollman's, and Bathrick's hotels and boardinghouses, legislators and jurists sat for dinner. As Hollman remembered:

> At this moment the sound of music was heard. Everybody was on the watch in an instant to ascertain what it could mean. The mystery was soon explained for a moment afterwards a wagon containing a band performing one of the national airs was driven into the village followed by Mr. Ernst and family. Immediately after them came three wagons full of women and children and sixty or seventy emigrant men on foot. I directed them to drive up to the State House where three rousing cheers were given for the legislature and the State of Illinois. The scene was affecting and I openly shed tears of thankfulness and joy after the long months of hardship and anxiety.[48]

Although technically founded in June and July 1819, Vandalia became an active and economically self-sufficient community during the winter of 1820 and 1821 when the state government first convened, when the first businesses opened, and when the Ernst colony arrived.

In Vandalia's old cemetery at Second and Edwards, the stones of several first settlers can be read: the McLaughlins, Charles Prentice, Robert Blackwell, William C. Greenup, William Lee, George and Sophia Remann Leidig, Frederick Remann, John Frederick Yerker, Elijah and Mildred Berry, William Berry, James William Berry, and Ferdinand Ernst. These people, and others who settled Vandalia from 1819 to 1821, laid the social and economic foundation for the second capital of Illinois.

2

Ferdinand Ernst and the German Colony

FREDERICK HOLLMAN's arduous work, the dramatic arrival at Vandalia of Ferdinand Ernst and approximately one hundred German immigrants, and the colony's breakup after Ernst's untimely death: these facts are well known, not only to Vandalia's history but also to that of Illinois. During its short existence, the colony was a benefit and boon to the new capital. Ernst was also one of Vandalia's most important figures, even though he lived there only about twenty months. The colony is a fascinating variance from midwestern colonies and utopias—the Mormons and Icarians at Nauvoo, the Jansonists at Bishop Hill, and the Rappites at New Harmony—in that the colony had no utopian or religious paragon for organization. The Vandalia Germans were simply a group of impoverished Europeans who temporarily obligated themselves to the wealthy Ernst in exchange for Atlantic passage and settlement in Vandalia. Ernst, however, did consider himself a leader who could command as well as provide. The colony's breakup was caused, in large measure, by disease and death. But what has not been known—because the colony's chief primary source, Hollman's autobiography, omits these details—is that the group's lack of focal organization created serious problems as well.[1] The colony, rather than being a shining example of community, became a sad example of community's fragility.

No paintings or descriptions of Ernst are extant. He was born about the year 1784—not in the 1790s, as his Vandalia tombstone indicates—perhaps in the ancient village of Trier in the Rheinland. He was the son of a rich tenant farmer from greater Algermissen near the city of Hildesheim in the northern German state of Hanover. Ernst's father accumulated several large estates for his children, and Ferdinand inherited the estate "Almstedt" in the district of Winzenberg. He married a woman whose first name was Mariane, or Mary Ann; their three children were Hermann (who married William Greenup's daughter), Augusta (who married Dr. Robert H. Peebles of Vandalia), and Rudolph (who died in the military). Ernst called himself a *Landwirt*, a farmer or agriculturalist; German-American historians call him an *Amtmann*, a judge or city magistrate.[2] At Vandalia, he both farmed and held city offices.

Little else can be said about Ernst's life before his twenty-fifth year. When he was about twenty-five, he first met the eighteen-year-old Frederick (in German, Friedrich) Hollman, who roomed with the Ernst family while obtaining agricultural education at the *Domäne* of Canton Mayer. (A "domain" was a government-owned area of land leased for agricultural purposes.) A later portrait shows Hollman as a square-faced, friendly man with a wide smile. He eventually moved from the Ernst household and took over a lucrative superintendency at the domain of Gutenstadt.[3]

About the same time, Ernst befriended Ludwig Gall, a wealthy young man like himself. By 1816 or 1817 Gall and Ernst discussed the possibility of collaborating as sponsors for Germans who wished to emigrate to America. The recent Napoleonic wars had left the German states and much of Europe in economic and spiritual crisis. Crop failures and inflation crippled the lives of so many middle- and lower-class Germans that emigration was deemed a viable response. As moneyed individuals, the two men elected to help these people by funding their crossing and establishment.

Gall finally chose to take a colony to Pennsylvania, while Ernst carried on plans for a separate colony.[4] In February 1819, Ernst went to Hildesheim searching for his friend, Hollman. A twenty-eight-year-old bachelor, Hollman still supervised the Gutenstadt domain; he came to Hildesheim on business one day when he happened into Ernst. "My dear Fred," Ernst exclaimed (in Hollman's account), "you are the very man I am in search of. I have sold my possessions for forty-five thousand dollars and I am going to America to found a colony, and I wish you to go with me and you shall have a good share of the enterprise. Make any sacrifices in order to be able to accompany me." In his autobiography Hollman does not elaborate on his own motives for making this extraordinary sacrifice.[5]

Ernst, Hollman, and some other men boarded the *Plato* at Bremen on March 29, 1819, and landed at Baltimore on June 16.[6] Journeying first to Washington, the Germans were greeted by Secretary of State

John Quincy Adams, who forwarded a letter of welcome to Ernst from Illinois congressman Daniel Pope Cook. The group then left Washington by stage and continued to Wheeling, Virginia. There they purchased horses and followed the course of the Ohio River. All the while Ernst recorded his impressions and observations in his journal.

In Ohio, Ernst separated from Hollman and ten other men. During his travels he interviewed immigrant Germans and commented in his journal concerning his experiences. He remarked about the unbearable heat and flies of the prairie, typical Illinois weather, and soil and crop conditions. American customs made him uncomfortable; American men, for instance, shook hands with a stranger but did not remove their hats. Governor Bond, however, provided him an elegant reception at Kaskaskia, which pleased Ernst.

Meanwhile, Hollman and the other Germans made the difficult trek to join Ernst at Edwardsville, Illinois. At one point when the axle of Hollman's wagon broke, two strangers walking from Baltimore came to his aid until he could locate a wheelwright. Traveling in the cool night and early morning, Hollman met Ernst on July 23.

Comparing the proposed site of Vandalia and the Sangamon River Valley, Ernst decided he preferred Vandalia as the site for his colony. At the September auction he purchased four lots, recorded his happy impressions of Vandalia, instructed Hollman, who did not speak English, to build quarters for the colonists, and shortly left for St. Louis. There he boarded a skiff to New Orleans and set sail for Germany on November 1. "With a feeling of sadness," he wrote, "I left a land which in such a degree met my wishes and hopes, and to which I intend soon to return forever."[7]

While Hollman toiled for fifteen months at Vandalia, Ernst set about his own work. All that is known about these months is that Ernst arrived in Hanover on January 1, 1820; that he published his journal; that (according to Hollman) on February 24 he wrote Hollman stating he had about a hundred persons enlisted to emigrate; and that Ernst, his family, and several colonists arrived at Baltimore on October 2, 1820. The Germans made their slow journey from Baltimore to Vandalia in five wagons. Near the Saline River in southeastern Illinois, a band of looters attacked the teamsters who carried the bulky German chests. Finding no cash, the thieves left the men unharmed but scattered bedding, clothing, utensils, and heirlooms. The teamsters gathered what they could and proceeded to Vandalia.[8]

Ernst's travel journal, *Observations on a Journey through the Interior of the United States of America in the Year 1819,* became a popular travel guide and went through eight German editions and at least one in Dutch. This is not surprising because the book is a remarkable chronicle of minutiae. Ernst preserved the adverse and favorable qualities of American life, terrain, and customs. Implicit throughout was his desire to prove that emigration was a workable opportunity. Along with helpful information, he provided success stories of Germans like Julius Bärensbach of Edwardsville, who had been forced by poverty to serve indentureships in exchange for Atlantic passage but who was now wealthy.[9]

With this hope, the Germans arrived at Vandalia in December 1820. Hollman tearfully joined the entourage and guided the three wagons to the statehouse. Vandalians and legislators spilled into the streets to greet the new arrivals. Ernst viewed with satisfaction and surprise the village which, when he last saw it, was a partially cleared spot in the forest.[10]

Many of the colonists worked out their indentures to Ernst in only four months and were then free to establish themselves in business, stay in Vandalia, or leave town. Vandalia's population in 1821 is unknown, but perhaps a third to a half were German immigrants, who included merchants, butchers, tailors, goldsmiths, and laborers. August Rosemeyer entered the blacksmith trade with Arthur Berry, and the two partners soon moved their business from opposite the Vandalia Hotel to Main Street "a few rods east of E. M. Townsend's tavern." George Leidig obtained a dram shop license in December 1821 and remained in the hotel or grocery business until his death in the late 1840s. He sporadically advertised not only whiskey but also gin, rum, cognac, brandy, and other fine liquors. Henry Wageman advertised clothing items for sale at the Columbian Hotel, a lodging place that Hollman himself operated.[11]

Some of the families provided Vandalia with a historical legacy and demonstrate the long-term success of Ernst's venture. After the death of his first wife, Leidig married Frederick Remann, Jr.'s sister, Sophia. Their son became Vandalia's mayor; their daughter Olivia Whiteman was later famous because her childhood playmate was Tad Lincoln. The Snyder family—forty-year-old Emanuel, a shoemaker, and his forty-nine-year-old wife Ann Eliza—had lived in Hesse before they sailed with Ernst. Their son Henry was by tradition Vandalia's first blacksmith and brickmaker. Snyder descendents still live in the Vandalia vicinity.[12]

The Remanns of Reiden in Hanover were Frederick, a thirty-eight-year-old butcher, his wife, and three young children. Frederick, Jr., was thirteen when the family came to Vandalia. When his father died about 1822, he set to work at age fifteen to save for and secure an education. He invested his $500 gratuity from the Black Hawk War in land and a merchandising business. At business, he thrived. An advertisement in an 1866 issue of the *Vandalia Union* reads: "To Arms! To Arms!! The Fenians are Marching! Their Cannons are Thundering! Ireland to be set free! England to be wiped out! Because F. Remann has filled his store, on the corner of the Public Square, with the largest and best selected stock of Goods ever offered in Vandalia, And at Such Greatly Reduced Prices as to Enable Everybody to Purchase for Cash or Produce at Wholesale or Retail!"

Remann died in 1873 while president of the national bank at Vandalia. His and his wife Julia's surviving child, Frederick III, served in the Civil War and was overwhelmingly elected to Congress in 1894. His son, Frederick IV, was a University of Illinois graduate and an attorney.[13]

Especially during the first year of the colony, the venture seemed quite successful. Ernst purchased several acres of farmland south of Vandalia, to which he brought the county's first improved stock of English cattle. He received the high honors of a chair on the village board of trustees and on the directing board of the state bank. Not long before his death he hired a local man, Moss Twiss, to construct a mill on the Kaskaskia for preparation of grain. In his autobiography, Hollman fondly remembered evenings with the Ernst family. Together, the family, along with Hollman and the Reverend Smith, enjoyed playing the music of Beethoven, Haydn, and Mozart. Smith, whose first name is unknown, was a Lutheran pastor brought to Vandalia by the Roman Catholic Ernst for the benefit of his predominantly Lutheran emigrants. Smith's German messages, delivered at services at the statehouse, were of such eloquence as to attract English-speaking locals to the services.[14] Such happy days for the colony were far too few, however.

Traditionally, the breakdown of the colony has been attributed to the deaths of at least twenty of the group, including Ernst. Fritz Wolff was overcome by the Kaskaskia in May 1821 while swimming after a runaway skiff. Frederick Remann, Sr., George Leidig's first wife, and Emanuel Snyder all died before 1823. Henry Yerker died in a prairie fire later that year. Hollman remembered that Reverend Smith died of a stroke hastened by despair concerning the Germans.[15] The names of other Germans who perished are no longer known.

When Hollman wrote his autobiography during the 1870s, he forgot or omitted other problems within the colony. One was faithlessness. For instance, in May 1821 an adult German tailor left Vandalia with three German teenagers. All four thereby defaulted on their indentures to Ernst; they were probably never found. Ernst placed a furious notice in the *Intelligencer* threatening to prosecute anyone found harboring the four. The editor inserted his own words of support for Ernst and his selfless venture.[16] Although not alluding to any examples, one German historian criticized Ernst for laying the foundation for such faithlessness: "In America, the emancipated dayworkers and farmers . . . after drinking from the fountain of freedom, did not want to tolerate any longer the absolute, peremptory commands of a German *Amtmann*, which Ernst should have considered beforehand."[17]

The second problem was Ernst's own personal affairs, which by 1822 were extremely vexatious. Moss Twiss and two other men separately sued him for nonpayment of work and building materials for projects.[18] The most alarming and inexplicable crisis occurred when the brothers John Frederick Yerker and Henry Yerker separately sued Ernst for trespass. They each claimed that Ernst broke into their homes, caused great disturbances, and detained them for several hours. John Frederick testified that Ernst took two featherbeds; Henry stated Ernst assaulted him before taking $100 worth of books. The jury found Ernst guilty but assessed damages at only 6¼ cents for Henry and $37.50 for John Frederick. Attorneys for both sides protested the decision.[19]

Ernst never paid the award, however. Hollman remembered his fatal illness as a sudden attack of "bilious fever" (possibly typhoid), but the Edwardsville newspaper termed it "a long and painful illness." In either case Ernst lived long enough to appoint William H. Brown, Hollman, and Elijah C. Berry as his administrators. He specifically asked Hollman to protect his family's financial future. Ernst died intestate on August 19, 1822, when he was approximately thirty-eight and was buried in the Vandalia graveyard.[20]

Livestock, farm implements, carriages, carts, furniture, two pianos, flutes, clarinets, French horns, bassoons, bass, tenor, and common fiddles, assorted music, table and glassware, thermometers and hydrometers, and many other items were sold at the sale at Ernst's farm on October 10 and 11, 1822. Judge John Reynolds, a future Illinois governor, assessed the estate. Two years after the sale, the estate was inventoried as worth $3,697.37½, including debts of $1,361 that Ernst owed the state bank, $800 on a mortgage, and $871 outstanding on his Vandalia lots.[21] Collecting debts owed by Ernst and those owed the estate proved difficult because by 1822 and 1823 the notes of the state bank had inflated greatly. Hollman testified by the end of 1823 that a dollar note was worth only 17 cents; he did not leave enough money to pay a proportionate amount.[22] After the state bank sued for recovery of Ernst's mortgage and debts, the case traveled from the circuit court to the state supreme court, which ruled in the administrator's favor. An 1823 law had released Ernst's estate from all debts due the state, and the court ruled that a debt to the state bank constituted a debt to the state.[23]

Sadly, Mary Ann Ernst had to rely upon the courts, not the administrators, for her welfare. She filed suit against the administrators to obtain proceeds from the estate, but the administrators wished to pay Ernst's debts first. The same 1823 law had instructed them to pay the proceeds of the Vandalia lots to Mary Ann, but they applied to the circuit court to pay her only after settlement with creditors. Finally, at the April 1828 term of the court, with James Hall representing Mary Ann, the court awarded her the proceeds of the lots. The administrators next took their case to the state supreme court, which also ruled in favor of Mary Ann.[24]

If Ernst specially entrusted the well-being of his family to the administrators, particularly to Hollman, these proceedings seem extraordinary. Additional circumstances might have arisen, which Hollman forgot after fifty years. For example, he remembered incorrectly that Ernst died in 1824, and his memoir never takes a self-serving or self-justifying tone. More extraordinary yet is the fact that Ernst died intestate because by all accounts he lived long enough to write a will. Whatever the circumstances of the estate and its difficulties, Hollman opted to leave Vandalia in 1827. He moved to Galena, never again returning to the town he helped establish.[25]

Mary Ann outlived her husband nearly twenty years. When she died unmarried in September 1841, her son Hermann Ernst petitioned the circuit court for relief in handling his mother's estate. He testified that he was the surviving family member (his sister and brother apparently having died by 1841), and that Mary Ann's estate consisted only of promissory notes. Her burial place is unknown. Surely it is beside Ernst, but the family monument erected after Hermann's death in 1874 does not include her name.[26]

Scattered around the Vandalia cemetery are markers for a few colonists: John Frederick Yerker, George and Sophia Leidig, Frederick Remann, Jr., and the Ernst family. Snyder descendents are also buried there. No one knows where other Ernst colonists are buried. Little evidence calls attention to Ernst's selfless vision for the betterment of his fellow Germans, but his legacy has always been the social conscience that gave his immigration venture a foundation and an impetus. In spite of failures that doomed Ernst's venture, what survives his colony, in addition to the American descendents of the hundred German immigrants, is this legacy.

3

By Their Strong Arms

Ferdinand Ernst had been deeply attracted to the Fayette County
environs. Later generations, too, loved those lands: the high hills
north and south of Vandalia, the steep dales, "the pasture lands rivaling
the famous blue grass region of Kentucky, . . . a rich alluvial deposit,
and of inexhaustible fertility," the sandy loam and flora of the Grand
Prairie; the timbered tracts of ceded Indian lands; the groves of apple,
peach, and maple trees in upland regions, the wild grapes, plums, and
mulberry; and the muddy, shallow, and swift waters of the Okaw, the
East Fork, Hurricane, and Hickory creeks.[1] Although Fayette County
lies in Southern Illinois, whether it belongs to the famous "Egypt" area
depends upon whether one applies the name to the entire region bounded
by the Mississippi, Ohio, and Wabash rivers or includes only that area
south of a line from St. Louis to Vincinnes (today, the region south of
U.S. 50). Fayette County's terrain does reflect both the beautiful rolling
hills characteristic of the southerly Illinois counties and the magnificent
prairie lands of Central Illinois. As the area of southern migration and
of the state's first center of power, Vandalia's and the county's early
history clearly belongs to that of "Egypt."

These prairie lands and hills attracted hundreds of settlers like Ernst
to Fayette County's boundaries. Unfortunately, traditions about early
Vandalia settlers are frustratingly few; no informative letters, diaries, or
contemporary accounts of everyday life in Fayette County are known
to exist, with the priceless exception of Frederick Hollman's autobiography covering from 1819 to 1827. Almost nothing is available from
the period, neither locally written depictions of everyday life, nor in-

dications of the fabric of social exchange. A later generation recorded memories and traditions.[2]

It is uncertain who the first white settlers were. Guy Beck, a teenaged Kentucky native in search of better hunting grounds, built a cabin on federal land in 1815 in the area of the present Fayette County. On that spot among rolling, timbered hills, he lived the rest of his life and died in 1871.[3] He is the first known white settler, a distinction that his tombstone, deep in the woods where he lived, commemorates.[4] Although this distinction is probably irrefutable, histories of neighboring Bond County indicate that white settlement there predated Fayette's by several years; Beck may not have been the first. Small settlements near Hurricane Fork, along the Kaskaskia River (including the county seat of Perryville), and within the present Bear Grove township west of Vandalia were established in 1816 or earlier. These communities are not reflected in federal land records; ownership of land in the present Fayette County area, by Bond County settlers, state politicians, as well as the Bank of Edwardsville, began in the Perryville vicinity (the present Kaskaskia and Pope townships) in 1816.[5]

Other evidence points to a much earlier settlement of the Vandalia area. According to the received tradition, Thomas Jefferson authorized Isaac Hill, a Bond County settler, to explore the Kaskaskia River Valley. Two of Hill's maps were passed down through the family; one map is a copy of a now-lost 1803 map on which the Vandalia site is called "vanne delai" and the Kaskaskia ("Okaw") River is "eau carré." The other map is Hill's 1810 work, on which the site is called "Vandla." French trading and travel during this period is possible; if authentic, the maps would help explain the origins of Vandalia's unusual name and the Kaskaskia's nickname and would establish white settlement, or at least activity, in the Fayette County area several years before Beck. The maps have been known for about a hundred years and contain colloquial French, but their authenticity has not been completely substantiated. They are now missing.[6]

Vandalia's verifiable pioneer history coincides closely with the town's establishment. The early, pre-statehood shortage of professional people, entrepreneurs, and large-scale farmers was solved once Illinois entered the union and settlement increased; this emigration also improved Fayette County and Vandalia. Southern Illinois was not merely a place to which the poor escaped hardship. "Thousands, it is true, have been driven here [Illinois] by want," wrote James Hall in the 1820s, "[but] we now find classes of people among the emigrants [who are] gentlemen of wealth and intelligence, professional men of talent and education, and respectable farmers and artizans."[7] Whether impoverished or wealthy, people's motives for coming to Vandalia varied. Some came specifically because of the town's economic benefits as state capital, including some of the original buyers in September 1819. Some came because of the attractiveness of particular land tracts, or to follow a family member who had domiciled earlier. Others came by accident; some Fayette County settlements have a quality (like the discovery of Reeve's Bluff in June 1819) of accidentalness or happy discovery. Guy Beck was one such settler; others in the Beck family came to the county because of his stories. Isaac Workman, traveling with a wagon train to Texas, camped overnight near the National Road. Looking for his lost horse the next day, he liked the county and settled there. His descendents still live in Vandalia. One extended Virginia-born family, my ancestors, traveled from Kentucky toward Central Illinois. According to family tradition, their wagons became stuck in the muddy Vandalia-to-Vincennes road; so, proceeding no further, they settled near Vandalia.[8] It was common for southern settlers to "just up 'n' move" then "settle down" with very little forethought.

The two county histories and modern Vandalia genealogists have accounted for many Fayette County settlers. The majority were of southern nativity, predominantly from Virginia, Tennessee, Kentucky, and the Carolinas, and some from Maryland. The list is extensive: the Brownings, Mabrys, Enochs, Brazles, Carsons, Blackwells, Berrys, Stapps, Gatewoods, Pilchers, Lovelesses, Mahons, Elams, Carrolls, Bones, Browns, Blankenships, Washburns, Evanses, Houstons, Hickersons, Depews, Duncans, and many others. Of the fourteen known Revolutionary War veterans who lived in the county, at least eight were southern-born. Other families came from Ohio, Pennsylvania, and New York, but not many from New England states.[9] "Like most of the other townships in the county," a county historian writes, "this [Wheatland] was settled first by families from Tennessee—some of that old pioneer stock that has helped to develop so many new countries; a people who were seldom known to refuse a stranger the hospitalities of their humble homes; men who are firm friends, but dangerous enemies. . . . At a later date there appears to have been a tide of emigration set in from Ohio—a class of people too well and favorably known to need any comment at our hands."[10] A majority of the county and town officials from 1819 through 1839—for example, John Enochs, Paul Beck, John A. Wakefield, Thomas R. Gatewood, William C. Greenup, W. L. D. Ewing, James W. Berry, James T. B. Stapp, Akin Evans, William Hodge, and John Whitley—were also natives of southern states or children of southern-born.

Some foreign-born traveled to the town and county. A handful of settlers of Irish background, like the Seftons, the Holins, and the Ma-

JABEZ

hons, settled in the Vandalia area during the capital period.[11] Ebenezer Capps, a successful Vandalia merchant, was among the county's few English-born residents. The German colonists at Vandalia are the best known of the European groups in the county, but most disappear from the primary sources after 1822, the year of Ernst's early demise. The Sonnemann family from Germany and a second group of Hanover natives, the Steinhauers and Dieckmanns, emigrated in the early 1840s. These people became examples of the successful, self-made immigrant, a myth that holds for these families—well-known in twentieth-century Vandalia—if not in the case of most of the Ernst colonists.[12] Other German families settled in Kaskaskia and Wheatland townships.

Two Polish agents, Baron Louis Clopitski and John Prebal, received a splendid Vandalia reception in October 1834. Several Poles, granted preemption rights by Congress, soon moved to town and, according to the Vandalia paper, were well cared for with services and local contributions. Some became citizens of the capital; an announcement in the *Illinois Advocate* informed Nicholai Browenski, Baron Clopitski, Upseki Polern, Konstantly Mezynki, Mzzynskiemu, and Kaminskeomer that they needed to pick up their mail at the Vandalia post office. Little else is known of these these people; the 1840 Fayette County census lists no Polish names.[13]

The predominantly southern nativity of Vandalia's and the county's early citizens implies a concomitant ethnic and cultural homogeneity. In fact, this homogeneity may explain the lack of stories of regional-based social or political conflict. One story from Vandalia's tradition suggests that a local distrust of "Yankees" did exist; a young northeastern teacher left town in disgrace when his ideas were perceived as too Yankee and liberal for students.[14] Stories like this are few, but New Englanders in Vandalia were also few. Certainly there was not the vociferous regional conflict of the kind observed in other Central Illinois communities. Politics of the era were based largely on western perceptions of Andrew Jackson's policies and on personal charisma of certain candidates like Daniel Pope Cook, Joseph Duncan, and Zadoc Casey. But at the same time, voting patterns of Vandalia and Fayette County indicate that the whig party, the stronghold of New England conservatism in the 1830s and 1840s, stood little chance of victory in either the town or the county. By the antebellum and Civil War periods, when the democratic party had become the "southern" rather than the "western" party, voting patterns, along with southern nativity and sympathies in Vandalia, coincided more explicitly. "He was a staunch and outspoken Union man," wrote a county historian of the German immigrant Frederick Remann, Jr. "At that period of the history of his county it cost something to be a Union man."[15] Antipathy toward and exclusion of blacks from the predominantly white settlement is discussed in chapter 7 and survived well into the twentieth century.

Decades before the Civil War, local political competition did not proceed along regional lines. Men who held leadership positions in Vandalia—William Berry, John A. Wakefield, Robert McLaughlin, Charles Prentice, William L. D. Ewing, James Black, and Robert Blackwell—vied for legislative seats. County residents vied for local governmental positions. Most of these men were strongly pro-Jackson and, except for the New Yorker James Black, unanimously southern-born. Political and economic competition arose due to conflicting claims and aspirations rather than regional prejudices and political divergence. The foreign-born—for instance, Remann, Sonnemann, Steinhauer, and Dieckmann—seemed to assimilate well into Vandalia society, perhaps because of the hospitableness of native-born settlers. Although some conflict and local gossip occurred among Ernst colonists and local native-born, in general the groups worked together toward common civic goals, and some intermarried. The Ernst colony dissolved, after all, through death and internal discord rather than regionalism.

That perception of hospitableness may or may not reflect a nostalgic desire to conceal hostilities and conflict. As a source of symbolic meaning, the first generation of settlers captured the imagination and admiration of later generations. "A spirit of concord and harmony, quite in keeping with the beauty of the surrounding landscape, seems to pervade [one township's] precincts. . . . By their strong arms the forests were felled, the tangled undergrowth cleared away, the stubborn glebe broken, and the primitive cabin, school-house and church erected."[16] Only occasionally do these ringing words commemorate a solitary woodsmen. James Hall's Pete Featherton—the man who (when drunk) was "bold and self-satisfied," "the best man in the country," and "could whip his weight in wild cats"—embodies the older "democratic" concept of the rugged loner who came West. But evidence indicates that groups of friends or extended families more often traveled together and settled a town or rural area in proximity. Having provided mutual support during the emigration, people continued to do so in material and spiritual ways and to provide hospitality for travelers and foreigners once they established their proximate homes and farms.

The presence of friendship groups and extended families around Vandalia and county neighborhoods suggests that the *mentalité* of county residents included the values of the linear family, which could include a rather large number of children, siblings and other kin, rather than the single person or the conjugal unit. If this larger family unit was typical, the hierarchy of power and economy grew from the man's legal ownership of the property, his labor (whether he worked a farm or operated a business), the woman's labor to maintain the household (a year-round task, whereas a farmer's labor was seasonal), and the children's ability to work until they attained maturity and could finally support their aged parents. Such a social structure among Fayette County farmers would have closely tied economic betterment with parental values, family consciousness with production, and might have encouraged (along with the similar geographic nativity of settlers) a deeply imbeded social conservatism among county residents. That familial conservatism would have been mitigated by the homogeneity of a male-dominated, white society. As one historian writes, "Linear family values did not constitute, by any means, the entire world view—the *mentalité*—of the agricultural population, but they did define a central tendency of that consciousness, and abiding core of symbolic and emotive meaning; and most important of all, they constituted a significant and reliable guide to behavior amid the uncertainties of the world."[17] The consciousness of settlers would thus have centered primarily around those family values, and around the larger issues of community involvement and community survival insofar as these issues affected the family. That granted, conflict of a violent, regional source would have been less common in Vandalia.

Men of the era were usually the wage earners, and only white males over twenty-one could vote. Men fought: the war with Britain from 1812 to 1815 was fresh in most people's minds, and military experience honored a man seeking election to office. Service in the Revolutionary War likewise gained respect for the aged veterans who lived in Fayette County, fourteen of whom are known and commemorated with a bicentennial courthouse monument. Although its utility was sometimes questioned, participation in the state militia was also conceived by some as a badge of honorable manhood. A Central Illinois farmer noted that local companies were closely "interwoven with the social life of the community." Two companies of Fayette County men rode off to fight in the ignominious Black Hawk War of 1832, under the leadership of William L. D. Ewing, John Dement, and Samuel Houston, a local man related to the famous Texan of the same name. Whether Fayette County men gained rank in the federal armed forces or the state militia, most prominent Vandalia men held the same rank. The merchant Charles Prentice's son remembered: "The male population of Vandalia, thirty years ago, was made up almost exclusively of gentlemen of a military mind. And the rank to which all seem to aspire and attain was that of Colonel. If there was a Major in town I failed to make his acquaintance.

We had two Captains,—Captain Eccles and Captain Linn, but, as all old settlers know, Captain Linn was a steamboat captain, and not a military captain,—and not, therefore, subject to 'the articles of war,' as was the balance of gentlemen in town."[18]

Depending upon his ambitiousness and need (travelers through Illinois commented on some men's extreme inertia), the man of a family might spend his day farming or hunting, stacking hay, thining corn, coaxing stubborn wheat to grow, removing small trees and bushes around fence rows or from ground to be planted, or he would plow fields with homemade or patent plows, keeping them cleaned of mud and grass. In the fall came hunting. "Almost every citizen made hunting his main business in the fall," wrote Governor John Reynolds, "by which he added considerable to the support of himself and family." Deer, fowl, bear, and rabbit were among the hunter's kills, obtained for immediate consumption or for storage with salt or in a smokehouse; buffalo and elk were plentiful only during the very earliest years of settlement. Single-trigger rifles of .30 or .45 caliber were less common among hunters after the 1820s, when double-trigger rifles became popular. Even locally crafted guns of scrap iron were costly at $25 to $40, but it was a necessary expense, not only for hunting but also for protection against hostile persons. "Probably he has killed more deer, turkeys, coons, foxes, &c., than any other man in the counties," it was said of the Sefton township settler Abraham Sidwell. "He has swam the Kaskaskia River many times while in pursuit of game, even in winter, when the ice floes were thick."[19]

A local farmer's stock would include cattle, sheep, or hogs. John Thompson, an English-born settler who came to Fayette County in 1844, purchased three hundred sheep in Cincinnati and recalled the effort needed to get them to Fayette County, where his family had already arrived. "It took us a month and a half to drive them through, and we landed in Vandalia over the Old National Road the first of July. I remember the bottom east of Vandalia was almost knee deep in mud at this time. We stayed all night with old Paddy Thompson, who kept a tavern, and put our sheep in his lot. The only sheep we lost was at Terre Haute; when we went to load them on the ferry boat, a man hit one of them on the head and killed it." John Thompson also recalled that his father traded a number of the sheep for thirty acres, and another portion for rails to fence them in. "The sheep were valued at a dollar a head, and three of them bought a thousand rails." Breed was rarely a consideration when a person obtained cattle or sheep—"Our husbandry is yet in a rude state," James Hall wrote in 1830—but new varieties were occasionally introduced around Vandalia. Ferdinand Ernst brought the first imported English-bred cattle to Fayette County, while another German, Augustus Snyder, brought the first Durhams. Most farmers could not afford or did not bother with well-bred or full-blooded stock. According to a contemporary historian, an 1835 Illinois law designed to improve cattle breeds in Illinois proved politically fatal to several general assembly members. The furor reflected both the common man's disinterest in agricultural excellence and the settler's petulant laissez-faire mentality.[20]

Although many settlers lived at a bare-subsistence level, others were remembered for their industry and success in the face of difficult odds. "Every man," wrote a Fayette County historian, "who has, by self-denial, energy and industry, risen from poverty to a position of prominence, is beyond question one whose life is worth perusing." John Enochs was typical. A native of Waterloo, Illinois, a son of southern-born parents, Enochs came to Vandalia in 1820, when he was twenty-six and already twice widowed, and set up a carpentry business. He subsequently served in respected county offices like sheriff, justice of the peace, and county treasurer; he was sheriff when two men were convicted of crimes punishable by "stripes," which he administered. Enochs, who was still alive when the first county history appeared in 1878, was "a man who started life with nothing but good health, willing hands, good morals, and a strong determination to succeed, and has gained by his industrious and persevering habits a competency; and for his manliness and honesty, a life of honor."[21]

Vandalia traditions rarely laud women with comparable eloquence—or even mention them—except as wives of sterling men. Glenda Riley identifies four stereotypical typologies of pioneer women: "(1) the Calamity Jane, (2) the sex object, (3) the frontier suffragist, and (4) the saint in the sunbonnet." Vandalia records do not indicate the presence of female outlaws in town, nor women of vocal political zeal. If the capital had prostitutes, not surprisingly the boosteristic primary sources and county histories do not mention them. The stereotype of the frontier woman with flowing calico dress, sunbonnet, and a horde of children is perpetuated by Vandalia's Madonna of the Trail statue erected in 1928 to commemorate the National Road. Many women fit this category, but individual cases offset the stereotype. Wives of state officials, for example, often came to Vandalia to observe the legislative proceedings and attend functions at the capital. While some women dressed in calico and sunbonnet, others shopped for better fashions advertised by Vandalia stores. At least one Vandalia woman, Mrs. Scantland, operated her own clothing business. Although some women were wholly dependent upon their husbands, some were widows who emigrated with their children from Ohio or Kentucky, unneedful of male protection. Not all remarried. Mrs. Thompson was one widowed settler. A Virginia native of English ancestry, she came to rural Vandalia about 1819 and established a farm with her children. Frederick Hollman mentions her as a friend of the German colony, and he married her daughter, Martha. Little else is known of her, even her full name, except that her son Benjamin Ward Thompson was a renowned pioneer of Fayette County.[22]

Isabella Bond McLaughlin and (as her name is spelled in the earliest records) Mariane Ernst were two of Vandalia's most intelligent and respected women. Unfortunately little is known of their lives and personalities. McLaughlin was characterized as "a woman of remarkable vigor and force of character." She was a niece of Governor Bond and married to merchant and politician Robert; a portrait attributed to James W. Berry shows an attractive, elegantly dressed woman. The 1878 county history says of Isabella: "While taking a lively interest in the affairs of the day in which her husband and relatives bore such a conspicuous part, she also cultivated those feminine graces that made her one of the most popular and beloved women at the capital." County histories' glowing descriptions of pioneer's personalities are usually more nostalgic than factual, and this account praises her for a subservient role. Perhaps McLaughlin, the life-partner of Vandalia's richest man, was indeed a force behind his successes and a well-liked hostess at their large downtown home. Had she been able to vote and serve office, her political and economic savvy might have been applied more fully than simply to help Robert.[23]

Mariane Ernst, who later became "Mary Ann," was thirty-five in 1820, the year she came to Vandalia, and seven years older than Isabella. Born and raised in the kingdom of Hanover, she shared a large farm there with her husband Ferdinand before they emigrated to Illinois. Life in Vandalia was apparently neither happy nor prosperous. After Ferdinand's death she did not remarry, she suffered the uncertainties of probate, and her own estate was negligable. What was life in Vandalia like for a German-speaking widow who had to force the just acquisition of her husband's property? All that is known is one German traveler's comment that she attained a position of leadership among those Ernst colonists who remained in Vandalia.[24]

Fayette County families lived up to twenty miles from the capital. Once Illinois entered the union, legislative and local interest resulted in establishment of better highways. Traveling to Vandalia from the county was undoubtedly inconvenient, however, due to time-consuming farm labor and inconsistently repaired roads. Jeremiah Evans, a Bear

Grove settler, established his own blacksmith stand because he did not have time to let a Vandalian do the work. When county settlers did ride into town, they did so for a number of reasons: to obtain goods and sell or exchange their produce; to attend organizational meetings, commemorative dinners, and social occasions; or to obtain services such as blacksmith work if they could not perform the tasks themselves. One apparently common reason was to participate in the settlement of an estate or to bid at an auction. Estate records list the names of settlers like Ezra Griffith, Thomas A. Gatewood, Paul Beck, and others who lived several miles from Vandalia but who frequently took part in probate administrative duties, crying at estate sales, or bidding on a deceased person's property. One might buy a promissory note from the decedent's estate and attempt to regain the debt for himself, a relatively easy way to obtain some cash.[25]

People rode to town to attend land sales. In 1819 the federal government set off the Vandalia land district at the center of Illinois, with an office at the capital. As auction day drew near, land officers widely publicized the date and location of the sale and advertised tracts for sale. Vandalia's boardinghouses and hotels soon filled with men interested in buying tracts, and men rode into town to purchase the tract on which their improvements were already built. But a land sale might also encourage settlers to stay home. Fayette County had its share of squatters, as well as those who exploited the government's liberality toward land purchasers.[26]

By caring for children, preparing food, ploughing recalcitrant soil, raising stock, and riding into town people passed the time. They spent the time with household and economic duties, and spent seasons without mechanical heat and coolness. They spent the time and refreshed themselves in familiar, sometimes primitive, surroundings of log or lumber. Without highly accurate timepieces, with hearth clocks and pocket watches prone to running down, with local clocks varying perhaps as much as a half an hour, people estimated time, measuring the days by light and darkness, by the position of the sun, by particular days, by the cycle of weather-related illness, and by the feel of the air as seasons changed, rather than by specific hours. Although mail (which came to the post office, not to homes) was scheduled by hours, high water and unfriendly weather made even this an irregular way to measure the time.[27]

The time was also paced by events like marriages. Among county families, almost no one stayed single very long. Within just a few months of their arrival, several Germans under Ernst's leadership married other colonists or American-born Vandalians. Young women usually married before they were twenty, and bachelorhood past twenty-five was deemed unusual. Recorded instances of men and women living together unwed are extremely rare. As if to provide a moral against fornication, the county histories' sole account of such cohabitation includes the woman's murder by the man, and the fact that his execution was in 1842 the first hanging in the county.[28]

Time was paced by births and by deaths. Couples often had many children, but not all children survived infancy. Some women were not strong enough to bear many offspring or survive serious illness, and a man might outlive two or three spouses. Reminiscences of settlers like Enochs provide this impression in lieu of mortality figures. George Leidig of the Ernst colony became a widower very soon after moving to Vandalia; Robert Blackwell, Leidig's fellow Vandalia merchant and newspaperman, survived two spouses.[29] In many families, however, the husband was more prone to dangerous sickness than the wife and to the risks of working land for hours. When a husband died, male-dominated historiography took over: a young son, thrown upon his own resources, would set to work, achieving his own fortune and education. The woman's plight or success is rarely documented. When Frederick Remann's father died shortly after the Ernst colony's arrival, the fifteen-year-old Remann "by his own indefatigable industry . . . succeeded in acquiring a good practical education" and achieved prosperity in later life through his Vandalia and Hagerstown businesses. Benjamin Ward Thompson, who went by his middle name, lost his father at age twelve. Ward consequently worked hard against this disadvantage, and "the fact of his having so repeatedly been elected to important positions is the best commentary that can be passed upon his life and character as a man and citizen." Another Ernst colonist, Augustus Snyder, was sixteen when his father Emanuel died; he soon worked in "hewing out his own fortune," did farm work, attended school for just three months, and left a sizable farm just northwest of Vandalia.[30]

When death occurred, a family usually would not ride to Vandalia for the burial. Vandalia's old graveyard must have aroused a dreaded feeling in the 1820s and 1830s, when horse-drawn wagons carried pine or oak caskets down Edwards or Second streets to the hill. Settlers of the county often buried their dead on their own property or in small family burying grounds, depending on where the person died and if weather conditions allowed for the body's transportation. For instance, Ward Thompson is buried at Vandalia; his wife Susanna is buried eight miles from town. Many of the small graveyards of Fayette County began when an infant or child died, or when a transient died and was interred by a farmer on his property, and within a few years other burials were made in the same small place.[31]

The time was paced by seasons of particular sickness. Some months of the year, especially those when disease-carrying insects became common, brought about certain fevers. Vandalia was probably an unusually healthy town; only one local woman (away from town at the time) succumbed to the dreadful cholera epidemic of 1833, a fact exploited by boosteristic Vandalia editors. But the nature of germs, the transmission of diseases, and vaccinations were revelations of a later time; some dangerous ailments, like typhoid, had not yet been documented. Even if dangerously ill, a person typically would not ride to town to consult a physician. Physicians, who often rode to see patients rather than vice versa, were poorly equipped to give effective treatment, let alone provide preventative medicine. People more often relied on home remedies and patent medicines instead of calling a doctor and treated ailments like fevers and ague with what now seems to be reckless disregard for health, for example, pouring cold water on a naked fever victim in the midst of winter. Tom Higgins, an early settler, once removed a bullet from his own leg with a razor rather than pay a physician. Given this situation, people feared early death and tried to take often ignorant precautions against it. One Vandalia man was paid in 1849 to burn the garments and fumigate the home of a smallpox victim, for fear of the disease spreading through town. In one Fayette County graveyard two children, smallpox victims, were buried several yards from other graves for fear of transmission of the disease.[32]

The time was also paced by great events of the past: the day when the family received a land patent from the U.S. government, the day of a local execution (a hanging in Springfield in the 1830s became a moorage in time there), or a particularly savage bout of weather. The famous 1830 "Deep Snow," which paralyzed life in many parts of Illinois, killing livestock and marooning people in their cabins, was one example of natural savagry. Especially vociferous political campaigns, like the gubernatorial race of 1830, also became references in time.[33]

But the time was also spent at quiltings, shooting matches, fights, gander pullings, horse races, leap frog, and town ball. Because very few settlers attended church, congregational activities figured far less frequently in people's social life. They did turn out for July 4 celebrations, even in towns with a very quiet summer civic life. Settlers gathered around hotel tables or in groups beneath shady trees, ate roasted food, listened to leaders read the Declaration of Independence, and offered toasts:

James M. Duncan: *The New Convention*—as it has been said, so let it be done.

Robert Blackwell: *The Convention*—To be or not to be, that is the question.

Capt. Waggeman: *My adopted county*—Where the rights of man are respected and made the basis of her government.

John Baugh: *The Clay of Kentucky*—The richest paint for the Presidential chair.

Abraham Starnes: *The People of the State of Illinois—Attention!* By solid columns for the Convention, march. [Yankee doodle][34]

People gathered for levees, "chicken," "I spy," "slap jack," and corn huskings. One traveler described an Illinois husking: "Yells of defiance, mingled with whoops and yells in Indian style, arose in one continued medley, and reverberated far through the woods, whilst an unceasing shower of corn streamed through the air . . . many of the ears flying wide the mark, and one now and then making a dubious tangential movement, which brought it into contact with a body of some unlucky wight."[35] And people gathered for singing and one French custom, "shiverees." At least once at Vandalia (and probably more often) a crowd banged their homemade instruments—cow bells, tin horns, pans, and drums—through the streets and "honored" a newly married or engaged couple with this boisterous epithalamion:

"Charivary!"
"Pour qui?"
"Pour Monsieur ———— [the groom], il est marie!"
"Avec qui?"
"Avec Mademoisle ———— [the bride], charivary!"

The crowd then sang the tune "Charivary" while beating their instruments. Afterward the groom had to treat "the whole populace rag, tag, and bobtail!"[36]

Benjamin Mahon was one of the few Fayette County settlers whose county biography included his propensity for fun. A hard-shell Baptist preacher whose yearly itinerary was legendary, a writer said of "Old Ben," "He is a fine specimen of the pioneer preacher; a rough diamond, loving his joke, but a kind Christian gentleman." The reference to his joyfulness is very quick, but it alludes to the fact that not all of frontier life was "self-denial, energy, and industry."[37]

These things—social events, July 4 toasts, spontaneous sing-alongs—typified community (what social historians have called *Gemeinschaft*) in and around Vandalia. Competition, on a political and economic level, certainly existed. But once the evidence is examined and qualified, the homogeneity, the self- and kin-centered worldview, and economic family-orientation of new settlers in Vandalia and Fayette County predominate.

"Wilderness, once the chosen residence of solitude or savageness, converted into populous cities, smiling vilages, beautiful farms and plantations!" wrote a newspaper writer in 1817 of the western territories. Fayette County still provided ample opportunities for solitude or savageness, but it did have a number of agricultural and small population centers, themselves extensions of the family and clan groups. Because county settlers lived thirty or more miles from Vandalia, the presence of small satellite economic bases, semi-independent communities of families and friends—like Perryville, Bowling Green, the Hurricane Creek community, Sharon township, Loogootee, Howard's Point, Wilberton, Jones Precinct, the Bear Grove community, and Ewington— indicate the need for proximate community and for stores and businesses in a more convenient location than the capital. This was a boon rather than an economic and social risk to Vandalia; Indianapolis, founded two years after Vandalia, was unpopular as a state capital because it was too far removed from any population.[38]

Contrary to William Oliver's dismissal of such towns as "a store and a spirit shop," many were active centers. (Oliver was, however, advised not to spend the night at Ewington.) Except for Shobonier and St. Elmo (both dating from after the capital period), however, few survived into the twentieth century because of insufficient industry for long-term survival. Perryville's village life succumbed quickly when the county seat moved in 1821; Independence and Pope's Bluff probably had little trade if any. Another village in the Vandalia area was Wilberton, called "Frogtown" because of the creatures that lived in the nearby ponds. The town, laid out in 1826, had about a hundred people and a small number of downtown establishments. Howard's Point, a minor village near the present St. Elmo, began as a store for the benefit of National Road workers who roomed in Vandalia; it too did not long survive. Ewington, named for William L. D. Ewing, was, like Perryville, a bustling county town in Effingham County until the seat was moved elsewhere. The first town called Loogootee was founded as Hickory Creek Post Office in 1836. Established as a tavern near the Vandalia-Vincennes road eleven years before, Loogootee (in the "middle Frogtown" area) became a sizeable residential area with lumber and flour mills, professional offices, and commerce. "Old" Loogootee disappeared when residents moved closer to the railroad; the newer village still survives as primarily a residential settlement.[39]

These early towns' legacies include popular appellations, family histories, and the most folklore of Vandalia's region. The name Frogtown survives in modern Vandalia vocabulary as the vanished town's vicinity, as does "Slabtown," the nickname for Loogootee and its mill's slabs of lumber. Otego township, with its Four Mile Prairie and the residence of prominent Vandalian John A. Wakefield, obtained its name from the New York area of some settlers' births. Bear Grove township contained groves where bears wandered; Pope township is the location of Pope's Bluff. Wheatland township takes its name from the area's propensity for growing wheat, a difficult crop to start. The Kaskaskia's several small tributaries, along which small settlements existed, were named during this early period: Hurricane Fork, Ramsey, Boaz, Beck, Hickory, and Big creeks.[40]

A small settlement south of Vandalia and west of the present Shobonier included the homes of Lemuel Lee's descendents. The extended Lee family arrived near Vandalia about the time of its founding; brother Abisha died soon after, but brothers Lemuel and Harvey operated an mill along the Kaskaskia. The sons ("sons" again) of Lemuel Lee, a veteran of "the late war," are said to have settled south of Vandalia along the Kaskaskia River and established sizable farms. The Evans family, which included a nineteenth-century Vandalia sheriff and later a twentieth-century hotel owner and benefactor, originally settled in the Bear Grove community. As has generally been true, a number of prominent Vandalia persons lived in the county areas. In addition to the Lees, Evanses, and Wakefields, Ferdinand and Mary Ann Ernst also lived outside the capital's city limits. Several men who served in local elective office—Paul Beck, Thomas R. Gatewood, Jeremiah's son Akin Evans, John Whitley, and others—were county rather than city residents.[41]

Although Fayette County is not a rich mine for parochial folklore and illustrative tales, the extraordinary—for example, the exploits of settlers like Tom Higgins and associations with notables like Lincoln— earned preservation and elaboration. Some of the lore concerns these outlying areas beyond Vandalia's limits. Higgins, for instance, was undoubtedly a remarkable fellow. A physically powerful man, an occasional minor official for the state government at Vandalia, and possibly a dangerous bully, he and his family came to the county in 1816 along with the Brazel family and settled in what is now Ramsey township north of Vandalia. Fond stories abound concerning his physical prowess and his reckless courage: that he survived a brutal Indian attack in 1811 (although one contemporary seriously doubted the facts of the account); that he chewed up shot glasses in Vandalia grog shops; and that he loved to fight and once planned a duel so that his opponent would be frightened away but not hurt or killed.[42]

The fact that county histories like Fayette's and Bond's record several tales of violence and death modifies the thesis that such histories are primarily boosteristic in intent. Such stories made for entertaining and easily recalled historical material, at the risk of providing an impression of soradic violence and viligantism in the county. According to one history, in 1820 a certain man caught horse stealing was taken to Perryville, tied to a tree and whipped, then driven out of the area. He then stole a horse at Vandalia and headed for Indiana, where he was finally overtaken and shot. Loogootee men captured two other horse thieves and promptly hanged them from a wild cherry tree; they were then "quietly buried beneath the tree by the calm, stern settlers who considered the whole matter a well-performed duty." The county histories have several stories of first township instances of violent death and unsolved murders. Such occurrences were probably not common; Vandalia's local newspaper editors almost never reported such events.[43]

More tenacious and apocryphal are tales of dignitaries associated with Vandalia and the county. Who originated the tales is unknown, probably the first or second generation of settlers, but descendents elaborated on the stories. For example, it is said that Lafayette stopped overnight at the Loogootee hotel when he was en route to Vandalia in 1825, although he did not come within a hundred miles of Vandalia during his American visit that year. It is also said that Lincoln stepped upon certain large stone near Loogootee when dismounting his horse, although one wonders why Lincoln was traveling several miles southeast of Vandalia during the busy legislative sessions. People were proud to have been associated in some way with Lincoln, even if the association was simply that of his proximity. Lemuel Lee's hotel on Gallatin Street was supposedly Lincoln's lodging place for a short time. The German immigrant Augustus Snyder remembered that he knew Lincoln in the Black Hawk War, and that Lincoln "could dust the back of any man in the regiment." A legend persists that Stephen Douglas rode a donkey up the steps of the third Vandalia statehouse in celebration of a democratic victory. The story has not been substantiated, but such an act would have been within Douglas's often boisterous nature.[44]

Structures, too, became subject of folklore. "There can yet [in 1878] be seen some of the primary cabins, and the remains of others, standing as relics of the past." The settler George Washington Jackson's log cabin, which still stood in Ramsey township in 1939, was said to have been a hiding place for Lincoln. This particular house attracted still another story that reflects later generations' romantic ideas about frontier life.

The legend that Lincoln jumped from a Vandalia statehouse window, although easily discredited, has long been known to Fayette Countians and thousands of tourists (chapter 9). According to one story, after his jump Lincoln walked sixteen miles north of Vandalia and concealed himself at the farmer's "humble log hut." "There is a legend that it was originally constructed by Indians, who at that period roamed the hills and angled for fish and hunted game down there in 'the sticks' of what is now Fayette County."[45]

Rather than crude fabrications, such stories reflect the symbolic quality that individuals like Lincoln, Douglas, Lafayette, and local rowdy, Higgins, made upon the identity and self-consciousness of persons from Vandalia and Fayette County. Most Vandalians today know at least one of these stories. Such legends verify the observation of one county historian: "There will always attach an interest to the history of the pioneer families of the West, which can never properly belong to others who came at a later date, as they have laid the foundation of our social and material status."[46]

This interest was, like other towns, an example of "parochial localism." When recorded, it was boosteristic and nostalgic. All the men of Fayette County were industrious and self-made; all the family groups were virtuous and harmonious; all the women were hard-working and good mothers; all overcame hardships through energy and perseverance. Conflict rarely occurred in those early days. The settlers gave honor to Vandalia through their strength, selflessness, and moral character.[47]

Unlike some other towns, however, Vandalia's local history does not seem to be the "inversion of boosterism," but rather of anamnesis. In the Old Testament, the Hebrew *zakar* can mean to remember something in order to provide direction or action: God "remembers" His covenant, acting in conformity to it. Although Vandalia failed to become a satisfactory and lasting state capital, it did not have the urban disappointments of, for instance, Jacksonville. In Jacksonville, "small-town failure" was portrayed in local histories as "chosen success." Vandalia's self-consciousness seems always to have been that of a small town, even as state capital, a town that grew slowly but steadily in population and industry from the 1850s through the 1960s. Therefore, when Vandalia's nineteenth-century historians portrayed the past with glowing nostalgia, the motive seems less that of civic failure (as in Jacksonville's case) than of a remembering the history for the sake of determining genuine small-town progress and community. The superior character of the first generation were seen as confirming, foreshadowing, and determining the progress of Vandalia by the late 1800s and early 1900s.[48]

Why some traditions were remembered and others were not remains an ultimately unanswerable question. Understandably, Lincoln, Lafayette, and relics of the past like log cabins were remembered. Somehow, Mary Ann Ernst, the Polish settlers of Vandalia, and, if true, an earlier French settlement of the Vandalia region were forgotten. The answer may be that later generations recalled their own. To borrow another biblical term, the Greek *mnemoneuein* means both to recollect the past and to center recollection on a certain person or thing, making beneficial mention of them (e.g., in prayer, or to "remember the poor of Jerusalem"). A similar thing happened in the writing of Fayette County's past in the concomitant process of recalling history in light of small-town industriousness. In the old county histories of Fayette County, both the present and future progress of Vandalia and the deferred remembrance involved in genealogy won the day. Direct forebears were remembered and honored in the remembering, but at the expense of whomever's descendents were unavailable for interview. Five and six generations later, historians still depend upon those recollections and still accord the honor.

4

High on the
Okaw's Western Bank

No contemporary drawings or written descriptions of early Vandalia's downtown are known to exist; the earliest photographs of
Vandalia buildings date from the 1860s or later.[1] Fortunately, advertisements in local newspapers and contemporary statements on local
economy, along with material from state and county histories and other
sources, contribute toward a composite picture of the state capital.[2]

Except for brick state buildings, Vandalia's downtown structures were
probably small frame buildings; no Vandalia building, even the third
statehouse at the corner of Gallatin and Third streets, impressed contemporary writers as special. Sidewalks were dirt paths or plank walk-
ways shaded by second-story porches.[3] Most businesses stood upon two
parallel west-east streets, Main and Gallatin, and on Third through
Sixth streets between the two; since the early 1820s most major businesses have stood along Gallatin rather than Main.[4] Vandalia's geography provides a striking view of the downtown. One may stand on
the hill at Seventh Street, above modern Vandalia's businesses, and look
down as Gallatin Street slopes gently east toward the Kaskaskia River
and as the tilled flatlands stretch out in a rural panorama. Transposing
the view to the 1820s and 1830s, one imagines a striking setting for
the capital even if Vandalia's frontier buildings were nondescript.

During the capital era, Vandalia had several hotels and boardinghouses for state officials and visitors—more than enough for any other
town of approximately eight hundred persons, but the crowds were too
great to be accommodated well. For instance, the editor John York
Sawyer reviewed local hotels in 1834 and concluded, "we trust the old

complaint of want of room will no longer be heard in Vandalia." Just four months later, a Beardstown, Illinois, editor wrote that the capital was "crowded to excess. . . . The number of applications for doorkeeper and clerks of the different Houses [of the legislature] is [itself] truly astonishing."[5] Vandalia's lodging places included a hotel owned by John McCullom, one of Vandalia's first settlers, who may or may not have been in collusion with a gang of thieves.[6] Other hotel owners were men from other towns like the attorney and legislator Thomas Cox and Edmund Tunstall, the Carmi man who constructed the first statehouse.[7]

The most important hotels were proximate to the capitol buildings. McCullom's hotel, Daniel Bathrick's Sign of the Bell, and Hollman's Columbian Hotel, along with some others, all stood near the first statehouse. Ferdinand Ernst's Union Hotel, which remained in operation during the capital period and stood until the twentieth century, was, at Third and Main, a longer walk away from that first capitol at Fifth and Johnson. Near the second and third statehouses stood McLaughlin's National Hotel on Third Street (taken over by John N. Johnson in 1834), Scantland's Sign of the Globe on Gallatin between Third and Fourth, Thompson's Tavern at Third and Gallatin, John Charter's (and later Thomas Redmond's) Sign of the Green Tree Hotel at Fourth and Gallatin, and Abner Flack's Vandalia Hotel (cater-cornered from Redmond's).[8] Flack, who came to the capital during the 1830s, hosted many receptions and parties at his Gallatin Street tavern. According to tradition, Lincoln attended a dance there; the shy young man awkwardly danced with a woman but stepped on her dress and tore it.[9] By the later 1830s at least thirteen lodging places operated in Vandalia.

In these hotels, state legislation was argued, planned, and written up for presentation; presumably the Illinois governors themselves stayed in these hotels and plotted course.[10] Unfortunately, legends about Lincoln's dancing ability, rather than boardinghouse conversations and political debates among statesmen, have been passed down. Local operators sang praises of their hotel's food and liquor, rather than of their crowded and cold rooms. Owen Kellogg proclaimed his establishment's benefits: "His Table, Bar and Stable will be furnished at all times with the best that the country can afford and the charges will be moderate." Thomas Redmond announced that he had a fine social hall, and that his "Bar will be furnished with the choicest liquors of every kind. His stable is large and extensive . . . constantly furnished with the best Hay, Oats, Corn, and the best of Fodder." William Redmond, perhaps Thomas's son, and George S. Tindal had a "house of General Refreshment in this place, long considered a great desideratum." They promised to serve partridges, prairie chickens, and wild turkeys in season.[11] In 1821 the Fayette County commissioners set local hotel rates at:

> Breakfast or supper, 25 cents.
> Dinner, 37½ cents.
> A night's lodging, 12½ cents
> Horse per night, 50 cents.
> Horse feed, 18¾ cents.
> Half pint of rum, wine or French brandy, 37½ cents.
> Half pint of peach or apple brandy, gin, cordial, or cherry bounce,
>   25 cents.
> Half pint of whiskey, 12½ cents.[12]

Officials and travelers might have met in the hotel's dining room, warmed themselves by the heat of the wood stoves there, and consumed meals of fruit and vegetables stored from the summer, wild or domesticated meat, and fresh pies and bread made by the owner's wife. Most of all, visitors enjoyed the warmth of drinking; there was no distinction between a hotel and a tavern. Places that sold only liquor were "groceries," "dram shops," or "grog shops." In contrast to the brutality of pioneer men at fight or sport, their behavior in places of alcoholic refreshment could be surprisingly affectionate; with their hats pushed back, men sat at the bar, arms around each other's shoulders, having a happy discussion about some legal case or a political issue, or singing tipsily together. James Hall wrote humorously of men's casual relaxation:

> With a coat to my back, that I'm able to pay for
>   Whether specie or paper prevail;
> And a wife who at church, I shall ne'er have to stay for,
>   And a brewer that gives me good ale;
> With a couch to recline on, a valet to wait,
>   And tobacco to puff away sorrow!
> I'd envy not Bony, his honor or state,
>   Nor exchange places with him to-morrow.[13]

Travelers noticed these inebriated gatherings. Edmund Flagg visited the capital in 1836. "As I drew nigh to the huge white tavern," he wrote, "a host of people were swarming the doors and, from certain uncouth noises which from time to time went up from the midst thereof, not an inconsiderable portion of the worthy multitude seemed to have succeeded in rendering themselves gloriously tipsy in honour of the glorious day."[14] One Alton man wrote that professing Christians should pay more attention to the caliber of individuals they elect to the state legislature; Vandalia, he wrote, was in serious need of a temperance speaker.[15]

Besides hotels, the town had a large number of other businesses and services. Several attorneys and physicians practiced at the capital.[16] Blacksmiths' stands operated along Main Street from early morning until late at night, as the capital's blacksmiths repaired or made locks, keys, bells, bits, saws, knives, traps, and gun barrels for customers.[17] The capital had also several grocery and hardware stores on Main and Gallatin streets that the local leaders Robert McLaughlin, William Kinney, Charles Prentice, Clement Fletcher, and Frederick Hollman operated. McLaughlin's niece and nephew, William and Polly Duncan Linn, lived in Vandalia during the capital period. Linn had a store on Fourth and Gallatin and at various times advertised a variety of clothing items, groceries, and hardware. Polly's brother, James M. Duncan, was another Vandalia merchant. During the 1820s and early 1830s he was active in cultural and civic affairs, culminating in his controversial term as cashier at the state bank when, fearing he would become a scapegoat by a legislative investigation, he refused to turn over bank funds to the government. Still another Duncan brother, Yale-educated Matthew, operated a local hotel and was remembered for his "fund of anecdotes [which were] inexhaustible as the sources of the Mississippi" and "his eccentricities [which] would have thrown gravity itself into fits."[18]

"He is a general locum tenens, the agent of everybody!" wrote a Missouri settler of a western merchant. "And familiar with every transaction in his neighborhood. He is a counselor without license, and yet invariably consulted, not only in matters of business, but in domestic affairs. . . . Every item of news, not only local, but from a distance—as he is frequently the postmaster, and the only subscriber to the newspaper—has general dissemination from his establishment, as from a common center; and thither all resort, at least once a week, both for goods and intelligence."[19] Nineteen-year-old Charles Prentice arrived at Vandalia in 1819. He worked as a clerk and bought out his business partner's interest a few years later. He apparently came to Vandalia alone and had no ties in town other than his wife and children. Prentice was unusual among successful entrepreneurs in that he was not a whig, but an active and vocal democrat. Did people gather round him for advice and information? Was he one of Vandalia's most popular individuals? Little is known about Prentice. When he died in 1837, his estate included a sizeable wardrobe, fur and silk hats, equestrian paraphernalia, valuable candlesticks, dishes, and many other items including portraits of Jackson and Van Buren (both purchased by another local merchant). Upon his death the Vandalia whig editor William Hodge reported sweeping East Coast whig victories and then irreverently proclaimed, "COL. PRENTICE, LET OFF YOUR THUNDERCLOUD!"[20]

John A. Wakefield, an early settler of the Vandalia area, ran for the state legislature from Fayette County in 1822, 1824, and 1826, winning a seat in 1824. His history of the Black Hawk War became one of the first accounts of that conflict. (Illinois State Historical Society)

Joseph Duncan, congressman from 1827 to 1834 and Illinois' sixth governor (1834–38). His brothers, James M. Duncan and Matthew Duncan, and his brother-in-law William Linn, were Vandalia businessmen. During his gubernatorial administration, and against his advice, the legislature initiated the multi-million-dollar internal improvements program. (Illinois State Historical Society)

William Walters edited Vandalia's *Illinois State Register* in 1836, following the death of John York Sawyer. A Vandalia editor until 1839, Walters became one of the state's principal spokesmen for the western style of Jacksonian democracy. (Illinois State Historical Society)

William H. Brown, a Vandalia resident during the capital era, edited the *Illinois Intelligencer* during the infamous Third General Assembly. He left that editorship during the height of the convention controversy. Interested in Vandalia's cultural activities during the 1820s and 1830s, Brown later became the Chicago Historical Society's president. (Illinois State Historical Society)

Shadrach Bond was the first governor of Illinois and the namesake of the county in which Vandalia was founded in 1819. This portrait may have been painted by James W. Berry. (Illinois State Historical Society)

"Plan of the City of Vandalia, Seat of the Government of the State of Illinois" was included in Ferdinand Ernst's *Observations on a Journey through the Interior of the United States of America in the Year 1819*. (Illinois State Historical Society)

Thomas Cox was a Union County attorney and legislator at the time of Illinois statehood. One of the five elected commissioners who selected the site of Vandalia, he operated a hotel there for a time and eventually moved to Iowa, where he was instrumental in establishing another state capital, Iowa City. (State Historical Society of Iowa)

Frederick and Martha Hollman, in an 1839 portrait. Hollman, the associate of Ferdinand Ernst, helped provide homes and quarters for Ernst's German colony in 1819 and 1820. Martha Hollman was a member of the Thompson family who settled the Vandalia vicinity about 1816. (Courtesy Elona Kindschi)

James Hall resided in Vandalia from 1827 to 1833. During those years he devoted himself to a variety of literary and cultural efforts that made him the foremost literary spokesman of the early West. (Illinois State Historical Society)

"Vandalia in 1836" by John Matthew Heller (detail). Dedicated in 1954 and destroyed in 1969, the painting authentically depicts the capital's downtown. (Illinois State Historical Society)

The earlist known photograph of the Vandalia statehouse. The undated picture, probably taken during the 1870s, is a carte-de-visite ("visiting card") photograph, a popular style so named because of the small size of each print. (Historic Vandalia Museum)

The third Vandalia Statehouse as it appears today. (Vandalia Leader-Union)

Any legislator or local citizen walking into Prentice's or McLaughlin's or Linn's or Fletcher's stores would at once be struck with a variety of sensations: the sudden change of light from the bright outdoors to the window- or candle-lit interior; aromas of perspiration, wood and wick smoke, whiskey and tobacco, and from the outside, animal and out-house odors. Here, people gained local news, gossip, farm reports, and political events. Items like camrick, calico, cloths of several kinds and styles, harnesses, sickles, combs, utensils, blades and scissors, seeds, fire-arms and ammunition, saddles, and ox yokes lay on the high shelves. On other shelves one would find bacon, butter, eggs and flour for baking, vegetables, hops, lard, tallow, wax, and hides. Because nearly every shop-keeper had a liquor license, regular customers could expect a drink, served from the bottle or one of the barrels of spirits against the wall.[21]

Other Vandalia businesses included Mr. Ross's hatting business, Dyer and Myer's tailoring firm, Tilghman Wright's boot and shoe-making business on Main Street near the river, and, for a short period, a brewery. According to contemporary accounts, Vandalia was among the leading communities in the state in the number of small-scale manufacturers, although its totals were far fewer than the larger towns of Central Illinois.[22] The German immigrants of the Ernst colony included mer-chants, butchers, tailors, goldsmiths, and laborers who worked and prac-ticed their trades in their homes, rented quarters, or their own stores. George Leidig advertised a number of imported liquors, as well as "good Kentucky whiskey" at his store.[23]

At the eastern edge of town, Ferdinand Ernst, Lemuel Lee, and Moss Botsford operated mills along the winding Kaskaskia. Ernst's mill was 38 feet long, 16 feet wide, with one eight-foot story and a large carriage wheel turned by the river waters. Such a mill, said the builder Moss Twiss who was suing Ernst for unpaid debts, cost $1,000 in labor and materials. Lee and his brothers operated mills on the river for several years. A small stream ran diagonally through the northeast portion of town; here Robert K. McLaughlin had a mill in the later 1820s.[24] The fact that Vandalia citizens petitioned the legislature in 1837 for a law relieving them of "clock peddlers" indicates that a certain number of itinerant retailers were common. Books, drugs, shoes, dry goods, hard-ware, clocks, and religious tracts filled their carts. In larger towns like Vandalia where the mercantile community developed more prosperously, these peddlers were less common than in smaller towns.[25] By the late 1820s, several new Vandalia establishments included Claibourne Berry's land agency, Thomas Redmond's new hotel—"convenient to the State-house"—and James Black's market. Black, who lived the rest of his life in Vandalia, came to the capital about 1825 from New York, wearing a very old suit. Mercantile success, however, provided sufficient prosperity to make him known for his excellent clothing tastes.[26] William Kirkman operated a tailoring business, with coats priced at $6, dress coats at $7, and vests and pantaloons at $2 each. The hairdresser John C. Pendergrass promised to yield "the palm of superior skill and excellence to no man, whatever may have been his practice."[27] By 1829, British-born Ebenezer Capps had opened his store at Fourth and Main. Like Prentice, Capps found great success with his Vandalia hardware and grocery store; unlike Prentice, Capps lived long enough (until 1878) to make his business a substantial achievement. The store was well known far outside of Illinois. According to one story, the store's inventory was so complete that two legislators made a bet whether Capps could supply a particularly obscure item: goose yokes. A box was promptly obtained; Capps said he kept them just for legislators.[28]

Besides these downtown business, Vandalia had three state capitol buildings, none of which impressed travelers and visitors (chapter 7). The first statehouse at Fifth and Johnson streets housed the Second and Third General Assemblies. This frame building burned in December 1823. Vandalians constructed a ramshackle brick building—part of which was reconstructed from a fire-gutted bank—near the northwest corner of Fourth and Gallatin to serve as a new capitol building. Through six general assemblies, legislators worked upon sagging floors, within bulging and cracking walls. From 1836 until 1839 the statehouse was a more stately unpainted brick building at the center of the public square facing Gallatin between Third and Fourth. But even this third statehouse was originally not an imposing and ornamental government hall; Vandalia's typicalness as a small frontier village was not mitigated by its state buildings.[29]

Vandalia's everyday character, too, was similar to all frontier towns. Horses stood at the hitching posts or rails along Gallatin, Fourth, and Fifth; horses and wagons traveled the unpaved streets. Small stray farm animals scurried through the streets. The streets were filled with smells of animals' waste, of human waste behind the public buildings, and of stagnant standing water. As in other towns, insects filled the air. "The fall musquitoe," James Hall writes, "is seen only at night . . . is more muscular and sprightly, with a good appetite and sharp teeth; it is also more dissipated, frolicking all night, and sleeping all day."[30] "The whole earth and air seems teeming with . . . mosquitos, gallinippers, bugs, ticks, sand-flies, sweat-flies, house-flies, ants, cockroaches, &c., [which] join in one continued attack against one's ease."[31]

In spite of such unpleasant conditions typical of the era, people gathered in downtown Vandalia to trade, talk, and sit lazily on chairs outside

hotels like McLaughlin's. Downtown Vandalia was probably characterized by the same hospitableness, closeness, and cultural homogeneity
as the county. News in town traveled quickly. Women "evince great
alacrity in attending and sympathizing with the sick, it matters not
whether strangers or friends."[32] Illness elicited helpfulness; a local death
left a perceivable vacuum in the fabric of local life. If someone had a
problem or was (in the language of the day) "uppta somethin'," he or
she could expect it to become public domain. Before 1836, Vandalia's
public square served as a common, grassy and tree-filled space. Locals
played ball, conversed, or danced and sang on the public square.[33] People
talked with accents from Kentucky and Tennessee, northern Germany,
Virginia, and New England. Their small-town talk concerned (again in
the popular language of the day) whoever in town was "tomcattin',"
about "them goll-darned houn' dawgs o' mine," and "d'you heered
'bout the racket over yonder and I guess them folks is all hatefuls an'
if they'r a-lookin' fer trouble they'll shore get a lavish of it." Or, they
talked about some candidate "who'z handsome as a picter [qualified]
but so darnation ugly [wicked]," someone else "who'z a clever [good-
natured] critter," and someone else "who'z right-well thoughted [intelligent]."[34] People discussed state candidates and praised the talents of
popular national leaders.

In winter, state officials, office-seekers, and lobbyists gathered downtown. Social exchanges particularly centered on issues and persons.
"There are no White men [Hugh L. White supporters] here from a
distance," wrote a Springfield correspondent from downtown Vandalia
in December 1835, "while the hotels are lined with ruffle-shirted Vannies [Van Buren supporters]. There is no one here whose sole business
is to puff Judge White; consequently, I seldom hear his name except
when I go among *the people*, where (God be praised!) I hear nothing
else."[35] Not only did people talk politics, but during certain Vandalia
winters they also quarreled openly. One person described a particularly
volatile political winter at Vandalia as "a running to and fro, about the
seat of government by day and night, as can only be equalled by a
swarm of bees when rudely attacked in their hive."[36] "There is great
strife and struggling," wrote Lincoln of another campaign. "[The whigs]
smile as complacently at the angry snarls of contending Van Buren
candidates . . . as the christain does at Satan's rage."[37] A few winters
saw harmonious legislative sessions and uneventful court sessions;
others produced much more contention. "Then peace and quiet reigned
until the next election." Governor Thomas Ford wrote this of political
campaigns in general, but it could also describe what happened at Van-

dalia once the sessions adjourned: from political contention to civic stagnation.[38]

Politics at Vandalia meant something other than discussion and volatility: it meant a seasonal economy. Frederick Hollman remembered that a sharp decrease of trade occurred whenever legislative and court sessions adjourned and nonresident consumers left town.[39] A feast-or-famine trend seems likely. Hollman, however, also remembered that Vandalia's economy was "almost entirely prostrate" in 1822 and following. This view disagrees with that of a contemporary writer, Lewis Caleb Beck, who observed in 1823 that Vandalia contained "about 150 dwelling houses, and 700 inhabitants among which are professional men, and mechanics of every description." Beck's account suggests an amazing rate of initial settlement if Vandalia's economy was "almost entirely prostrate."[40]

Many new businesses, in fact, advertised in the *Intelligencer* up until 1825, when the number of new ads dropped dramatically. Whether the decrease is an accurate indicator of economic decline is debatable; possibly businesses simply failed to advertise. Barber John C. Pendergrass, for instance, only published an advertisement in 1830, although he was still employed in Vandalia in 1838. Ebenezer Capps also seldom advertised in the local papers except for his occasional specials on patent medicines. But a slowing of local economy during the mid-1820s seems likely in light of another contemporary account. An 1834 citizen's committee report states that "the spirited improvement which marked the commencement of this place should have slacked and at least wholly ceased for a time, is what the experienced might have anticipated." Until 1828, Fayette County farms were not yet productive and the surrounding area not settled extensively; the report blamed the lack of county support for the village's decline following initial improvement. But after 1828, farms became productive, and, according to the report, "there has been a steady and healthy improvement which has been annually increasing."[41]

Barter transactions between consumers and producers—a good hog in exchange for blacksmith work, or grain for dress cloth—must have predominated during the capital's first several years; the success of merchants like Prentice was perhaps based upon their shrewd use of barter and informal transaction. The newness of Vandalia's market economy, the shortage of circulating media, and what must have been subsistent county production would also have encouraged many promissory transactions. The note issuance and loan liberality of the first state bank must have assisted and diversified Vandalia's economy; by the mid-

1820s, as the local market developed and as statewide economy suffered, some Vandalia merchants specified cash.

A probable economic decline in Vandalia during the mid-1820s would have been precipitated by two factors. First, the economic malaise following the 1818–19 Panic struck Vandalia late. One land officer wrote in 1819 that the area was the only place where land sales were still brisk. Then, as the shortage of good currency and low agricultural prices took their toll, land sales in the Vandalia area fell off. This could have discouraged establishment of new local businesses and new settlement and trade.[42] Second, the first state bank, authorized by the Second General Assembly, helped and then hurt the economy. Reacting to the adverse economic situation in Southern Illinois, the legislature authorized a state-owned bank. Such a bank, according to prevalent wisdom, would fill the state with badly needed currency. But within a few weeks the bank's notes depreciated to 75 cents on the dollar; a month later they were worth 62.5 cents, and down to 30 cents by 1822. Without sufficient backing in gold, the notes were never destined to remain at par. Certainly the depreciation was disastrous for Vandalia creditors; when Hollman was sued by the Ernst estate for a debt of $400, he testified that dollar notes were so depreciated that he could not afford to make proportionate payment. Ironically, while Vandalia hosted the general assemblies, those assemblies occasionally enacted legislation detrimental to Vandalia as well as other local economies. Legislation focused on relief of debtors rather than long-range solutions. A review of suits brought against debtors in the second circuit court at Vandalia reveals the same situation: thanks to legislative favoritism, creditors had difficulty collecting from debtors. That same relief legislation made payments on Vandalia lots easy to delay. Whereas the state hoped for high yields on Vandalia lots, the government finally lost money on Vandalia as debts were stayed and property values decreased. In 1823 almost $26,000 was still due the state from the September 1819 auction.[43]

In spite of tenuous state economy, Vandalia had a nucleus of permanent businesses: the stores of McLaughlin, Prentice, and Black; the hotels of McLaughlin, Charter, the old Union Hotel, and the Columbian Hotel (renamed the Sign of George Washington). Linn, Leidig, McLaughlin, Dr. R. H. Peebles, Prentice, Robert Blackwell, Henry Snyder, E. C. Berry, James M. Duncan, and William Greenup comprised the core professional community throughout the capital period. Peebles died in 1835, Prentice in 1837, and Linn and probably Duncan moved to Springfield around 1839; the rest stayed in Vandalia after the capital period. The merchantile class, as Lewis Atherton has described it, achieved success as western settlement increased, and the success of these Vandalia businessmen reflected the town's and county's success. Therefore, the apparent economic well-being of men like Black, Prentice, Capps, and McLaughlin tends to substantiate the report that Vandalia's economy rallied by about 1828.

Probate records shed light on these men and their economic worth. McLaughlin, who died in 1862, left an estate of more than $800,000. The capital-era physician Nathaniel M. McCurdy also left a comparably large estate when he died in 1876. These later records are less illustrative than those of Prentice, for instance, whose estate in 1837—more than $4,300—was much greater than that of the well-to-do Ferdinand Ernst's estate appraised fifteen years earlier. Ernst's wealth was both self-made and inherited, whereas Prentice's seems to have been self-made only.[44] Compared to Prentice, the estates of two other Vandalia merchants who also died in 1837 were worth $350 and $328. Fayette County records reveal that Prentice's success was common among Vandalia businessmen. James Black, who died in 1843, left a sizeable estate; Dr. Peebles left money and holdings of about $15,000, worth accounted for by participation in other businesses rather than his medical practice—not a lucrative calling in those days. Hotel owner McCullom left $834.25 "in state paper" and property totalling just under $1,145 when he died in 1823. Not all Vandalia men, of course, achieved prosperity, shown by probate files for less wealthy settlers like Paul Beck, who was inventoried at $78.30, Thomas Higgins at $38.56, editor John York Sawyer at $249.28¾, and the murdered bank cashier James Kelley (p. 92) at $386.25. The quoted figures imply that Vandalia was not so depressed from the seasonal consumption by the state government that men like Capps, Prentice, McLaughlin, Peebles, or Black could not overcome the economic vicissitudes through shrewd use of barter, liberality in note acceptance, or good investments. The figures also imply the obvious; one would not get rich simply by living at the state capital.[45]

Sales of Vandalia's city lots provide an incomplete picture of the tides of local economy, but the deed records do show that Vandalia did not attract great numbers of immigrants. Not surprisingly in view of the 1819 Panic and the extreme slowness of frontier people to purchase improved land, almost no one among the original September 1819 bidders finally obtained deeds; they apparently never paid up. Also not surprisingly, lots in the outlying areas of the original town (blocks 1–16, at North [now Jefferson], St. Clair, and Randolph streets, and blocks 55–62, at Edwards and South streets) were in little demand during the capital period. Lots in the downtown area, especially between Madison and Johnson streets to include Main and Gallatin, saw greater demand and frequent turn-over of ownership. Unreflective of the boom years of land, the peak years of Vandalia lot trading were from about 1828 through 1832, while the slowest years were 1820–22 and 1838–39; meanwhile the county saw a great increase of purchases during Vandalia's initial settlement and during the boom years from 1834 to 1838. Even in 1830, the large sales were more reflective of large property acquisitions by people like the successful businessmen James Whitlock, George Leidig, and Charles Prentice than an influx of new residents.[46]

It is nearly impossible to locate residences of Vandalians during this early period. The only extant tax list for early Vandalia is very short and comprises only the early 1820s. Also, the census records for 1820, 1830, and 1840 do not yet differentiate county and village residents; by the time they do so, the capital period had passed and many new residents had moved to town. The approximate population of Vandalia, too, was also far greater than the numbers of actual land owners listed in deed records, suggesting that property was rented out or that persons squatted on state-owned town lots.[47]

Sales of county land, while behind figures for northerly Illinois counties, continued to rise slightly year by year. While Vandalia merchants and creditors were hurt by the laws benefiting the state's debtors, many Illinois farmers benefited (if unethically) from the situation. In this, Vandalia was typical among other Southern Illinois towns; both town and county experienced slow growth. That typicalness, in turn, hurt the town's reputation as state capital. Travel authors and visiting dignitaries expressed ambivance concerning Vandalia's quality and population.[48] Although some authors expressed displeasure at Vandalia's ordinariness, most complaints had to do with crowded accommodations and shortage of certain goods.[49]

Vandalia's economy improved during the 1830s, after farms became productive, after the economy rallied following destruction of state bank notes by 1830, and during the national optimism of that decade. Not everyone condemned local businesses and services. Writing of Vandalia in October 1834, John York Sawyer noted that among the capital's businessmen were three blacksmiths, two bakers, two shoemakers, six tailors, a gunsmith, and a wagon maker.[50] Two years earlier, James Hall wrote that Vandalia had four merchants, two girls' schools, a boys' school, a Sunday school, a resident Presbyterian minister, and a visiting Methodist minister. Hall stated that the capital was healthy and attractive, was favored with pure spring water, and was surrounded by tracts of excellent soil. He also noted the abundant coal and wood in the Fayette County hills.[51] The Baptist preacher and social chronicler John Mason Peck recorded that Vandalia had five lawyers, four doctors, a land office, three taverns, several stores, and eight hundred people.[52]

Five years later he wrote a directory for travelers: Vandalia had four doctors, four taverns, eight stores, one clothing store, four lawyers, two schools, two printers, a steam mill and a water mill, and about 850 people.[53] Although these descriptions do not describe all the same Vandalia characteristics, the accounts suggest a growth of certain services and cultural facilities in the capital during the 1830s.

One other Vandalia profession was the town's public printing office. Vandalia's printers often won the state's business and published legislative journals and official documents, and until the late 1830s, Vandalia's newspapers enjoyed monopolies. With reportive proximity to the state government, the *Illinois Intelligencer* was arguably the state's most important newspaper. Founded in 1816 at Kaskaskia, the paper was moved to Vandalia in 1820 by owner William Berry. At Vandalia, William H. Brown served as editor. After Brown left in February 1823, Berry ran the paper until financial distress forced suspension of publication in March 1824. Until 1824 the editors supported John C. Calhoun and Henry Clay, and John Quincy Adams thereafter. The firm "Robert Blackwell & Co., printers to the state and publishers of the laws of the United States" began publication of the *Intelligencer* in 1825. Blackwell and James Hall, both Adams supporters, operated the paper together from 1829 until 1832, relinquishing it due to Hall's political and financial woes (chapter 6).[54] The paper was, like others of the era, a four-page, five-column weekly that sold for $3 to $4 a year. Congressional or state legislative proceedings and speeches occupied pages one and two, along with pseudonymous letters and commentaries. Miscellaneous national and world items, poetry, and lurid stories of infidelity and murder filled space. Editors seldom reported local news, devoting less than one column on page three to community happenings. Advertisements and notices about stray animals and runaway slaves completed each issue.

Once John York Sawyer arrived in town, politics and hilarity joined. After its sale in 1832 the *Intelligencer* survived only a short time.[55] However that same year Sawyer moved his *Illinois Advocate* from Edwardsville to the capital and presented, for the first time in Vandalia, the pro-Jackson editorial point of view. Sawyer, who weighed between three and four hundred pounds, was known both for his hair-trigger temper and his uproarious laughter; one traveler remembered hearing him in a local bar, laughing loudly enough to be heard in the streets, before meeting him. Sawyer had edited an agricultural paper in Indiana, and one of his interests was reporting Fayette County farm conditions.[56] When he died suddenly in 1836, Sawyer's paper came under ownership of the fiery William Walters, a young District of Columbia editor who had been encouraged to move to Illinois by the state's congressmen. By that time the paper was renamed *Illinois State Register*. Walters's talent for biting political commentary was matched only by his Vandalia rival, William Hodge, who dared to break Vandalia's newspaper monopoly by establishing a whig paper, the *Free Press*, in 1836. Hodge had lived in Vandalia for several years, serving in county offices and participating in civic events; he was one of the men who designed the third state capitol. Hodge, about whom little else is known, is buried in Vandalia's old cemetery. Walters, driven out of the business by financial and political failure in the 1840s, died while en route to the battlefields of the Mexican War. At least in print, the two men became quick enemies. Hodge once referred to Walters as "our Locofoco-Fanny Wright neighbor," while Hodge emerged, in one memorable outburst from Walters, as "a wretch, whom no charity can soften, no religion reclaim, no miracle convert . . . cold as the snows of Russia and putrid as the dead." No record exists of the two men's face-to-face encounters.[57]

Even before the affairs of the first state bank came to a close, state leaders called for another attempt. Following Andrew Jackson's veto of the recharter of the Bank of the United States, Illinois politicians became favorable to a new state bank, especially in the wake of an upswing of trade and land speculation. The Ninth General Assembly consequently passed a charter for a state bank. Stock subscriptions opened in April 1835, and branches, including one at Vandalia, opened around the state. Like the first state bank, the new system lacked important restraints on note issuance, loans and subscriptions, a central authority, and accountability among the branches. The special session of the Ninth General Assembly in January 1836 and the Tenth General Assembly (1836–37), too, enacted policies to make the bank more speculative. The government also connected the bank with the $10 million internal improvements project—railroads, highways, and other public projects—passed to statewide acclaim in February 1837.[58] The future of Illinois seemed assured by this state-funded adventure.

During this optimistic mid-decade, William Walters wrote in a March 1837 *State Register*:

> Since the passage of the [internal improvements] bill, the Land office here has been literally crowded with persons desirous to enter and occupy public land. We have no doubt that the passage of the bill has already increased the value of the land in the State more than 100 per cent, and every day is adding to its value. We have the utmost confidence that every acre of the public land will, in a few years, be settled by emigrants, who will add to the population of the State, will increase its wealth, its influence and power among the other States of the confederacy. If the present Leg-

islature had done no more, they would have deserved the thanks of the People for the passage of this law.[59]

Walters seemed unconcerned with the bill to relocate the state capital to Springfield, passed within days of the internal improvements bill. Vandalia's capital period drew to a close in the heady excitement of the state's promised prosperity. Several new Vandalia businesses opened in 1836, 1837, and 1838. Inspired by the project, Dr. Nathaniel McCurdy and General J. D. Whiteside secured contracts for several mail routes to Vandalia, including a daily line of four-horse post coaches from Salem via Vandalia to Springfield.[60]

The Vandalia of 1836 seemed a very different village than the Vandalia of 1823. New businesses were licensed; services were more varied and readily available. William Linn, brother-in-law of Governor Joseph Duncan, advertised dry goods, cutlery, queensware, saddlery, and shoes, while W. S. Marshal & Co. also advertised "pure wines for medical purposes." Prentice promised to sell goods at "St. Louis prices," "for cash or in exchange for wheat, live hogs, pork, bacon, butter, beeswax, tallow, beef hides, deer skins, furs, etc." The same year, Robert Blackwell and J. T. Eccles advertised ladies' kid "run rounds," spring kid walking shoes, men's laced stitched calf boots, childrens' run-around morocco ankle ties, and other items. [61] Stout and Johnson operated a book shop opposite the Green Tree Hotel on Gallatin; they offered Blackstone's Commentary, Vattel's and Toller's laws, Jefferson's and Franklin's works, and a "new and elegant" assortment of books and stationary. E. S. Phelps had a watch repair and jewelry shop a block east on Gallatin between Third and Fourth. His competition in 1838 was W. H. Robbins, who opened a clock, jewelry, and silverware store. A retail clothing store owned by Allen McPhail stood between Flack's hotel and Phelps's shop. Moses Phillips, grandfather of Fayette County historian Robert W. Ross, and Evert Westervelt owned a cabinet warehouse on Fourth Street south of Gallatin opposite the Methodist Church; they manufactured bedsteads, bureaus, tables, washstands, and took special orders for furniture. Abner Johnson and Jesse W. Curlee, also in 1838, announced their partnership in the cabinet making business. William Luther and A. G. Herron opened a shoemaking shop in an upstairs room of Stolle's hotel.[62]

Following the nationwide Panic of 1837 and the eventual collapse of the improvements project, both the project and the state bank created a mounting state debt that vexed legislators into the 1840s. These events affected Vandalia in at least two ways. First, although the direct reason for the decline after 1839 was the relocation of the state government, the economic decline caused by the failed bank and project did not help and surely hurt local economy further. Second, an examination of circuit court records reveals that the state bank's suits against debtors were as frequently successful as the first bank's suits were not. The court decided in favor of the bank in cases against William L. D. Ewing, William Linn, Lemuel and Harvey Lee, Joseph Hall, Zela F. Watwood, William Hodge, the estate of Charles Prentice, Akin Evans, Harrison Thompson, and others. Circumstances of these cases vary, but local debtors in the late 1830s were unable to take advantage of the kind of relief and stay laws that helped keep persons solvent during the early 1820s.[63]

Throughout Vandalia's capital period, little state revenue came from Illinois citizens. Taxes on nonresident land holders, injudicious loans, and speculation on the Vandalia lots prevented the government from initiating a system of taxation. The Eleventh General Assembly, the last at Vandalia, passed a general taxation law that levied a 20 cent per $100 property tax. During the spring and summer of 1839, opposition to the law was statewide and vociferous. Here again, the adverse economic situation requiring taxation came at a time when Vandalia, having lost its greatest economic boon to Springfield, was ill-equipped to address the crisis.[64]

Long-time Vandalia businessman James M. Duncan closed his store in 1838, moved elsewhere, and far fewer businesses advertised in the papers in 1838 and 1839. Many of the new operations surely faced grave difficulties after 1839. Vandalia's future became less certain. James Black and William Greenup attempted a navigation company in 1838 and 1839. They ordered a boat from Cincinnati, hired a captain, and hoped to obtain state aid for improvements on the Kaskaskia. Greenup predicted that steam boats would navigate the river six months a year and flatboats and keelboats for nine months a year. The aid never came, however, and the business never began. Boosters like William Hodge pressed the completion of the National Road to Vandalia as a means of community revitalization.[65]

The earliest account of Vandalia's downtown, written by historian Robert Ross for 1904 publication, describes the area in 1850. By that time Vandalia had declined seriously and several capital-era businessmen had moved or died. Ferdinand Ernst's hotel and adjacent structures were in 1850 lawyers' and doctors' offices. Along Gallatin Street stood capital-era buildings such as Robert Blackwell's house, the old Thompson Tavern, a two-story building—the old State Bank of 1835—with its massive pillars and brick facade, Abner Flack's hotel, and the old Charter's hotel. North of the public square was Capps's store and the home of the McLaughlins. Mike Lynch's wagon shop and Colonel Greenup's home both stood to the west of Capps's store. The third statehouse stood in disrepair. Vandalia's population had dropped from about eight hundred to about three hundred.[66]

Thanks to the advent of the railroads during the 1850s, the town recovered. "New enterprises sprang up," Ross recalled, "induced by the increased facilities for carrying on industries and trade. . . . As an inducement to prospective settlers along the route of the railroad, the Illinois Central offered half-rate transportation to those who desired to visit the lands it offered for sale. . . . Thousands flocked to the State to take advantage of [the reasonable] terms, and Fayette County received its fair share."[67]

With revitalization, Vandalia entered the time of small-town progress that has characterized its existence ever since. The capital era passed into the most distant part of local history, the pioneer period. As reflected in Ross's account, local histories centered local memory upon structures that remained. But probably because of local emphasis upon small-town progress, Vandalians have seldom been farsighted in historic preservation. In my lifetime, some of the last important historic buildings like Alexander P. Field's home, the Flack hotel, and the house purported to be William L. D. Ewing's home were razed for parking lots. Incredibly, the destruction of the third statehouse was contemplated in the early 1900s. Besides a few other buildings, now private homes, the statehouse remains Vandalia's most notable existing historic site. In the 1950s the Vandalia Historical Society also erected plaques at the sites of twelve more important capital-era buildings: Capps's store, Charter's hotel, the Vandalia Inn, Ernst's hotel, Flack's hotel, the public printing office, the first and second statehouses, the second state bank, the McLaughlin home, the house of public worship, and the old city cemetery. During the 1970s, the same society erected commemorative biographical plaques upon the graves of pioneers in that cemetery: Blackwell, Greenup, Leidig, Black, Prentice, Remann, Ernst, the McLaughlins, James W. Berry, Elijah C. and Mildred Stapp Berry, Mary Posey Hall, and the supposed original plot of five officials who died during Vandalia general assemblies. The graves of editors William Hodge and William Berry should be memorialized in the future. In addition to Vandalia's museums, a tour of the quiet downtown and original burying ground can provide a brief lesson in local pioneer history and local memory.

5

"Boosting" the State Capital

V ANDALIA'S DOWNTOWN history invites a larger issue: the character of a town's internal dynamics concerning how best to "boost" a community's economic potential. In Vandalia's case, participatory democracy for the sake of community progress grew from its largely homogeneous population; this town spirit seems to have been largely spontaneous and cooperative. In light of its failure to become a thriving capital, however, Vandalia's cultural sameness may have hurt rather than enhanced its participatory and problem-solving dynamics.

Stanley Elkins and Eric McKitrick's 1954 article "A Meaning for Turner's Frontier" portrays the creation and development of communities as a source for American frontier democracy rather than the individualistic, independent tendencies of the frontier. The authors postulate that in new communities, civic difficulties arose due to that newness, for example, irregular law enforcement, poor roads, inadequate food supplies, and a lack of good housing, schools, churches, and municipal organizations. From the challenge of these difficulties, young men spontaneously created civic roles, mobilized concerned citizens, and applied pressure upon government for improvements. Frontier democracy was a cooperative venture, emerging from the cultural and political vacuum of new towns.[1]

When certain Vandalia phenomena are examined, the Elkins-McKitrick model becomes a helpful framework to understand the town's social dynamics. This "cooperative" model describes, if in oversimplified terms, the establishment of Vandalia: the first provisions of necessary services in the social and civic vacuum of Reeve's Bluff; the cooperation between German-born and American-born; and the initiative taken by young men like Ewing, Prentice, and McLaughlin in assuming civic and leadership roles. As in Elkins and McKitrick's model, nearly all of Vandalia's leaders were young men in their teens, twenties, and thirties when they arrived at the capital. Too, many spontaneously assumed the reins of leadership once they moved to Vandalia.[2] This model describes the activity of collective boosterism in Vandalia: public meetings calling for local improvements and publicizing Vandalia's benefits. The model describes the cooperative activity of establishing churches, schools, and cultural organizations during the 1820s and 1830s (chapter 8). In Vandalia, humanitarianism and religion evolved as local leaders (usually the established leaders like McLaughlin, Hall, Prentice, Peebles, Blackwell, Black, and William H. Brown, and certain nonresident officials like Thomas Lippincott and John Mason Peck) took over opportunities where no cultural precedents existed. Their efforts apparently were aimed at enhancing rather than criticizing or controlling local social structures; for instance, the two Vandalia churches were effectual only on an evangelistic and not a prophetic, socially vocal level.

Most of all, the model describes the cooperative effects of Vandalians in erecting public buildings. If cabin raisings and barn raisings were Elkins and McKitrick's classic examples of frontier cooperation, Vandalians' initiative in financing and constructing the second and third statehouses is the cooperative equivalent. Now-anonymous individuals took the initiative in quickly subscribing $3,000 for the second statehouse. It was a spontaneous, word-of-mouth, effort; no Vandalia paper ever made a blanket appeal for support of that construction effort. Again in 1836, Vandalia leaders like Lemuel Lee took the initiative, obtained gubernatorial permission, and arranged with local builders and contractors for the construction of the third statehouse (chapter 7). Here again, the effort was spontaneous and word-of-mouth.

Vandalia's local leaders took different kinds of initiatives. Once the survey of the National Road reached Vandalia in 1828, local leaders like Robert McLaughlin, William L. D. Ewing, Alexander Pope Field, William Linn, William H. Brown, James Black, James T. B. Stapp, Elijah Berry, Nathaniel M. McCurdy, and William Hodge held public meetings to press Congress to complete the road. The poor roads east of town were not the only reason the highway was necessary; an interstate road from the East through Vandalia to Alton or St. Louis would greatly increase Vandalia's trade and population. By the early 1830s, many of the same leaders became vocal for statewide internal improvements, another potential plum for Vandalia's growth. A few—especially Black, Prentice, Brown, Peebles, McLaughlin, Stapp, and Blackwell—were also active in cultural, religious, and civic work. Some, notably Ebenezer Capps (at least during the capital period) and Thomas Redmond, do not seem to have participated in local boosteristic and cultural projects at all. In spite of their differences concerning the presidential aspirations of Adams, Clay, Jackson, or Crawford, nearly all of the men convened to support the constitutional convention proposal of 1823–24. The unanimity was not simply among the southern-born men, as most were, but also included Frederick Hollman of the Kingdom of Hanover and Robert H. Peebles of Pennsylvania. Apart from the slavery question, which some of these men, honestly or not, dismissed as irrelevant, it may be speculated that their support of a convention's supposed reforms indicated a kind of boosterism because certain proposed changes in the constitution, like an annual rather than biennial general assembly, would have assisted Vandalia's economy.[3]

Community in Vandalia was essentially based on the common background and similar local interests of its citizens. Community was not based on religion (most people were unattached to an organized denomination), nor ethnocultural divergences and conflicting traditions. The basic homogeneity of citizens meant that when local challenges arose, they rose to the occasions and attempted answers to local needs. Vandalia community ("*Gemeinschaft*") was also based on the hope for a better, more prosperous local existence, and as far as the "when" of the last sentence is true, Vandalians' dreams translated into actions.

These examples point toward the cooperative model of frontier community. The self-contained, quiescent communities of Southern Illinois were not vital centers of migration, sectional rivalries, and statewide commerce. If the predominance of Fayette County settlers from the South encouraged a worldview of the linear family (chapter 3), a small-town neighborliness might have ruled the day, in turn influencing the cooperative shape of Vandalia's participatory democracy.

The Elkins-McKitrick thesis has been criticized for overemphasizing cooperative community decision making and omitting factors of divisiveness, sectional rivalry, and social conflict in the creation of roles and the making of community decisions. Robert R. Dykstra, in his study of Kansas cattle towns, disputes the linking of participatory democracy and cultural homogeneousness, arguing instead that solutions to community problems necessitated differing responses and creative social conflict.[4] Don Harrison Doyle, too, disagrees that frontier decision making was necessarily peaceful and cooperative. At Jacksonville, Illinois, a high rate of population turnover, the large diversity of ethnic and regional cultures and classes, and religious and political differences created a partisanship and social conflict. Not only did this conflict underlay the social structure, but conflict was also necessary for decision making and innovation. True, Jacksonville, like the majority of other frontier towns, did not attain the civic greatness desired by boosters. Leaders resigned themselves to a communal, small-town existence—as if that were the goal all along—and preserved that resignation in the form of nostalgic, boosteristic local history. Nevertheless, Jacksonville's heterogeneity resulted not only in lively decision making and sporadic, outright turmoil, but also in mechanisms of social control and community, voluntary organization.[5] A similar situation existed in early-nineteenth-century St. Louis; rapid population growth and a vocal new citizenry threatened the local elite, resulting in participatory government and progress through compromise among factions.[6]

In Vandalia's case, does the impression of social cooperation and spontaneous participation arise from surface phenomena preserved by boosteristic editors and nostalgic, postbellum county historians? Did serious conflict, political maneuvering, and civic competition exist beneath appearances? Certainly local editors shied away from criticism; the 1878 and 1910 county histories, as well as Frederick Hollman's autobiography, overlook much of the dark side of the capital's formative years.

Vandalia differs from Jacksonville, St. Louis, and the Kansas cattle towns in that it was not a center of sectionalism, migration, and commerce. The capital was not peaceful and untroubled, but conflicts were familial and did not create new roles or enhance decision making. They did not arise from social heterogeneity, nor were they intended to advance Vandalia. Unlike situations in other cities, Vandalia's conflicts were only disruptive rather than allying and constructive. The conflict apparent in the Ernst colony or confrontations between locals over supposed insults were not catalysts for new leadership, but were private (although publicized) disputes. Likewise, when local men publicly came into conflict, conflicts typically had nothing to do with civic decision making but reflected frontier attitudes of honor and retribution. William L. D. Ewing was constantly at odds with others, but his conflicts resulted more from the machismo of a hothead than the machinations of a competitive town father.

Because Vandalia's conflicts were disruptive rather than allying and constructive, it is possible that a different kind of conflict existed than in other communities. Community conflict can be seen as the obverse of cooperation, an allying force for positive competition; absence or suppression of conflict results in fewer allying and binding forces. Vandalia's leaders surely competed among themselves, but if deeper conflicts existed in early Vandalia, they may have existed less as Hobbesian turmoil and new leadership dynamics than as failed boosterism or even civic complacency.[7]

Here, Dyksktra's critique provides clues about conflict in a culturally homogeneous setting.[8] If the familial worldview of Vandalians hid community conflicts, then evidences of Vandalia's cooperative spirit indeed concealed community discord. That discord would have been different than that of high-mobility towns because Vandalia's slow growth rate would have in turn provided no challenge to social elitism or factionalism. Civic inertia would have coexisted with spontaneous participation and cooperation, discouraging creative conflict and masking a divisiveness or a resentfulness expressed less in emergence of new leaders, fresh ideas, and civic vision than in lack of communication and isolation from leadership efforts. Because this theory is in this case hypothetical, future frontier community histories should determine whether this mentality existed in other communities in a testable way.

One of the mysteries of Vandalia's capital period concerns the town's economy. Why did Vandalia not thrive, given its undoubted benefits? A failure on the part of local leaders to unite behind long-range goals, or even to dispute over such goals, would have delayed good solutions until opportunities passed. A significant example is the call for a new state capital. Vandalians protested the removal of the government to Springfield, but in local meetings a few months after the law was passed in February 1837. A few meetings also convened, and their minutes and recommendations were published before the passage; the participants were unanimous in their pro-Vandalia convictions. However the most vocal protests were reactive, defensive, and sporadic rather than constructive and thoughtful. In spite of their city's long unpopularity as capital, Vandalians seemed caught off guard when the legislature voted for Springfield. Consequently, the most strident local protests for Vandalia's benefits occurred after that vote. Did now-unknown conflict and divisiveness among local leaders cause this delay, or was the reason simply civic indolence?[9]

Failed public spirit was not unknown during this era. James Hall complained, "The merchants and gentlemen of Philadelphia are liberal and high minded men; but they are in the habit of attending more to *their own*, and less to *public* business, than the same class of society in almost any part of the United States." Hall also complained that political contention eroded public spirit. "*Party spirit* has raged in that devoted land [Pennsylvania], with ungovernable fury; the bitterness of contention has been permitted to inflame and corrode the public mind; the gall of political enmity has been infused into the cup of social intercourse, and the interests of the state have been too often forgotten, in the tumult of schemes to raise or to defeat a party, to prostrate or to exalt an individual."[10] Because this description would serve well for state politics during the Vandalia capital period, Hall's account offers another clue about Vandalia's lack of effective boosterism. The political climate was such that leaders' interest in state factional contention may have obscured issues of community survival. If so, Vandalia's distinction as state capital hurt its need for a satisfactory reputation; local leaders diverted their attention from community problems. Vandalia's editors, conforming to the concerns of the era, paid more attention to political rumblings than to local problems (chapter 6).

One more phenomenon of frontier boosterism must be mentioned: the man who nearly embodied the town because of his activism. Dr. Conrad Will of Brownsville, Elijah Iles of Springfield, and John Russell of Bluffdale are examples. Vandalia did not have such a booster whose name along with Vandalia's was synonymous. James Hall was atypical in that he was passionate for the betterment of the West rather than Vandalia specifically (chapter 8).[11]

Boosterism and political activism are not necessarily alike, but Vandalia's greatest booster was probably its most politically active citizen. William Lee Davidson Ewing was an intriguing individual. He lived in Vandalia from its founding, when he was twenty-five, until 1840, when he moved to Springfield. He was an attorney, married to Caroline, the daughter of Elijah and Mildred Stapp Berry. He is said to have been a short, muscular individual; it is not known whether the portrait of Ewing, first published in Davidson and Stuvé's history of Illinois, was drawn from life.[12]

One local history calls Ewing "a man of fine education and polished manners." The records show that second part to be pure sentiment. He was convicted of assault and battery as early as 1821, and was indicted on similar charges several other times; in 1831, inebriated and armed, he stabbed and critically wounded an unarmed man with whom he had a minor difference of opinion; he was convicted by the U.S. Treasury of negligence in his office as receiver at the Vandalia land office; and he was once indicted on a charge of adultery and other times on affray charges.[13]

But—and this is what raises intriguing points concerning Ewing's character, Vandalians' preferences in a leader, and the nature of the era— his record of antisocial and violent behavior did not at all detract from his community and political standing. The same year as the first assault Ewing was appointed village trustee and soon gained the appointment as receiver of the Vandalia land office. He served variously as village trustee, as clerk of the house of representatives, as state representative from Fayette County, and as the speaker of the house. He was, for two weeks and a day, the governor of Illinois (p. 82). The legislature elected Ewing U.S. senator to complete an incumbent's term, and he served as auditor of public accounts. During his term as state legislator, he took a leading role to defend Vandalia's claim to the seat of government; as such, he was Lincoln's first serious political antagonist (chapter 9). He died in Springfield in 1846, and, according Robert Ross, was buried in Oak Ridge Cemetery although that graveyard was not established at the time. Ewing was never a major politician, but he was, as the Springfield paper called him, Vandalia's "strong man," its most active booster.[14] For this he should be remembered.

The data from Vandalia's capital era resists neat formulas and sure conclusions. In the 1830s, Vandalia's place in "mass society" was symbolized by the state government, a presence destined to go to a better, more centrally located community.[15] On one hand, Vandalians never seemed able to exploit the town's benefits in any effective way. On the other hand, one man remembered that William Ewing stood ready to challenge Lincoln to a duel to keep the capital at Vandalia. Such a sentiment among Vandalians could not have been isolated.

6

On the Track
at Vandalia

THE HISTORIES of Vandalia and of Illinois state politics can be paired insofar as political debate, editorial declarations, and legislative procedure happened in downtown Vandalia. Had the government been hosted by another town—Kaskaskia, Pope's Bluff, Covington, Carlyle, or elsewhere—the issues and candidates of 1819 through 1839 surely would have been the same. Because the government resided temporarily .at Vandalia, its presence effected the daily course of events, and much early history there cannot be understood without an awareness of key issues and participants.[1]

Kaskaskia hosted only one state general assembly, the first, in October 1818 and January through March 1819. In 1820 the government documents moved by ox cart through the rolling hills of Southern Illinois; the general assembly first convened in Vandalia in December 1820. In a real sense, the political squabbles of the era also moved to Vandalia. Ninian Edwards and Jesse B. Thomas, the great political rivals of the Illinois territory, sat in Congress while their partisans came to Vandalia. Edwards, who had served as territorial governor and whose son and namesake was Lincoln's associate, was a wealthy land-owner who possessed an aristocratic mien as he strolled around the capital. Nevertheless, he devoted his life to political service and died heroically giving medical aid to cholera victims in 1833. Thomas was large man whose features were startlingly bold. By contrast he was soft-spoken and gentlemanly. Disagreements between him and Edwards in 1812 concerning the structure of territorial government became great enough to effect territorial politics as two factions, for and against Edwards's administration. When Shadrach Bond and Elias Kent Kane became the first governor and secretary of state, Thomas's friend Kane nearly succeeded in obtaining Edwards's defeat for a second senatorial term.[2]

When Vandalia became capital these factions still reverberated, but to a lesser degree. John McLean, Daniel Pope Cook, and Elias Kent Kane were a trio of younger men whose political careers at first revolved around these factional lines. All left careers unfinished. McLean, also a friend of Thomas's, won the first seat in the U.S. House of Representatives in 1818, only to lose it to Cook, the former territorial attorney general. McLean was remembered as a strong, manly individual; Cook, by contrast, was small, homely, and fragile. Both men possessed magnetic personalities and political acumen. Defeated by Cook in 1819 and 1822 for Congress, McLean served as three-time state legislator at Vandalia from Gallatin County and later as twice-elected U.S. senator. He died suddenly in 1830 at age thirty-nine. Cook himself died at thirty-three from tuberculosis. But before his early demise, Cook assumed reins of influence from his friend Edwards and wielded great national and state power as a four-term congressman. Kane was a Yale graduate who probably wrote most of the 1818 state constitution, served as Bond's secretary, then represented Randolph County in the legislature at Vandalia, and finally sat in Congress three times. His portrait shows a stylishly dressed man with a handsome, square face, dark curly hair, and a reserved expression. Unlike Cook, Edwards, and Thomas, who left Illinois in 1829, Kane survived the state's factional era and became a Jacksonian spokesman before his early death in 1835 when he was about forty-one.[3]

Other men also impressed themselves upon state politics at Vandalia. Men who served on the state supreme court—Samuel Lockwood of Westchester County, New York, the portly and hilarious Thomas C. Browne, the transparently ambitious John Reynolds, and the sober and skilled jurist William Wilson—as well as the brusque federal judge Nathaniel Pope ostensibly favored Edwards. Thomas Cox, the young attorney from Union County who helped found Vandalia, pressed Thomas's cause in the legislature. Conrad Will was perhaps more beloved than distinguished, although his legislative career (he served in the First through the Ninth General Assemblies) was unusually long and active. A notorious practical joker, Will once sent people scurrying to win his reward for every eagle killed in the county, provided the hunters brought him the gizzards, which eagles do not have. It may have been Edwards, an opponent, who published a bogus obituary for Will in 1821. Alexander Pope Field, a younger relative of Pope and Cook, came to Vandalia when he was twenty-two and became prominent in the Third General Assembly's passage of a constitutional convention proposal. Edwards appointed him secretary of state in 1828, a position Field held until 1840 and that brought him to Vandalia as a resident. Theophilus W. Smith, another legislative leader and a supreme court judge, is best remembered as an indefatigable schemer. He once confronted Edwards at Vandalia with a loaded pistol; a much larger man, Edwards broke Smith's jaw as he knocked away the weapon. Smith sullied his judicial career as he kept one foot in politics. Other men, like William S. Hamilton, son of the statesman Alexander, Thomas Mather, Alfred Cowles, Samuel McRoberts, the future governors John Reynolds, Joseph Duncan, and Thomas Carlin, and the future congressman Zadoc Casey, all began careers of public service at Vandalia during the 1820s in either the legislature, the courts, or both. Even the Methodist circuit rider Peter Cartwright served as a legislator from Sangamon County; he married at least one Vandalia couple while lodging at the capital.[4]

While politics centered loosely around the older territorial factions, most political discussion in Vandalia, if local newspapers are an indication, concerned the national scene. Vandalia editors were interested in preventing a state "monarchial" government wherein "the people" had less voice, as during the territorial era, and the concomitant need for good programs of western internal improvements and sound banking and currency. One of the advocacies of editors William Berry and Robert Blackwell, for instance, was the plight of settlers wanting to buy federal lands. Congressman Cook and his soon-to-be father-in-law Ninian Edwards received considerable criticism when in 1820 they voted against the Public Land Act, which lowered land prices from $2 to $1.25 an acre. Each man justified his vote because the bill abolished the system for buying land on credit, but they were dogged for years by the charge that they had voted against the bill to protect their own speculative holdings. One letter in the *Intelligencer* accused "Mr. Cook and his *party* (I will not call it a faction)" of being "perfect federalists" in this disregard for the needs of their nonaristocratic constituents. The letter, and others in the same issue, deplored the local nature of Illinois politics and asked whether officials such as Cook and Edwards were truly Jeffersonian when their record of support on western issues and national candidates was examined. On the other hand, the *Intelligencer* editors supported the two men, but not because of their common factional allegiances. The paper disputed the charge of personalism while praising Edwards and Cook for seeking a system for the West that would not oppress land purchasers; their opposing votes, according to Berry then Blackwell, were rightly motivated. James Hall pseudonymously attacked

Cook in the Shawneetown *Illinois Gazette* on just this point; a portion of the letter exchange was printed in the *Intelligencer* along with supportive communications for Cook.[5]

The *Intelligencer* frequently contained arguments (clipped from Ohio and Indiana papers) in favor of the National Road and the opening of river and lake trade between the Mississippi and the Great Lakes, also sought by Cook through federal land grants to Illinois for a future canal between Lake Michigan and the Illinois River. Even downstate the issue remained of interest because the development of Northern Illinois trade routes potentially spelled economic gain for Southern Illinois. In 1823 a letter upbraided the state senator from Bond, Fayette, and Montgomery counties for opposing the canal and therefore "the wishes of a great majority of his constituents." During the 1826 campaigns, the *Intelligencer* praised Cook's general efforts in Congress in support of internal improvements and of President Adams, a friend of improvements; in particular Robert Blackwell praised Cook for the "able manner" with which he pressed a land grant for the canal.[6]

These issues of beneficial policies for the West led the editors of the *Intelligencer* also to support a liberal program of federally funded internal improvements, especially the proposals of Congressman Henry Clay. In the July 26, 1823 issue "Jonas Plainway" applauded Clay's support of improvements as superior to that which "has been done by his predecessors, or is likely to be done by some of his competitors." In the August 23, 1823 issue another writer called Clay "a decided and consistent democrat, an able and upright statesman, a warm and zealous friend of domestic manufactures and internal improvements, an enemy to all encroachments upon the rights of the states by the general government, or upon the constitution by the executive or judiciary, and at the same time that he is of ripe years and mature judgment[.] *All these important requisites centre in Mr. Clay, and in him alone.*" The author continued by comparing other contenders for the 1824 presidential elections as lacking in one or more of the essential, pro-western traits.

After William Berry left the *Intelligencer* in March 1824, Robert Blackwell continued to praise these traits against the growing state enthusiasm for Andrew Jackson. Blackwell perceived President Adams's policies as heir to Clay's endeavors. He noted in 1827: "To the zeal and eloquence of Mr. CLAY, we are indebted for the commencement and progress of this great national work. . . . The people of this state are . . . mainly interested in the permanent establishment of the AMERICAN SYSTEM, as it is aptly termed, appropriating our surplus revenue to the improvement of the country, by roads and canals, and protecting our citizens in their exertions to rival our natural enemy, Great Britain, in the manufacture of cotton and woollen goods." In subsequent issues he attempted to "give our readers the reasons which induce us to support the present administration, in preference to Genl. Jackson . . . our motto always has been, and we trust ever will be, '*measures and not men.*' " The measures were the same—encouragement of domestic industry and federally sponsored internal improvements—and Blackwell feared that a Jackson administration would consider such appropriations as unconstitutional. To Berry, Blackwell, and their letter-writing subscribes, William Crawford was seriously deficient as a pro-western candidate, considering his Bank of the United States policies while treasury secretary under Monroe. Judging from toasts at local celebrations, Vandalia merchants and manufacturers similarly considered Clay and Adams to be friends of the West:

"Let Old Kentuck and Yankees agree, and our next President will be Clay."
"Old Massachusetts and John Quincy Adams."
"Of all the nags that run the Presidential races, give me the *Clay*-colored horse of Kentucky."[7]

However, referring to Cook's 1824 vote in Congress to elect Adams president, Vandalia sheriff Joseph Oliver, at the July 4, 1825 celebration, gave a prophetic dissent: "[A toast to] General Jackson—may he be our next President, Daniel P. Cook, to the contrary, notwithstanding."[8]

One contemporary described the state's factional politics as not "between Federalist and democrat, but between those in office and them who want their places." "As for principles and measures," writes Thomas Ford, "with the exception of the convention question, there was none to contend for." Theodore Calvin Pease puts the matter more scientifically: "The decaying federalist party never existed in Illinois, and all her aspirants for office professed themselves republicans. So far as they grouped themselves for their political combats on partisan lines, they rallied around favorite measures in state and national legislatures, favorite candidates for the presidency and most important of all around the banners of state political factions."[9] Although the *Intelligencer* occasionally referred to factions like "Cook and his friends," "Mr. Kane's party," the "slave party," and the "bank party," readers of the Vandalia papers did not learn of these factions except in polemical terms against political factionalism. Unless factional disputes also involved larger issues of western benefit, editors tended to disregard these disputes until a campaign was in full swing. More important to editors, and perhaps to voters, was the distinction of the pejorative label *federalist*, with its connotations of "monarchial" government, and Jeffersonian republicanism, which connoted pro-western or democratic policies. Thus it is a fine distinction on one hand to repudiate the term *federalism* to describe the state's early parties, and on the other hand to recognize that although no adherers to that party existed in the state, the term, with its implied worldview, was used by political observers in contrast to an acceptable, pro-western republicanism. It is also a fine distinction to say that candidates in the early 1820s competed on no party platforms comprising clearly articulated "principles and measures"; certain economic measures—banking, internal improvements, and western lands— were articulated clearly in the Illinois press, issues that eventually became the western brand of Jacksonism after the 1820s.[10]

The campaign of 1826 was fateful. Daniel Pope Cook was too ill to canvass personally in his bid for a fifth congressional term in 1826. His opponent was Joseph Duncan, a thirty-two-year-old pro-Jackson legislator. Cook's handbills called attention to his efforts at improvements. Ninian Edwards, distressed by his 1824 resignation from the U.S. Senate under a cloud of charges of suspicious ethics, sought vindication when he launched into an acrimonious 1826 gubernatorial campaign. But he and Cook still suffered under the charge of federalism and personal interest in voting against the 1820 Public Lands Act. Because father- and son-in-law were simultaneously running for state office, Vandalia handbills charged the two with seeking to be "a family of rulers," out of step with the people's wishes. Similarly, amid the controversy surrounding the 1824 presidential election, Cook was also blamed for supporting Adams although Jackson had won a plurality in Illinois. Cook and Edwards countered with charges of nepotism: Duncan's uncle and brother, Robert McLaughlin and James M. Duncan, were principal campaigners for Joseph. However the countercharges carried less weight because the Duncans and McLaughlin were not simultaneously seeking office. The *Intelligencer* supported Edwards but printed critical open letters to him by "Tyro" (George Forquer) and "A Fayette Farmer." Edwards barely won the governorship, while Duncan defeated Cook, who died the following year.[11]

The 1826 campaign was the last in which the older territorial factions played a part; it also marked the growing weakness of the Illinois Adams–Clay ranks as Andrew Jackson's hopes grew. The campaign ended older politics in Fayette County, which had once sent consistent majorities to Cook but which gave a 67 percent majority to Duncan in 1826 and a 61 percent victory to Edwards's Jacksonian opponent. From 1826 on, majorities consistently went to Jacksonian candidates.[12]

Editorial observations alone are not thorough barometers for early Illinois politics, no more so than the behaviors of individual politicians like Cook and Edwards.[13] Insofar as Vandalians cared for politics and followed the local paper, they knew from the *Intelligencer* in the 1820s about "measures, not men"—and the measures of Adams and Clay rather than Jacksonian perceptions—but little about personal and intercounty factional groups.

Vandalians, however, knew, or could have known, a great deal about the politics of slavery. During the early 1820s popular consciousness concerning Illinois slavery grew, transcending factional disputes. The 1818 constitution prevented the future introduction of slavery and servitude but preserved the property rights of existing slave owners and retained slavery until 1825 in the salines of southeastern Illinois. Following Missouri's application for statehood as a slave state, this constitutional compromise failed to satisfy either those in favor of or against slavery. Edwards and Thomas in the U.S. Senate supported Missouri's application; Thomas in fact led the fight for compromise. Cook became an active restrictionist spokesman in the House. When twenty-two-year-old representative Henry Eddy of Shawneetown (near the salines) arrived at the newly cleared Reeve's Bluff in December 1820, he introduced resolutions in the Second General Assembly for the increase of Illinois slavery. Legislators at Vandalia rejected his resolutions.[14]

The *Intelligencer* tended to oppose slavery, although publisher William Berry was implicated in *Edwardsville Spectator* reports of a plot to increase Illinois slavery. Throughout 1820, 1821, and 1822, Berry and editor William H. Brown published letters on both sides of the question, however. The issue had not yet crystalized as strong public opinion, so Vandalia talk on slavery probably constituted a smaller portion of boardinghouse exchange. The talk took a different turn when state supreme court justice Joseph Phillips announced in 1821 his hope to succeed Shadrach Bond as Illinois governor. Phillips supported slavery, unlike his rival Edward Coles, a thirty-five-year-old bachelor from Edwardsville. Coles, in whom haughtiness, loquaciousness, and public service uneasily conjoined, was Virginia-born and a personal friend of Madison, Lafayette, Monroe, and Jefferson. Berry supported Coles for his opposition to William H. Crawford's presidential hopes; as it was widely believed in Illinois, Crawford opposed western internal improvements, and his banking policies as Monroe's treasury secretary hurt states' economies. Internal improvements and Illinois economy, rather than slavery, typified this comparatively mild campaign. Candidates expressed support or disapprobation of the proposed Illinois and Michigan Canal at Lake Michigan and of a state highway system.[15]

Coles won the election without a plurality in August 1822 and arrived in Vandalia in November 1822 convinced that the slavery issue should be clarified. His first address to the Third General Assembly, convened in December, urged prompt legislative disapproval. Instead, the largely pro-slavery legislature took the opportunity to effect a resolution calling for a constitutional convention. Senators achieved the required two-thirds majority and approved the proposal. Advocates believed a similar two-thirds majority existed in the house, but at the last moment Nicholas Hansen from Pike County changed his vote, defeating the measure, it seemed, by that single "no."[16]

That night, Vandalia's streets filled with angry convention supporters. They approved a secret agreement to oust Hansen, who had won his seat earlier in the session after a contested election. Later that evening, a mob formed in downtown Vandalia. According to an *Edwardsville Spectator* correspondent, one supreme court justice and several legislators, all drunk, burned an effigy of Hansen, gathered a crowd of about two hundred persons, and marched through downtown, yelling insults at anti-convention officials like Governor Coles.[17]

The next day, February 12, 1823, the house reconsidered the Pike County election issue, voted to replace Hansen with his pro-convention rival, and, thus achieving the two-thirds majority, passed the convention proposal. When William H. Brown passionately decried the proceedings, one source maintains that an angry crowd gathered outside the *Intelligencer* office and threatened to toss the printing press into the Kaskaskia River.[18]

The measure had to be approved by the voters in the August 1824 elections. For the next year and a half, advocates and opponents waged a furious campaign to turn public opinion. The Illinois press published articles and speeches from both sides. Committees met at Vandalia and elsewhere throughout 1823 and 1824 to plot strategy, effect precinct organization, and recruit leaders. Convention advocates argued that slavery was a peripheral issue; the state constitution had been congressionally but not popularly approved and had long been criticized as seriously flawed and undemocratically enacted. A convention, advocates claimed, including nearly all of Vandalia's local leaders, would redress the constitution's defects and would provide voters a long-awaited opportunity to vote on their government. Robert McLaughlin and others published point-by-point reasons why a convention should be approved.[19]

"Go the Whole," in a July *Intelligencer*, had typical "democratic" words from the pro-convention side: "*Slavery* and many other *bug-bears* are made objections to voting for a convention—but this is all stuff. Can the people be *equally represented* in *convention*, is the grand consideration on which the question should turn. I affirm they can—*Disprove it who dare!*" A topic not usually considered by historians of this campaign is whether many convention supporters sincerely wanted equal representation and democratic participation in the drafting of the constitution. One of William Berry's editorials was also typical: "If, the constitution is defective, it should be amended regardless of any *scare-crow* which have been brought to bear against it by those un-friendly to a convention. If the people of Illinois are opposed to a change in our constitution so as to admit of slavery in this state, we are certain they can prevent it, although a constitution be called. The same voters who declare themselves in favor of an alteration in the constitution can . . . in electing members to the convention, vote against slavery." Because of the covert and violent campaigns of many convention supporters, including the ouster of Hansen, the evasion of the slavery issue by convention supporters such as editor and legislator Berry strikes one as naive at best.[20]

Opponents charged that convention supporters avoided their real in-tentions: unlimited slavery in Illinois. Because the legislative journals were not yet published, widespread disagreement existed about what really took place at Vandalia during the Third General Assembly, which adjourned in March 1823. This ambiguity proved a detriment for anti-slavery spokesmen and an opportunity for pro-slavery spokesmen to express outrage at this "bug-bear." But the violence of some pro-con-vention supporters and the moral zeal of opponents eventually turned the tide toward the latter's cause. The legislative tactics and the Vandalia mobs of February 1823 finally became publicized. Thanks to Coles's secret funding, his friends purchased William Berry's ownership of the *Intelligencer* and, beginning in the spring of 1824, established the Van-dalia paper as an anti-convention forum.[21]

Just three weeks before the end of 1823, the first statehouse became engulfed in flame. Because the legislature was not in session (and there-fore the stoves were not lit) the cause of the blaze remained unknown and suspicious (chapter 7). The next night after the conflagration, a mob allegedly headed by a "Col. Berry" burned an effigy of Governor Coles and yelled "State House or Death" while marching around Vandalia's blocks. The *Spectator* correspondent noted only that "Col. Berry" was not Elijah C. Berry.[22]

The coincidence of the statehouse fire and the mob impressed on people's minds the maliciousness of many convention supporters. In-formal polls taken of men visiting Vandalia during the winter of 1823–24 to purchase federal land revealed growing opposition to the con-vention. David Blackwell's opposition editorship of the widely read *In-telligencer* strongly influenced the outcome, a 57 percent rejection of the convention proposal. A Vandalia poll gave a 113 to 91 victory to the proposal, and a 12 to 30 rejection at the county poll at John Wake-field's house. Illinois histories have called attention to the strange fact that convention opponents' political fortunes fared less well than convention supporters. This was also true of Vandalia's editors: David Blackwell and William H. Brown discontinued their association with the paper, while pro-slavery Robert Blackwell and William Berry ran the press for several years. The state supreme court became the instrument for defining slavery's extent in Illinois. Governor Coles left Illinois eight years later and moved to Philadelphia, where he lived until 1868, well after the Civil War decided for the nation an issue he helped to decide for Illinois in 1824.[23]

Adams's controversial election to the presidency and Andrew Jackson's prospects for 1828 disassembled the older political factions into rival groups. James Hall of McLeansboro, Illinois (not the author who lived at Vandalia), sketched an often-quoted genealogy of no less than five rival factions that vied for supremacy at Vandalia. These groups ostensibly supported Adams, Clay, or Jackson for 1828, with the exception of the satellites of Ninian Edwards, who preferred playing his politics close to the vest, and lingering supporters of the once-powerful Jesse B. Thomas, disenchanted with the new movement. The *Intelligencer* followed with interest the fortunes of Adams and with alarm the popularity of Jackson. "They hope," commented Blackwell on Southern Illinois Jackson meetings, "by this mean, not only to discover their own strength but to give tone to public feeling; and, if possible, induce a belief that Jackson is a strong candidate." Blackwell expressed irritation at the attacks on the president's internal improvement and protection policies and at the claims that Jackson favored the same policies. He conceded defeat after the November 1828 elections but continued to press for internal improvements and federal policies beneficial to the West.[24]

Blackwell was a minority voice, however; the tide toward Jackson sent former Crawford supporters into the president's camp, while Clay and National Republican partisans (i.e., the anti-Jacksonites) found themselves and their policies eclipsed. Two campaigns followed by the *Intelligencer* illustrate the confusion in Illinois politics until the mid-1830s. The first concerned two Jacksonites, between whom there was little to choose. In 1829 John Reynolds and William Kinney announced their candidacies for the gubernatorial elections of August 1830. Reynolds, a politically motivated forty-one-year-old Illinois judge whose ambition was ill-concealed by an odd, self-justifying humility, was a vacillating "milk and cider" Jackson man in contrast to "whole hog" Kinney. Kinney, forty-nine, was sturdily built, a handsome Baptist minister with auburn hair. He may have been the same William Kinney who, early in Vandalia's history, operated a local store. He served in several political capacities during the capital period. However his lack of education and his tactless, sectarian remarks (he supposedly likened Methodists to blacksmiths' dogs: used to sparks of fire they could tolerate the fires of hell) cost him political effectiveness.[25] Reynolds became known for the state histories he wrote during the 1850s.

Both Reynolds and Kinney worked tirelessly for a year and a half. Reynolds flattered Governor Edwards into political support. "We must head our opponents in this own way. . . . I will do my part. I was placed on the track at Vandalia for this purpose. . . . The office I go in for with the wishes of our friends is not the only one." With that last remark, Reynolds implied that his governorship might spell a regained senatorship for Edwards.[26] Among candidates and editors, the campaign rivaled and perhaps exceeded the 1823–24 convention canvass in its divisiveness and controversy. The lion's share of this contention stemmed from James Hall's strange support of Kinney. Hall, who lived in Vandalia and who became editor of the *Intelligencer* in 1829 (while Blackwell retained ownership), was an Adams partisan but backed Kinney as a favor to those Jacksonian legislators who elected Hall as state treasurer. One wonders, in the face of the ensuing newspaper war, what pause Hall gave to this supposedly altruistic maneuver.[27]

Hall had enemies; he must have known it. Ninian Edwards resented his editorial flaying of Cook in 1822. Certain influential editors and legislators, including Alexander F. Grant, the twenty-four-year-old Scottish-born Shawneetown editor, had been engaged by Hall in 1828 in other public controversies. Grant, who is buried at Vandalia, Edwards, and other Reynolds supporters like Sidney Breese turned their attacks from the campaign's issues (such as they were) to Hall's perceived hypocrisy. Hall was termed "an ultra federalist and an up to the nub Clay man." Edwards, with malicious glee, accused him of calculating "upon being the *actual* should Mr Kinney have the good luck to become the *nominal* governor." To a lesser extent, Hall was reproved for filling the *Intelligencer* with his own prose and poetry and for supporting his friend James M. Duncan, Joseph's brother, when James refused to turn over bank funds to the state pending a more satisfactory investigation. Hypocrisy? Duncan recalled, in print, overhearing Edwards express desire for the impeachment of judges Reynolds and James Turney. Finding them sitting outside McCullom's tavern, Duncan had warned the judges of Edwards's threat. Now Edwards and Turney were speech writers for Reynolds, exclaimed Duncan![28]

Mudslinging editorials, letters, and handbills continued, as the *Intelligencer* and *Gazette* became figurative armed camps toward the campaign's end. At the August 1830 elections, Reynolds received 58 percent of the state vote; Fayette County gave his Jacksonian opponent Kinney 58 percent. At the next general assembly, Hall was defeated in a third bid for state treasurer and was brought to trial by political enemies for a supposed discrepancy in state financial records. Hoping for political reward, Edwards waited in vain for the legislature to return him to the U.S. Senate. The campaign also marked the end of the *Intelligencer* as a major state political organ; Hall's financial difficulties necessitated the paper's sale.

The second campaign, the first gubernatorial canvass in which the still-nebulous and informal terms *democrat* and *whig* come to fore, concerned Joseph Duncan's fortunes.[29] Except for the Black Hawk War, Reynolds's four-year term as governor passed unauspiciously and, under the constitution, he could not immediately succeed himself. Many Illinois Jacksonians supported "Old Hickory's" reelection in 1832, but some like Duncan reconsidered their former zeal. Jackson had not supported western improvements, as had been hoped, and his choice of New Yorker Martin Van Buren as vice president indicated a perceived change in administration attitude concerning the West. Pro-Van Buren men and partisans of war hero and westerner Richard M. Johnson for the number-two seat divided a Jackson meeting held at Vandalia on January 2 and 3, 1832. Duncan, Alexander Pope Field, and John Dement, all pro-Johnson, assumed leadership of the meeting after William L. D. Ewing and Samuel McRoberts, pro-Van Buren, withdrew in disgust.[30]

Congressman Duncan's support of Johnson reflected his growing disenchantment with Jackson; he voted to override the president's veto of the Maysville Road bill, expressed no sympathy for Jackson's war on the bank, and consistently voted contrary to administration policies during the 1833–34 Congress. Disgusted with national politics and estranged from his former political friend Elias Kent Kane, Duncan resolved to end his congressional term and to run for the Illinois governorship. A small announcement to that effect appeared in the new capital paper, the *Vandalia Whig and Illinois Intelligencer*.[31]

Most anti-Jackson newspapers in the state portrayed Duncan as a commendable public servant and a friend of the people. Some Jackson men, loathe to believe in his apostasy, continued to support him. Realizing Duncan's popularity in the state, others like the new Vandalia editor John York Sawyer took the threat of his candidacy seriously and searched for able opponents. Robert McLaughlin, Duncan's uncle and a Jackson man of demonstrable integrity, launched his campaign in October 1833. Kinney, unchastened by the 1830 canvass, ran again, as did an Adams-Clay candidate.

Duncan was unable to leave Washington personally to canvass Illinois. With his campaign conducted second-hand and without a clear repudiation of the administration from Duncan himself, many voters assumed Duncan still favored Jackson. Like many Illinois democrats, McLaughlin supported both the president and a new state banking system; he also favored liberal state internal improvements. The Springfield anti-Jackson paper supported McLaughlin. Jackson advocates, like those at a Vandalia caucus, praised the president while criticizing the latter's "impolitic war" on the Bank of the United States; some Jacksonites praised both Duncan and Jackson. "We should suppose that there are few, if any," Sawyer wrote on September 4, 1832, "whose eyes are not sealed with impenetrable *Clay*" who would object to Jackson's veto. The leading pro-Jackson paper, Sawyer's *Illinois Advocate*, supported both Jackson and McLaughlin. The people "want a plain, sensible, independent and honest man," wrote Sawyer in the June 28, 1834 issue, "who will watch over their interest [i.e., McLaughlin], instead of providing offices for family connexions, or mere partisans [i.e. Kinney and Duncan]." Furthermore, Sawyer noted, Duncan was supported by Adams and Clay people. Whig meetings, including one at Vandalia at which Alexander Pope Field and then-county coroner William Hodge spoke, consistently attacked both the president and his policies.[32] Duncan won in August 1834; Kinney came in second, while McLaughlin and James Adams trailed. Fayette County gave its own man 81 percent. Duncan's sympathies became clearer once he reached Illinois during the fall of 1834.

By a fluke of office, Vandalian William L. D. Ewing was Duncan's gubernatorial predecessor, not Reynolds. During the same campaign year of 1834, Reynolds had successfully run for a seat in Congress. But the death of his wife in 1834 prevented him from resigning the governorship until the eleventh hour. Lieutenant-Governor Ewing, forty, ascended to the governor's chair for a total of two weeks and one day. His only duty was to address the state legislature, the Ninth General Assembly (December 1834–February 1835). Ewing echoed the prevailing democratic opinion in praising Jackson's veto of the Bank of the United States charter but stressed the need for a new Illinois bank to fill the resulting economic vacuum.[33]

The political scene of the 1830s was very different than that of the early 1820s. Different men held power in Vandalia and as Illinois congressmen; of the first political giants, only Kane survived. Now, Thomas

Ford, James Shields, John T. Stuart, Orlando Ficklin, John J. Hardin, Usher B. Linder, James Semple, William L. D. Ewing, Richard M. Young, John McClernand, E. D. Baker, Orville Hickman Browning, Stephen A. Douglas, Abraham Lincoln, and others comprised the state's political talent. After beginning political careers in the legislature, Semple, Stuart, Young, Ewing, McClernand, Ficklin, Hardin, Shields, Douglas, and Lincoln later served in Congress. Browning became interior secretary under Andrew Johnson; Shields became the only person to service in the Senate from three different states. Newton Cloud, Usher Linder, and Jesse K. DuBois also had significant state careers. During the 1830s talented politically minded men like Semple, Browning, Adam W. Snyder, Levi Davis, Ferris Forman, and John S. Greathouse defended cases in the various Vandalia courts. Ford, elected Illinois governor in 1842, is remembered as one who helped solve economic problems following the state's internal improvements collapse, as failed mediator in the Mormon crisis of 1844, and as the author of a classic state history. He and his half-brother George Forquer had long been jurists and participants in state politics.

The Tenth General Assembly at Vandalia (1836–37) initiated that ill-advised improvements system; paradoxically, it was also a gathering of great political talent. Of its members, Lincoln became president; five became U.S. senators (Douglas, Semple, Shields, Browning, and William Richardson); eight became congressman (Robert Smith, McClernand, Douglas, Hardin, Richardson, Abraham Lincoln, E. D. Baker, and John Hogan); and one became governor (Augustus French). The assembly included past and future Illinois attorneys general, state treasurers, and state auditors. John McClernand became a Union general; John Logan was the father of another Union general, John A. Logan; Lincoln, Baker, and Hardin, notable whigs at this session, died in service to their country. Rarely in the Illinois legislature's history, and only this once during Vandalia's capital period, were so many legislators also noteworthy Illinoisans.[34]

The five state officials buried at Vandalia—John B. Emanuel Canal, William McHenry, Benjamin A. Clark, John Thompson, and Alexander F. Grant—were by no means major politicians. All died in the 1830s while visiting Vandalia on official business. Little is known about Wayne County representative Clark or Thompson of Randolph County, who both died in January 1836 during a special legislative session. McHenry, like Will, was a renowned "character" (he once killed a bear with a knife) and member of the 1818 convention. Canal, a twenty-one-year-old freshman legislator when he died at Vandalia in 1830, was already touted as a valuable member of the state bench and bar; his high accolades suggest that he may eventually had taken his own place among notable Illinois statesmen. Grant, only thirty when he died in Vandalia (the same evening as Thompson), was a circuit judge, popular friend of several politicians, and editorial associate of Henry Eddy at Shawneetown. Given its ill-starred reputation, it is strange that the proximate deaths of Clark, Thompson, and Grant did not create new accusations that Vandalia threatened the health of state officials.[35]

The political scene in the 1830s was also reflected in new issues and national personalities. Senate and house debates and resolutions during the Ninth General Assembly reflect both the intensity of the campaign for President Jackson's successor and the continuing preoccupation among editors like Sawyer and William Walters for western improvements. It was this dual concern, Jackson's successor and internal improvements, that preoccupied editors during the remainder of Vandalia's capital period. Orthodox democrats favored Vice President Martin Van Buren, but others perceived him as one who influenced the president to adopt economic policies more favorable to eastern workers than to western farmers and manufacturers. Both Sawyer and Walters, who purchased the *Illinois Advocate* following Sawyer's death and incorporated the paper with his own *Illinois State Register*, favored Van Buren and opposed the candidacy of Hugh L. White. Disenchanted Illinois Jackson supporters—enough to split the Harrison vote in 1836—favored White, a Tennessee senator, as a true Jackson man who held to pro-western policies like paper currency, sound banking, and federally funded internal improvements.[36]

In the wake of a national economic boom, democrats interpreted Jackson's recent veto of the Bank of the United States recharter as an endorsement for the establishment of state banks. "It therefore becomes the point of wisdom to prepare to meet the event [the end of the bank] in a becoming manner," wrote Sawyer in the January 21, 1835 issue, "and not wait, as the people of this state formerly did, when the old *humbug* state paper had fallen to 50 cents on the dollar, and make no provision to meet its depreciation." In his December 1834 gubernatorial address William L. D. Ewing stressed that an Illinois bank, solidly based on specie, would greatly benefit the region with circulating currency. With the Bank of the United States in decline and most notes of the first Illinois bank destroyed, money was, after all, scarce in Illinois. The Ninth General Assembly adopted a new state banking system, with $1.5 million capital and a charter designed to avoid the mistakes of the first bank.[37] Sawyer viewed internal improvements in the same way: the state must seize the opportunities now and not "stand with folded arms, but plunge in at once, into the stream of business."[38]

The economic boom culminated in Illinois in 1836. Early that year, the general assembly passed charters for railroad companies across Illinois and, finally, authorized construction of the long-delayed Illinois and Michigan Canal. Two hundred people crowded into Vandalia's decrepit statehouse and toasted with wine and champagne the passage of the canal bill. The next general assembly, the Tenth, authorized a massive internal improvements program, at state expense on loans made on the state's credit. Vandalia's editors wholeheartedly approved this measure, designed to encourage immigration into the state and improve commerce. Bonfires and fireworks in Vandalia and other towns greeted passage of the bill. One legislator walked to Capps's store and purchased $223.50 worth of champagne, food, and party favors.[39]

But President Jackson's "Specie Circular"—applauded by Walters— his restriction of land office money to small bills, and his curtailment of redemption policies braked inflation but reacted with 1835 crop failures to make the economy falter. The expansion of state banks across the West created a shortage of specie reserves in the country, and when New York City banks ceased redemptions in May 1837, state banks followed suit. The Illinois bank, the charter of which depended upon continued redemption, and the entire internal improvements project were thereby threatened.[40]

Walters at the *State Register* blamed the Bank of the United States rather than Jackson or Van Buren for the panic and suggested that the government should divorce itself from all banks. Political dialog on the economy varied. Walters and other democrats blamed speculators, unchecked banking policies, the business cycle, and the cession of borrowing from Europe. Whigs laid the blame at Jackson's feet for recklessly tampering with the national economy, in one man's words, attempting to fix a broken watch with a sledge hammer. Governor Duncan's July 1837 address at Vandalia reflected the general whig idea that the circular and the bank veto were policies Van Buren had convinced President Jackson to uphold, and from which President Van Buren now must suffer. In a letter James Shields more cynically added that many former bank advocates in Illinois, both whig and democrat, now opposed the state bank.[41]

Many Illinois democrats accepted the orthodox view of the panic but would not accept eastern solutions such as advocacy of hard money and distrust of all banks, national or state. One politician had written to Elias Kent Kane that he believed the motive of Jackson's bank veto was poorly understood in Illinois. Too, because of the perceived discrepancy between Jackson's "true" policies and those into which Van Buren supposedly enticed the president, democrats found greater difficulty maintaining party unity than did the whigs. William Walters supported Van Buren's plan to divorce the government from the deposit bank system and to control national currency through a subtreasury. However, whig papers took Walters and other editors to task on the heterodoxy of the state's disillusioned democratic senators, and finally caused Walters to favor repeal of the specie circular and to criticize Illinois Senator Zadoc Casey, whom Walters defended until he voted against the subtreasury in 1838.[42] "Died in this place [Vandalia]," wrote Hodge of orthodox democrats, "of the disease Politico Chorea . . . an eccentric stranger . . . named Loco Foco, a deformed and dwarfish, and squalid looking creature, and apparently destitute of intellect." "The people ought to take warning in time," wrote Walters of Hodge's attacks, "seeing the efforts which the Federalists are taking to break them down."[43]

The system that perhaps saved the democrats from fragmentation was new: the political convention. Informal or countywide meetings had long been a staple of state politics; witness the organizing zeal of the pro- and anti-conventionists in 1823 and 1824. At an 1832 pro-Jackson meeting at Vandalia one man expressed the wish that electors be officially instructed by a state committee to vote for a Jackson–Johnson ticket at the national convention. The idea captured attention. An October 1835 democratic meeting led by surveyor William Greenup approved Van Buren and the new convention system and adopted the campaign motto "union and harmony." The system developed in Illinois in response to the vacuum left by the demise of bi- and multifactional republicanism since the 1820s. For democrats in Illinois, the system became a guiding force for political unity, even if the system was mismanaged to the extent that some democrats like Ewing and Casey refused its conveniences.[44]

Whigs in Illinois, those former Adams–Clay supporters or those new politicians averse to Jackson, refused the convention system altogether and condemned it as "a Van Buren *party* measure." "*Harmony* is a word that ought never to be in your mouths," Walters chided Hodge, "as it is not among the virtues of your party."[45] The whigs, indeed, had difficulty living down democratic perceptions of the party as that of the aloof, anti-egalitarian business and banking establishment. For example, Vandalia attorney Ferris Forman, a dapper and well-to-do individual but a democrat, was, thanks to his fine clothing, nearly driven from town by a group of hostile Jackson supporters at an 1836 poll.[46] Walters sent bitter retorts toward his rival, William Hodge, at the new *Free Press and Illinois Whig*, concerning that party's federalism and antidemocracy.[47] On the other hand, the image oversimplifies the Illinois situation. For instance, Charles Prentice, the moderately wealthy Vandalia merchant, was an outspoken democrat. Rodney O. Davis, who is well-versed in the legislative voting patterns of the Ninth through Twelfth General Assemblies, finds that although whigs and democrats conflicted on issues of national import and on distribution of power in state measures, the two Illinois parties were similarly interested in such state projects as the state bank and internal improvements that bettered the welfare of the entire citizenry, especially before 1837.[48] This was also true of Walters and Hodge and of other local leaders. Although averse to the convention system, whigs achieved sufficient unity in Illinois to keep alive their pet project, the Illinois state bank, for several years and grew in unity and assertiveness throughout the late 1830s. Whigs and democrats at Vandalia displayed common interest in state improvements and economic betterment; Walters and Hodge, for instance, were one in their advocacy of the National Road's completion to Vandalia and westward.

Vandalia's capital period drew to a close as democratic confusion, greater whig resolve, and a deteriorating economy filled the columns of the state's newspapers. Thomas Carlin, probably the least competent of the first seven governors, won the office in 1838, publicly recommending prudent measures on salvaging the internal improvements system, by now a major drain on the Illinois treasury. The last legislature at Vandalia, the first session of the Eleventh General Assembly, should have curtailed the system and cut the state's losses. Instead, the legislators made substantial additions to the previously enacted projects.[49] Meanwhile, whigs took on the "common man" trappings of earlier Jacksonism and grew in assertiveness. Their campaign in 1840 became a brilliant manipulation of frontier enthusiasm and propaganda, in which many Vandalia whigs took their place. But whigs bungled two issues before the election: the controversy over immigrant suffrage, which some opposed because immigrants tended to vote democratic, and the Alexander Pope Field debacle in 1839 and 1840. Vandalian Field, secretary of state since 1828 and a whig since the mid 1830s, refused to leave office when Carlin desired a democratic secretary. Missing the absurdity of a secretary of state acting independently of gubernatorial appointive power, whigs supported Field and thereby hurt their party at the 1840 polls.[50]

The move from Vandalia to Springfield simply made for a change of governmental setting; Walters's newspaper went with the seat of government. However new policies made the move symbolic, in a way, of an era in Illinois other than that of the Vandalia capital period. Would the state have to repudiate its state debt from the improvements act, approaching $17 million in 1841? The governorship of Thomas Ford

(1842–46) provided the answer: the final divorce of state bank from state finances, a progressive tax to pay interest on the state's enormous loans, and a 1 mil property tax. These and other measures made possible the completion of the canal by 1848, the prevention of defalcation (unlike neighboring Indiana and other states), full payments on state bonds by 1857, and payment in full by 1880. Historians have observed that Illinois, by paying rather than repudiating its massive debt, earned the respect of the nation and took its place as a state competent to engage in the national trials of subsequent decades.[51] Thus, the resolution of the problems incurred by the fantastic, optimistic dreams and programs of leaders in Vandalia during the 1830s, rather than the dreams and programs themselves, gained for Illinois its high stature among states of the Union.

Once state politics has been traversed, less can be said about the character of Vandalia's politics; extant records make thorough analysis impossible. Factions did exist, evidenced particularly in 1836. Alexander Pope Field cried foul when, he charged, someone in a Vandalia faction (membership unnamed) intercepted his mail at the Vandalia post office and sent it to democratic newspapers.[52] During the 1820s, for several elections in a row, William Berry, Robert McLaughlin, and John A. Wakefield vied among themselves and others for seats in the state legislature. The recurrence of these same candidates implies some extent of local rivalry among these well-known Vandalians. McLaughlin even took charges of corruption against Wakefield to the house after he lost the 1824 election by a four-vote margin. The race between McLaughlin and Ewing in 1832 was comparably close; although McLaughlin received wholehearted support for governor in 1834, he was less well supported by local businessmen in 1832, who tended to go for Ewing.

The fact that some in leadership positions—Berry, Wakefield, McLaughlin, Prentice, Black, Ewing, and Blackwell—won seats in the legislature implies a connection between political success and local status, and perhaps a certain amount of local back-scratching during the 1830s. Not until the mid- and late-1830s can any party affiliation be placed beside the men's names.[53] Berry died in 1828, and Wakefield left Vandalia before the delineation of Illinois parties during the 1830s, but Blackwell remained favorable to the Clay, and then the White and Harrison, position, while the others transformed from convention-supporting "republicans" to Jacksonian democrats. Again, a connection between the southern nativity of these men (excepting Black, from Van Buren's New York, and German-born men like Leidig) and a strong pro-Jackson orientation is apparent In fact, after study of the miasma of extant poll books, illegible handwriting, lists of voters undifferentiated between town citizens and county residents, and mere lists of voters without their votes, it is apparent that Vandalia's prominent citizens consistently held to the Jacksonian orientation.[54] From large property holders like Prentice and McLaughlin, to local blacksmiths, those downtown professionals who voted followed the pattern of predominantly pro-Cook, pro-Clay–Adams orientation before 1826. In 1822 and 1824, locals split; German immigrants favored Coles for governor and then opposed the convention proposal, while southern-born businessmen favored Browne for governor and subsequently supported the proposal. After 1826, the orientation was pro-Jackson–Duncan–Casey. Only during campaigns that offered little choice, like the Kinney–Reynolds canvass of 1830, or a race between popular Jacksonians like McLaughlin and Wakefield and McLaughlin and Ewing, did significant divergence occur among voters. Why the change of orientation took place in 1826 is not known because no known large-scale turnover of population occurred around that date. Vandalia professionals followed the inconsistencies of the era.

Politics was a catalyst for civic unity, especially in the political meetings that predominated during the 1823–24 campaign and the later 1830s, and in the yearly July 4 local patriotic festivals.[55] Economic issues connected to politics, such as advocacy of a banking system, the National Road and local improvements, and the proposed constitutional convention, also called Vandalia leaders together for betterment of the town and the state.[56] State politics also hampered the town's need for a satisfactory reputation, however. Hooper Warren's appellation, "Vandalism," points to the popular perception that government is a hindrance rather than a help.[57] Vandalia was, in the eyes of many, guilty by association; in one instance (the 1830 gubernatorial campaign) politics drove from town Vandalia's outstanding organizer and intellectual, James Hall. This guilt by association did the town harm, and local leaders were slow to respond. Newspaper editorials are inadequate for the task of full political analysis,[58] but making allowance for editorial practices of the era, insofar as local editors were also local leaders, they were more interested in these issues than the community phenomena, the characteristics of local parties, and even relocation of the capital. Especially in this sense, politics distracted local leaders from the issues of local betterment.

Of politics, like local culture, Fayette County traditions included the anecdotal. Stories of major legislation like the internal improvements bill, and of individual characters like James Whitney ("Lord Coke") of Pike County, legislators like Justin Butterfield, Stephen A. Douglas, and especially Abraham Lincoln were remembered. Although Lincoln was one legislator in hundreds, his subsequent growth and achievement made him legendary among thousands of Fayette Countians. The fact that the greatest U.S. president began his political career in this town renders, in local folk traditions, the remainder of the capital period needless pretext. As fascinating as Lincoln's maturity and destiny is, however, politics at Vandalia meant a great deal more, both for the town and for the transition of Illinois from territorial immaturity to antebellum greatness.

7

Discord and Concord

D URING THE CAPITAL period, Vandalia leaders frequently exhibited civic cooperation. They conscientiously effected local improvements, convened for discussion, and publically countered Vandalia's uncertain reputation. Reflecting the era, they were concerned about two groups perceived as problems: runaways and Indians. Concerns for community improvement, minority issues, and law and order seemed more pressing than concerns for the kinds of cultural and social advancements discussed in the following chapter, but Vandalia's civic characteristics included both: those everyday aspects of community and the extraordinary efforts for cultural advancement. Aspects of community were several and varied.

In nearly all frontier communities, citizens contended with violence and social disruption; the kinds of discord existing in a community reflects upon the social character of that community. In keeping with Vandalians' similarity of background, local eruptions of acrimonious behavior and outright violence do not reflect regional or cultural rivalries. Such events involved personal disputes; during only one year, 1823, did extraordinary violence erupt at the capital because of political controversies. Unfortunately, the worst personal and political violence happened during that year. Although Vandalia appears to have been much less violent than other towns, it retained an untoward reputation because of 1823.

In September 1822 a new brick banking house stood ready on Fourth Street between Gallatin and Main, a structure that also housed the offices of the state auditor, the secretary of state, and the federal land officials. The bank was surely the finest and most stately building at the capital during these earliest years.[1] On the evening of January 28, 1823, bank cashier James Kelly worked late into the supper hour. (Kelly had purchased land at the September 1819 auction and was one of Vandalia's first civically active residents.) Before leaving the bank for supper he secured the fire in the stove, but while he was absent a spark flew out into a bundle of bedclothes kept (for unknown reasons) beneath the counter. Around 6 o'clock someone observed smoke pouring from the bank. Several people forced the front door open and while supreme court justice Theophilus W. Smith and several others bravely fought the blaze with a bucket brigade, someone ran upstairs to save documents.[2] Within an hour the bank was a gutted ruin. Bank books, some money, and most of the auditor's and secretary's documents were saved, but mortgages, several law books, the receiver's papers, and the December 1821 term decisions of the state supreme court were destroyed.

Bank funds retrieved must have been transferred to temporary quarters elsewhere in town. On March 26, 1823, Kelly again worked late at the office. He stepped away to go down the street for a moment. When unlucky James shortly returned, he found the locked door pried open and, inside, the bank's iron chest vandalized and three boxes and several bags of money gone. He shouted, and soon people were in the street at the scene of the crime. No one confessed to having seen anything. The next day a box containing $1,000 was found a hundred yards away, covered with brush in a ditch. A two-day search for the rest of the money proved futile. An estimated $4,200 in specie was gone, including $2,814 of the state's funds and funds of individuals and the receiver of public moneys. Six months later more funds were discovered buried in the manure of a downtown stable.[3]

Two months after the robbery Kelly and a few other men dragged hotel keeper Moss Botsford into the woods, tied him up, and tried to whip a confession from him. Kelly was later acquitted of the assault charges, but not before being accused of treating two jurors to a round of drinks. A month after Kelly's trial, he found Russell Botsford sitting inside a Vandalia store reading a book. Botsford, a local school teacher, had testified for his brother at the trial. As Russell read, Kelly paced in front of the store, openly carrying a loaded pistol and a whip. When after a half-hour Botsford finally emerged from the store, Kelly turned upon him with the whip and beat him. Struggling, Botsford knocked the pistol away, produced a large knife from under his coat, and plunged it into Kelly's body six times. Witnesses stated that Kelly, bleeding badly, chased Botsford several yards down Vandalia streets before falling dead.

Botsford's manslaughter trial at Vandalia inspired much local gossip and speculation. Edward Bates of St. Louis, later President Lincoln's attorney general, was called in to prosecute the case. Sidney Breese defended. Parts of the attorneys' speeches found their way into Vandalia gossip. The court once cited Botsford for contempt. Around midnight of July 31, the jury returned a not-guilty verdict after only a few minutes' deliberation. Judge John Reynolds, writing years later, implied that he did not agree with the jury's verdict.[4] After July 31 Botsford disappears from Vandalia records.

Sixteen days after the trial there occurred one more tragic shedding of blood: Kelly's assistant, Matthew Branch, cut his own throat with his razor, reportedly because of "an avowed disbelief in a future existence." Left among the victims of the robbery was William L. D. Ewing, found accountable by the U.S. Treasury for the stolen land office funds. As receiver he had been required to deposit the land office money at the Bank of Illinois at Shawneetown, but due to illness he had been behind several payments when the robbery occurred. The decision plagued him financially for years.[5]

Amid the tragic circumstances surrounding the bank's conflagration and robbery, unrelated violence occurred in Vandalia during the convention campaign. This violence, typical of Jacksonian-era rioting, was calculated, politically motivated, and involved several individuals in leadership positions.[6] Mob action broke out the night before passage of the convention resolution in February 1823; Nicholas Hansen was burned in effigy and Governor Coles was harassed by the crowd. Again in December 1823, following the mysterious conflagration of the statehouse, a mob marched around Vandalia's blocks (chapter 6). Not surprisingly, these incidents damaged the community's reputation. The Edwardsville editor Hooper Warren had long termed the mobs at the capital "Vandalism," and the pun, referring to the intrigues of the pro-slavery contingent, denigated the capital. The passion of both pro- and anti-convention advocates kept Vandalia agitated for a year and a half. One Kaskaskia correspondent eventually called for a constitutional convention with the aim of moving the state capital. The correspondent sought to prove Vandalia's untowardness by alluding to the events of 1823, as well as Vandalians' failure to remove the six-month-old debris of the burned capitol building.[7]

Vandalia had a reputation for violent occurrences and unsavory characters, apparently idlers who came to town during court or legislative sessions. Local court records serve as the best reference for the extent of crime but alone cannot account for all crime in Vandalia and the county. Besides missing cases and crimes not reported, the court records do not differentiate crimes committed in Vandalia and those committed in the circuit court jurisdiction outside of town.[8]

Vandalia's law enforcement and court system was similar to those of other towns. The capital had no police force as such; sheriffs pressed some cases and grand juries and justices of the peace heard other complaints.[9] The Second Circuit Court, held at Vandalia, tried major cases from the town, county, and the circuit. Assault and battery cases predominated the court's docket; other common cases included (in descending order of frequency) affray and riot cases, larceny indictments, cases concerning the granting of divorces, indictments for fornication or adultery, cases concerning illegal gaming rooms, and highway obstruction. One rape indictment from 1830 is on file, but the case's outcome is missing from the records. Only two manslaughter cases—that of Russell Botsford in 1823 and of John Robb in 1835—appear on the books. The 1823 bank robbery was Vandalia's major theft crime; others were sporadic and less serious break-ins.[10]

Most cases during Vandalia's capital period—an average of almost one a year was recorded for the capital period—involved assault and battery. Perhaps many more cases were not pressed. Most defendants were men like Thomas Higgins and William L. D. Ewing with reputations for such violence, but even Robert McLaughlin was fined $15 plus costs in an 1826 assault and battery case. (He pleaded not guilty.) "Affrays" and "riots" were the next most frequently tried crimes; nine and five cases, respectively, appear in the books. Again, men like Higgins, Ewing, and other repeat offenders occupied the docket. Besides the February 1823 mobs, rioting in Vandalia does not to follow the pattern of politically motivated riots in Jacksonian America in that, with the exception of Ewing, rarely were major town leaders indicted and rarely, with the exception of the 1823 mobs, were such outbursts tied specifically to Jacksonian issues.[11] Likewise, assaults, affrays, and riots occurred more often during the early and mid 1820s than in the late 1820s and the 1830s, a pattern unlike Indiana's capital, Indianapolis, where the town's first years were tranquil.[12]

The crime of larceny was punishable by whipping; Wilson Parks, found guilty at the court's April 1830 session, was one of only a few men punished with "stripes." Gambling—keeping "gaming rooms" and billiard tables—was prohibited in stores and taverns, and taverns were prohibited from opening on Sunday. At least four gambling cases came before the court from 1819 to 1839. Keeping "disorderly dram shops" was also a misdemeanor; Ebenezer Capps and Frederick Remann suffered revocation of their licenses in 1832 after they allowed drunkenness in their Vandalia groceries. Other local grocers occasionally came to trial including James T. B. Stapp, whose indictment was later quashed.[13]

Vandalia's newspapers seldom reported fights and crimes. Settlers later remembered that a special area near Madison and Fourth streets—the famous "bull pen"—provided space for recreative pugilism a safe distance from the comparatively refined public square. However serious confrontations sometimes did occur. In 1829 James M. Duncan and Dr. Peebles publicly fought; an open exchange of letters resolved the conflict. Two years later, William L. D. Ewing stabbed and seriously injured a man during an argument. Two state officials nearly dueled in Vandalia during the winter of 1836–37; a second intervened to resolve the conflict peacefully.[14]

One classic dispute in Vandalia occurred in the second statehouse among state officials. Abner Field, a minor state official from Southern Illinois, had been voted out of his state treasurer's office. While the house was in session an ill-humored Field stomped into the chamber and demanded of John Reynolds whether Thomas Reynolds had taken $10 from Field at Kaskaskia. When Reynolds hesitated, Field drew a dirk, yelled profanities, and kicked him. Thomas Reynolds haplessly appeared, and Field turned on him. He picked up a chair to defend himself but then fled Field's knife. During this exchange, David Blackwell danced on the house desks to ease the tension (to "create mirth") in the room. Later that day Field, dirk in hand again, approached John Reynolds in a Vandalia tavern. This time Reynolds took a loaded pistol from his coat and pointed it at Field's head. The enraged former treasurer backed down quietly. One observer wrote that the legislature subsequently elected Field to a new political office in Jo Daviess County more than 250 miles away.[15]

Violence and criminal activity hurt the town's reputation because public expectations demanded a more refined state capital. Any crime or rumor of crime placed local editors on the defensive. For example, in December 1837, William Walters, the democratic editor, received a letter complaining of troublemakers brawling and disturbing the peace nightly then cursing judges when brought to trial. The letter's author stressed that strangers in town, not Vandalia citizens, were causing the trouble, but the author worried about the severity of the situation. Friends advised Walters that advocates of moving the capital to Springfield would use the letter to their advantage, but in the interest of stopping the trouble, he printed it in the *Illinois State Register*. John Russell, a former Vandalia school teacher, made full use of the letter in his Grafton, Illinois newspaper. Then William Hodge of the Vandalia *Free Press* editorially upbraided both Russell and Walters, the former for exploiting incidents at Vandalia that occurred in almost all towns, and the latter for not sufficiently defending Vandalia.[16]

Future research concerning frontier communities may shed additional light on another phenomenon of early towns: the existence of subsurface discord manifested in pettiness, bickering, meanspiritedness, and social impropriety rather than overt and covert factionalism among leadership. Only one, dubious, source reflects such discord in early Vandalia. The *Busy Body*, dated Sunday, February 18, 1838, was a gossip sheet edited by "Joel Peep," who wrote, "Vandalia is our hobby, and our motto is— Each man prys into our acts and we pry into his." Examples of this paper's "news" that would not have been preserved in other contemporary accounts were:

We think that the law in relation to a certain gentleman of this town is rather too severe. He was fulfilling the Scriptures to the letter—'twas zeal—zeal in a holy cause "to multiply and replenish." But the laws of God and the laws of Illinois are different.

State of the Market

Impudence—market overstocked.
Bullyism—do.   do.
Courage, real—very scarce.
Pot—do-plenty, rather stale, we expect a new supply from Washington soon.
Instructors in the art of dancing—plenty; the best has left town for Ewington—returned.
Chesterfieldism—any quantity can be had near the *Grave*-yard.
Quackery—do.   do.
Politeness—very scarce.
Hides—very scarce; what there is—is bad.
Loafers—market overstocked.

War! War!! War!!!

It seems strange to us that of the thousand and one newspapers that are published in the United States, we cannot pick up one that has not some account of the war in Florida, in Canada, in Texas, &c.; but not one ever breaches a word of the horrible scenes that daily occur in Vandalia. Why should we speak of the wars at a distance! We have wars at home. It would seem that the warrior-god had entered into every soul in this vicinity—even children, ladies and all—yes, reader, the ladies!—The battle of which we are about to speak occurred a few days since at the Vandalia Inn, about two o'clock, P.M.; the two belligerents, Miss ——, and Miss ——, met and after a parley of some few minutes, and a variety of language which is too high-flown for us to repeat, one LADY says to the other LADY: "I suppose you don't recollect nothing of no chickens, eggs, ropes &c., no how." "Now, by holy Paul," says a neutral, "I would'nt

take that—stop her up;"—and at it they went—fist and scull, and the way
the "*har*" flew aint nobody's business. But *nous verrons*.[17]

Reflective of the era, relations between whites and blacks and between
whites and natives were poor. One clue to the situation is found in the
reminiscences of state official Usher F. Linder. Supreme court justice
Thomas C. Browne upbraided his Vandalia roommate:

> "My friend, I am not opposed to taking a social glass, but if I were
> you, from the way it affects you, I would either quit drinking or kill
> myself."
>
> "The devil you would!"
>
> "Well, no. I don't know that you will be driven to that necessity, for
> there are a hundred negroes and mulattoes in this town that you can hire
> to kill you for a quarter of a dollar, and thus save you from the crime of
> suicide."[18]

Scanty additional evidence suggests such racial tension.[19] Free blacks
in Fayette County included one of Governor Edward Coles's emancipated slaves and a number of freed slaves in Bear Grove township after
1840. George Dixon came to Vandalia in 1822 from Washington, D.C.,
to establish a small beer manufacturing company. "Cupid" Smith
crossed "wagons of any size" over the Kaskaskia. John Roy, a "man of
color," owned a dram shop near Vandalia. When he died around 1829,
his estate of $62.68¾ and 480 acres was comparable to those of some
white settlers.[20]

Other blacks lived in a situation of oppression, distrust, and poverty.
Most were servants or slaves; according to the federal census the Elijah
Berry family had six slaves and one free black in their household, Matthew Duncan had eight slaves, and John Dickerson four. Many free
blacks in town were impoverished and served indentureships to survive.
The vagueness of Article VI of the state constitution concerning slaves
and indentured servants led the legislature and courts to follow their
own standards concerning the poor and the nonwhite. The 1819 legislature gave county commissioners power to appoint overseers of the
poor and to apprentice impoverished persons. Although in 1823 Governor Coles questioned the effectiveness of such laws, many counties,
including Fayette, invoked them. In 1828 the Fayette County commissioners apprenticed three siblings to James M. Duncan and William L.
D. Ewing because the children's father had no means to support them.
Indentures were also common.[21]

The state supreme court interpreted indentureship laws. Cases like
Cornelius v. Cohen, *Fanny v. Montgomery et al.* involving a local black
woman, *Nance v. Howard*, and *Phoebe v. Jay* resulted in strict inter-

pretations of the Black Codes, limiting the scope of involuntary servitude but not eradicating slavery altogether. Other cases like *Boon v. Juliet* and *Choisser v. Hargrave* freed many blacks who had been indentured contrary to the letter of the constitution.[22]

Abolitionism was a radical and highly suspect political stance; colonization was the popular alternative among white intellectuals and politicians. An 1821 letter in the *Intelligencer* argued against any form of slavery but also argued against a free black population in Illinois. When abolitionist editor Elijah Lovejoy was assassinated in Alton in 1837, William Hodge, the only Vandalia voice raised in protest of the killing, condemned the mob violence but disavowed any sympathy with Lovejoy's convictions.[23]

In this racial climate, blacks of Vandalia feared incarceration as runaways. Jonathan Ward is an example. A bright, blue-eyed Maryland native of one-eighth Negro ancestry—and a free man—Ward was arrested as at least four times during the 1820s alone by Vandalia sheriffs and justices of the peace. He was jailed yet again in 1828 for harboring two "slaves" named Cherry and Peter, but he was released when the complaining parties failed to appear in court. When Ward came to Vandalia is not known; but he lived in town until 1869 and is interred near the graves of capital-era leaders.[24]

No one publicly supported the cause of Indians, upon whose ceded lands the white pioneers resided. Mutual distrust kept natives and whites separated; therefore, local trouble between the two groups was rare. Distainful of natives and therefore quick to attribute moral inferiority, settlers recalled for the 1878 county history that Indians visited rural grog shops like John Wakefield's on Four Mile Prairie, then held loud, inebriated dances near white settlements. At one July 4 celebration Frederick Remann made a toast (to hearty applause): "Any man that would not follow an Indian after he gets on the track is a white-hearted coward." Such bravado was typical of white frontier men.[25]

In 1832 Governor John Reynolds called for men to take up arms and travel to Northern Illinois, where Sauk and Fox Indians had crossed the Mississippi into Illinois and frightened settlers. Three companies of Fayette County men, excited at the prospect of "shootin' some Injuns," shortly rode to the fighting. The Black Hawk War was characterized by lack of military discipline, serious misjudgments on both sides concerning each's intentions, white hatred of Indians, and the natives' sad defeat. "Until 1832," writes a county historian in 1878 with a touch of pathos unknown to whites forty-six years earlier, "there was quite a number [of Indians] within the county, who left to participate in the war, never to return; and probably few, if any, of the present generation have ever seen a member of the race that a few short years ago were the owners and occupants of the soil they call their own."[26]

Besides the experiences of individual white and Indian men, the greatest effect of the distant conflict upon Vandalia was the opening of Northern Illinois for white settlement. Following the Indian–white conflicts of 1832, northern areas experienced a dramatic population growth. A study of land records from Illinois land districts reveals that the offices in north central and Western Illinois and Chicago showed the greatest increase of sales during and after 1830, while the Vandalia land office showed the least dramatic increase. The several new counties created by Illinois general assemblies in the 1830s, and by the greater representation at the capital following the reapportionment of 1835, also reflect this growth. That Shawneetown bankers refused a loan to Chicago investors because the former could not imagine any future for a town so distant from Shawneetown is probably only a legend. However the legend reflects the reality of population distribution during this period and the downstate's loss of its former progress. Vandalia, no less than Shawneetown, was victim of this population shift.[27]

Community improvement for Vandalia took several forms. The county court of commissioners in 1821 established annual street-clearing weekends. The legislature took some initiative to aid Vandalia in the early 1820s. A bill passed in February 1821 authorized local persons to drain the insect-breeding ponds in the timbered sections of town. The Third General Assembly (1822–23) passed other acts, one of which conveyed 1.5 acres to the town as a burial ground. The conveyed acreage included the knoll already used as a cemetery; before the law was passed, Ferdinand Ernst and perhaps other local citizens were interred there.[28]

Another act granted five lots to the village trustees, four of which were to be sold to pay for an interdenominational chapel on lot 16 of the North Square (Third and Main). Today, a plaque commemorates the chapel's construction. According to county deed records, the donated lots were not sold until the late 1820s and early 1830s. The July 12, 1828 *Intelligencer* mentions an upcoming meeting to consider the sale of lots for the projected "house of public worship." The issue covering the meeting is not extant, but a year later an identical meeting was called. The group appointed James Hall and William H. Brown as solicitors for funds for the house. By November 1829, the six-year-old plan was reality.[29] The chapel still stood in Vandalia during the twentieth century.

The Third General Assembly also followed the example of Indiana and established several roads from its state capital. The assembly authorized twelve roads, each four rods wide, and each to radiate from

Vandalia to major Illinois towns. Local county commissioners authorized maintenance on the roads. The roads were among the many authorized throughout the state by the legislature during the capital period.[30] Authorization and actual construction and maintenance of roads were different things, however, and travel authors complained about the poor roads into the capital. The roads east of town were particularly prone to inundation by the Kaskaskia and flooded in rainy seasons. As the song went:

> The roads are impassable—
> Hardly jackassable;
> I think those that travel 'em
> Should turn out and gravel 'em.

The unsurfaced country roads now in the rural areas of Illinois are probably equal in quality to the very best macadamized roads around Vandalia during the 1820s and 1830s.[31]

The National Road is the best-known an example of the difficulty in obtaining and maintaining good highways. Once the road was surveyed to Vandalia by 1828, people expressed hope in the town's future, but progress was painfully slow. "Will the people of Illinois submit to this?" wrote John York Sawyer in December 1834 when work on the road had delayed. Sawyer voiced the complaint of many Vandalians; local committees during the 1830s sent petitions to Congress for the road's completion. Vandalia advocates like Ewing, Prentice, Peebles, Alexander Pope Field, Linn, Black, James T. B. Stapp, Blackwell, William H. Brown, and others hoped that the road would be completed to Alton or St. Louis and thus place Vandalia on a major trade route with those river towns. By the late 1830s, work had progressed, but not quickly. "Most part of this road is nothing more than a track . . . the timber cut down and removed, the stumps being left," wrote a traveler in 1841. The road was never constructed further west than Vandalia. It is, in one sense, ironic that a Madonna of the Trail statue commemorates the highway's termination there; in the 1830s and 1840s, Vandalians badly wanted the road constructed further west for the sake of the town's economy. In another sense, however, the statue is quite appropriate because the National Road, once historic, exerted a powerful influence upon Vandalia's memory of pioneer settlement.[32]

Transportation into and from Vandalia was complicated by the path of the winding Kaskaskia River. Bridging the river was difficult; the best early bridge was probably a covered one constructed in 1840. Several men earlier promised to span the river, but a sound bridge was slow in coming. Flooding rendered skiffs and ferries useless during wet seasons, but the swift currents, sawyers, and ice in winter made swimming an extremely unadvisable alternative. Fritz Wolff, a German tailor, was the first known of many subsequent Vandalians who did not survive the Kaskaskia. Judges William Wilson and Samuel Lockwood and attorney Henry Eddy once had to swim the Okaw in the dead of winter. They made it across, but Lockwood nearly died of exposure. Whatever the most-used means of crossing the river, most travelers and stage lines apparently crossed over to Vandalia in relative safety. As early as December 1819, a ferry operated over the river.[33]

In the early days local people hoped to make the river a trade route for the capital, but the winding and shallow Okaw, the second longest river wholly within the state's borders, resisted efforts to improve its navigatory potential. In 1829, a group of Vandalia men traveled down the river to determine its capacity for improvement and navigation. Not until 1840–41, when William H. Lee (Lemuel's son) began a cargo business on the river, did Kaskaskia River travel realize a profit.[34]

Transportation was usually by horseback or team and wagon; occasionally people made very long journeys on foot. Others took the stage. When the daily stagecoach rumbled into Vandalia, its horn or whistle blew, and everything stopped so people could gather for their mail and the latest news. Travelers paid dearly to ride the stage; when a stage service was established from St. Louis through Vandalia to Vincennes, the price per passenger was $13 per 190 miles. This cost compares to $2 for one acre of land and $4 for a legislator's daily pay. Travel costs unfortunately precluded civilities. "They seemed to me," wrote Timothy Flint of stagecoach teamsters, "to be more rude, profane, and selfish, than either sailors, boatmen, or hunters, to whose modes of living theirs is most assimilated." Legislators traveling to Vandalia by stage may have become as critical of the capital because of the trip there as for the town's accommodations. Nevertheless, passengers were promised a comfortable ride, personal safety, and convenience. Baggage was not insured against theft or damage, nor were pedestrians promised safety: "Look out for the stage!" was a common expression because the stage "looked out for no one." Considering its importance for the state, Vandalia always needed good stage lines, and several Vandalians rose to the occasion and the potential profits. In addition to Dr. McCurdy's and General Whiteside's contracts in 1838 for several mail routes to Vandalia, other Vandalia men established or sought good lines for the town beginning in the early 1820s.[35]

Small-town talk could exaggerate the risks of travel. The seasoned traveler James Hall, in his typically wordy and lighthearted prose, wrote that during the 1830s better modes of travel encouraged people to travel west "who a few years ago, would as soon have thought of going to China. . . . Fashionable parties have made the adventure, and returned without being gouged, scalped, knocked into a cocked hat, or used up to a mere grease-spot, and a visit to the west is ascertained not only to be safe but in good taste. . . . What with railroads, macadamized turnpikes, and canals, one may whisk off from the seaboard to Cincinnati in six or seven days, at an expense not worth naming, and with ninety-nine chances to one, against the mishap of a broken neck, or even a dislocated limb."[36] Although internal improvements remained a dream to many when Hall wrote, hazards such as the Ernst colony had faced in 1820 were considerably less by 1830.

Mail came into Vandalia at least once a week. The *Intelligencer* and later the *State Register* periodically noted the times of its arrival and published lists of unclaimed letters. Mail was delivered at the post office—which was possibly on the south side of Gallatin Street between Fifth and Fourth streets—and picked up there by the recipient.[37] The receiver, not the sender, paid postal costs, at steep rates ranging from 6 cents a letter from thirty miles or less to 25 cents a letter from four hundred miles or more. Weather often delayed delivery, as did the muddy low ground east of the capital. "It has been asserted," quoted James Hall, "that nothing is so uncertain as the female—except the mail." As early as 1820, however, William Berry proudly announced that a new mail route would bring eastern news to Vandalia a week before it reached St. Louis.[38]

Although the Second and Third General Assemblies passed legislation aiding Vandalia, the state government tenaciously failed to provide adequate public office buildings there. The temporary statehouse constructed in 1820 was the only state building authorized by the legislature. If Vandalia's community improvement efforts seem rudimentary and the town's social structure typical, Vandalians' cooperation and initiative proved exemplary in providing the state government its own facilities.

After the first statehouse burned down mysteriously in December 1823, Vandalians faced the problem of obtaining suitable quarters for the legislature before the general assembly convened again the following winter. In February 1824, John Hull advertised in the *Intelligencer* for two brick moulders and eight laborers to make two hundred thousand bricks for the new statehouse by spring. Local attention shifted from the charred beams and flues at Fifth and Johnson to the burned-out, brick hulk between Gallatin and Main on Fourth Street. During the spring and summer of 1824, workers cleared the remains of the old state bank building of rubble and fire damage and raised a new statehouse from the remains. Townspeople probably contributed $3,000 to the building project. Governor Coles in his November 1824 address told the legislature that the Vandalia citizens who built the statehouse "doubtless should not be disappointed in their just expectations of being reimbursed for the expenses they have incurred in thus providing for the public accommodation." On December 1, 1824, the representative from Fayette County, John A. Wakefield, made a successful motion for the appropriation of funds to cover construction and labor costs.[39]

The homely new statehouse stood centrally in Vandalia's downtown area. Facing the public square along the west side of Fourth Street, it was sixty feet four inches long in front and thirty-two feet wide. With two stories, the building's downstairs contained the house chamber, and the senate convened upstairs. Between sessions the capitol's rooms often were used as offices for the state treasurer, public printer, and attorney general. The first floor also contained the supreme court chambers. No drawings or paintings of this building—the capitol of Illinois for twelve years—are known to exist. The fact that state documents and travel books often refer to the "banking house" suggests that the building was a two-part structure, the north section being new rooms and the south, office section being the renovated 1822 state bank. Six general assemblies convened there, and Lincoln began his political career in the building in 1834. The building was, for that reason alone, significant.[40] But what might have become an historic structure was unsubstantially and hastily constructed on low, moist ground and with inadequate cement. By the summer of 1836 local congregations refused to convene there any longer for fear it would collapse upon them. William Walters predicted the building would not stand until winter.[41]

The legislature had consistently defeated bills that would have authorized major improvements or a brand-new building. The capitol was repaired of extensive wind damage in 1828; in 1831 and 1832 several Vandalia men were authorized to construct additions, but the building remained dangerous and inadequate. The supreme court room was a crowded firetrap, as were the offices of the auditor and treasurer. Some officials rented offices from George Leidig and John Charter.[42] Realizing that the statehouse was no longer usable, and perhaps acknowledging legislative disregard for the public buildings, Vandalians Asahel Lee and Levi Davis wrote Governor Joseph Duncan in Jacksonville about the matter during the summer of 1836. Duncan replied that if possible they should repair the statehouse or find rentable quarters for the next general assembly. He believed a new building could not be constructed by December, but he allowed the men to use their own judgment and wrote that he would draw from the state "contingent fund" for whatever amount they might need.[43]

Lee hoped to perform extensive interior work, but the building could not tolerate it. The northwest corner bulged eight to ten inches for ten feet. A crack extended up the north wall and in the chimney on that side. The senate floor had sunk seven inches just since 1834. The west and north walls seemed near collapse. William Walters, in the August 12 *Register*, expressed his support of the suggestion that the old public buildings be razed.

Alexander Pope Field, Harvey Lee, William Hodge, Charles Prentice, and William Greenup sent letters to the governor testifying to the building's condition, remarking that there was no understanding between Vandalians and contractors for work if the legislature did not pay for the building. Lee assumed that the legislature would eventually pay or he would not have contracted on the terms that he did, because labor costs had risen 100 percent since 1835, he said.[44] For the next four months local companies and workers contributed time, labor, and materials for construction of the new state capitol on the public square. David B. Waterman and Co. handled the masonry. William Hodge and John Taylor & Co. drew up the plans, did the second-story carpentry, and built the stairs. John Hull was commissioned for lime and rock, the Lee brothers and William Linn furnished white and yellow pine planks and labor. William C. Greenup razed the old statehouse, delivered clean bricks to the public square, dug the foundation, and saved imperfect bricks for use in streets. (Two-thirds of the bricks for the structure were new, costing $7 per thousand.) Local merchants like Linn, James Black, Ebenezer Capps, Robert Blackwell, Charles Prentice, Robert McLaughlin, and Frederick Remann provided sundry materials and tools; Moses Phillips made a table. Timber was taken to a nearby mill and sawed to make window frames. Other timber for beams was hewn. State treasurer John Dement and county farmer Winslow Pilcher hauled lumber to the public square. Thomas B. Hickman laid 3,250 feet of rough tongued-and-grooved flooring; Maddox, Waterman and Company did masonry, laid the foundation, and did brick and plaster work; Johnson and Graves provided labor for construction of the cupola.[45]

The new statehouse was 150 feet by 50 feet, located in the center of Vandalia's hitherto-unoccupied public square. The building, completed at a cost of more than $16,000, had a cupola, a gabled roof, and exterior walls of unpainted brick. Its front entrance faced Vandalia's "main" street, Gallatin Street, and its rear entrance faced north; two other doors faced west and east. Downstairs were offices for the auditor, secretary of state, treasurer, and a courtroom for the supreme court.

Upstairs were the senate chamber, the house chamber, a committee room, and a lobby. Spectators' galleys overlooked legislative halls. Although a daguerreotypist rented a room in the building during the 1850s, no photographs of the statehouse in its original appearance have been discovered.[46] Artist John Matthew Heller's representation showed an imposing structure positioned grandly upon the public square, surrounded by smaller and less imposing structures of the era's downtown: the McLaughlin residence, Capps's crowded store, the public worship house, Charter's busy Sign of the Green Tree, George Leidig's old hotel, now operated by Abner Flack, the new State Bank, the Globe, the Vandalia Inn, and "Union Hall," still standing and in business years after Frederick Hollman built it from logs for Ferdinand Ernst.[47]

The building was sound and larger than the previous capitol, but still far too small. The builders misjudged the size required for a legislature expanded and reapportioned following the 1835 state census. Unimpressed with Vandalians' motivation, one writer complained the building resembled a Pennsylvania barn.[48] Legislators were also unimpressed with the fact that some interior work remained. It is uncertain when the downstairs offices were first used. During this session the council of revision rented a meeting room for $19 a month from Augusta Ernst Peebles; the auditor Levi Davis and Secretary of State Alexander Pope Field rented offices from Robert Blackwell for $20 a month during the 1836–37 session; likewise, the clerk of the supreme court and the treasurer rented offices from William Walters. The new statehouse had been constructed to provide state officials with adequate quarters rather than to entice the legislature to keep the seat of government at Vandalia. Had the latter been the motive of the builders, it would have been an unsuccessful effort.[49]

Legislators may have complained, but Vandalians' cooperation had provided them with essential quarters. During the capital period, many Vandalians cooperated to effect local improvements. Some were boosteristic and translated that sentiment into local programs and new services. Some did seek a greater tolerance among Illinoisans concerning Vandalia's social climate; only occasionally did Vandalians descend into Hobbesian turmoil. Most Vandalians were people of their times, as shown by the antisocial behavior of a few and in the widespread, shameful contempt for blacks and Indians. They succeeded best in cooperating for the provision of state buildings, a task which, after all, was beyond reasonable expectations and earned them few popular thanks.

8

Like Oxford or Cambridge

Predictably, James Stuart in 1830 noted the horrible road east of Vandalia, but, nearly alone among travel writers, he mentioned Vandalia's better qualities. He described hospitable meetings with Matthew Duncan and Robert Blackwell, who informed him of the several cultural organizations that convened at the capital. "It is an extraordinary fact," concluded Stuart, "that in this town . . . three meetings of an antiquarian and historical society have already taken place, and the whole of their published proceedings are as regular, and as well conducted, and as well printed . . . as if the seat of the society had been at Oxford or Cambridge."[1]

Concerns for law and order and for community development do not exhaust a town's social identity. More than a typical frontier village and a controversial location for the seat of the state government, Vandalia possessed a substantial cultural identity that began in the late twenties. The traditional interpretation of the social history of Illinois is that by the late 1820s the older manners of the territorial period succumbed to new values, better habits of dress, a greater demand for education, and a deeper religious sentiment. The change of cultural perceptions made possible the religious and educational organizations at the state capital during the late twenties and early thirties and laid the first foundations of the town's educational and religious institutions. But during the same period, anti- and non-intellectual qualities of the local social structure and Jacksonian politics also spelled disaster for some of the educational and literary projects carried on by James Hall, probably Vandalia's greatest capital-era citizen.[2]

From its beginning, Vandalia was center of Illinois state organizations. As early as December 1820, such an organization, the State Agricultural Society, convened at the barely completed capital city. The society's membership included several members of the bench and the legislature, as well as locals Elijah C. Berry, R. K. McLaughlin, and then-Gallatin County resident James Hall. Other organizations, such as medical societies and a state Masonic lodge, also met periodically at the capital.[3] A few locally organized societies also existed before 1827. A "Vandalia Polemic Society" came into being April 1821; at the first meeting local physician Dr. Van Vleck gave a speech. A Vandalia Masonic lodge was organized in 1821 and 1822, with members E. C. Berry, James M. Duncan, John Warnock, Moss Botsford, William L. D. Ewing, and others. The group met regularly until 1828, disappeared during the anti-Masonic prejudice of the 1820s, and reorganized in the later 1830s.[4]

Vandalia's social life included the July 4 celebrations common in frontier villages, many commemorative dinners that honored a visiting politician or dignitary like Daniel Pope Cook, and dinners that drew attention to a cause such as the convention campaign. Justice John McLean, a Jackson appointment to the U.S. Supreme Court (remembered as the sole dissenting vote on the Dred Scott case of 1858), presided over the federal court at the capital in the fall of 1837, and sat at the honored chair of a public dinner at Abner Flack's hotel. Other social functions included cotillions, candlelight suppers at the homes of the McLaughlins and Alexander Pope Field, levees, waltzes, dances on the public square, and perhaps ice cream socials.[5] The legislature frequently sponsored guest speakers for evening candlelit presentations. During the Eleventh General Assembly alone, speakers on temperance, phrenology, and Prussian education, an officer in Napoleon's army, and a guest from the newly founded McKendree College in Lebanon, Illinois all gave lectures at the capitol. Mrs. Sarah Hardin of Morgan County wrote her legislator husband in 1839 that she missed the "intellectual feasts" at the capital; she had attended the Tenth but not the Eleventh General Assembly.[6]

Two Yale students, Theoron Baldwin and John F. Brooks, assessed Vandalia's spiritual potential in 1830. Baldwin, appalled at Vandalians' irreligiousness, wrote to a friend, "But three years since the sabbath was frequently spent when the weather was pleasant by large companies in playing ball on the public square. It has been famed far and wide for its dissipation and wickedness. . . . Congregations are large for the place and very attentive, but the Western people are more fickle than the Eastern. They do not generally go to meeting either from habit or principle like tens of thousand in N. Eng. If things happen to take you will have a full house if not you may preach to the walls." Baldwin's observations can be verified; Zophar Case wrote a friend that a crowd singing "Charivary" once disturbed a Vandalia church service. However Brooks, Baldwin's associate, was pleased with Vandalia and considered its spiritual potential better than some other communities. He wrote to a friend that a church house in Vandalia was almost finished, a subscription had been made for a $200 a year salary for a minister, and a young Vandalia lawyer had recently been converted at a church service.[7]

Brooks probably referred to the Presbyterian church, one of the two present-day congregations founded during this period and the first continuously worshipping congregation in town. Only two Christian denominations met regularly during the capital period, although several churches existed in the county as early as 1817. After the end of the Ernst colony in 1822–23, Lutheranism was not organized in Vandalia until the early 1840s. Until 1845 Vandalia Roman Catholics rode to St. Louis for mass. Although rural Fayette County contained several Baptist congregations during the 1820s and 1830s, no known Vandalia congregation existed until after the capital period. Two Quaker families—the Peter Shaffers and the John W. Hocketts—lived in Vandalia, but it is not known whether a Friends meeting existed in the area, nor is it known if Jewish settlers lived in or near Vandalia.[8] By 1828, Solomon P. Hardy of the American Home Missionary Society organized a Presbyterian congregation in Vandalia. Seven persons placed their membership on July 5, 1828. Thomas A. Spillman guided the church after Hardy, followed by Theron Baldwin in 1830 and 1831. From 1832 to 1836 the secretary recorded thirty-two additions to the church, five deaths, nine dismissals by letter, and three elders elected and ordained. Among the church's members were James and Mary Hall, Mary Ann Ernst, Henry C. Remann, Joseph T. Eccles, William H. Brown, Angeline Blackwell, and James Black. Romulus Riggs, a wealthy Pennsylvanian who had extensive property holdings in Illinois, honored the church with the gift of a bell in 1830. It was the first bell to ring in an Illinois Protestant church and honored Riggs's young daughter, named Illinois.[9]

Methodist camp meetings must have been occurred in Fayette County during the 1820s, but in July 1831, J. P. Benson organized the first Methodist church in Vandalia. Like the Presbyterian church, the Methodist church has met continuously since its founding. Seven members comprised the first congregation, including Dr. and Mrs. Nathaniel McCurdy and the furniture maker Moses Phillips and his wife. After a short time county official (and later editor) William Hodge and some others placed their memberships.[10] At first the Methodist and Presbyterian congregations of Vandalia met together in the house of public worship on Main and Third. During this period, however, Methodism and Presbyterianism conflicted in Illinois due to the widespread charge that nonsectarian societies, established by the Presbyterians, were actually anti-Methodist and pro-"New Haven theology." Furthermore the Presbyterians were divided among themselves, between Calvinist "old school" and "new school" that favored the "New Haven theology" of Yale professor Nathaniel W. Taylor. Several churches and synods were denounced by the 1837 Presbyterian national assembly for subscribing to the new theology.[11] Whether these conflicts affected the Vandalia congregations is unknown. Records of the earliest Methodist meetings did not survive the 1899 church fire, and the Presbyterian record book betrays no theological conflicts, but after 1833 they met together no longer. In the fall of that year building commissioners R. K. McLaughlin, Robert Blackwell, and Jesse W. Curlee drew plans for a Methodist church building; McLaughlin donated the lot on Fourth Street south of Gallatin. The church was forty-feet square and sixteen feet high. Until it was completed in 1835, Methodists often worshipped within the unplastered walls, perhaps singing familiar Kentucky hymns:

> The Lord Our God is clothed with might,
> The winds obey his will;
> He speaks, and in his heavenly height
> The rolling sun stands still.
>
> O for a faith that will not shrink,
> Though pressed by every foe,
> That will not tremble on the brink
> Of any earthly woe!

That church building served until 1867, when a new church, constructed through a sizable gift from Dr. McCurdy, was built on Fourth and Madison, the site of the capital-era jailhouse.[12]

Sunday school unions and bible societies, popular throughout the region, combined the needs of education with those of religion. The Illinois Sunday School Union met for the first time at the Vandalia statehouse in December 1830. Theron Baldwin, James Hall, Governor Ninian Edwards, John Mason Peck, Samuel Lockwood, and Thomas Lippincott were recorded among the members. The society's goal included formation of Sunday schools throughout the state, and the members soon raised $100 for this purpose. A related predecessor to this organization was the State Bible Society, the goal of which was the distribution of Bibles throughout the state. Vandalia Presbyterians like

Jeremiah Abbot, James Black, and William H. Brown joined Peck, Lock-wood, Lippincott, and others in this organization. James Hall, J. D. Gorin, Robert H. Peebles, and others joined later. By June 1830, new branches of the organization had been founded in Marion and Jefferson counties.[13]

Cultural work in Illinois gained impetus through a group of several young men. Brooks and Baldwin were members of a group called the "Yale Band," which also included Mason Grosvenor, William Kirby, J. M. Sturtevant, Elisah Jenner, and Asa Turner, and later Edward Beecher and Jonathan Baldwin Turner (whose grandson was county farm adviser for many years). These students from Yale Theological Seminary, as members of a Yale group called the Society of Inquiry Respecting Missions and of the American Home Missionary Association, came West to influence the region's educational and religious potential, and especially to found a western equivalent to Yale. They achieved the latter goal when the group joined J. M. Ellis to found a college in Jacksonville. At the stockholders' meeting in December 1829, James Hall made the motion "that this institution shall hereafter be called and known by the name of ILLINOIS COLLEGE," a motion the trustees accepted.[14]

The exemplariness of the cultural advancement in Vandalia, particularly in the area of education and literature (although Baldwin and Brooks assisted in the town's religious life as well), was due to a great extent to the labors of Hall and the mutual inspiration of Hall and the Yale Band. Hall, former Shawneetown editor, attorney, and a writer of growing reputation, had moved to Vandalia in 1827 following his election as state treasurer. When the band first visited Vandalia during the winter of 1829 they found an enthusiastic friend in Hall and stayed for a time at his home. The thirty-six-year-old Hall acquired interest in the local paper, the *Illinois Intelligencer*, in 1829 and therein communicated his outspoken educational ideas for the benefit of the western public. James Hall's name stands behind most of the cultural endeavors at Vandalia in 1827 through 1833. The group from New Haven also assisted with several other organizations.

Throughout his career Hall advocated free schools for students and lyceums or Sunday schools in areas where schools had not yet been established. He probably wrote the constitution of the Vandalia high school, a new school that opened in November 1830 with John Russell of Bluffdale as instructor. Courses offered were reading, writing, and arithmetic for a fee of $3; these subjects plus grammar and geography for $3.50; plus higher math, Latin, Greek, and French for $4. Hall printed the constitution in the *Intelligencer* as a model for other villages to found their own high schools.[15]

The first Vandalia school began in 1819. Joseph T. Eccles later taught classes in a two-story frame house near the river bridge, and teachers occasionally conducted classes at the Presbyterian church and in a log school house just north of the corner of Gallatin and Fifth. In 1828 Mrs. Reid opened a "Female School" in Vandalia, charging $2.50 a quarter for spelling, reading, writing, and plain and ornamental needlework. The older system of private schools was used in Fayette County until 1834, when a public school system was adopted. Levi Davis, a young attorney who had just moved to Vandalia, was named the first county school commissioner; his principal duty was to sell sixteen sections for revenue. Two more schools opened in 1837, the Vandalia Academy and Free School and the Fayette County Manual Labor Seminary. Harvey Lee, Robert Blackwell, and William Linn were involved in the government of both schools; Charles Prentice, Moses Phillips, Dr. McCurdy, William Walters, and others were trustees of the latter school, so named because students worked to reduce their educational costs. Both schools advertised an impressive list of courses.[16]

Education was still quite rudimentary in Illinois. Robert W. Ross, who attended Vandalia schools in the 1850s, remembered that the popular books of the day included Smiley's and Smith's arithmetics, the old English reader and the New Testament for reading, Webster's Elementary Speller, Kirkham's text for grammar, and Weem's Life of Washington for history. "Oftentimes these few books were all that were to be found in an entire neighborhood, outside the few the teacher tried to accumulate and which he generously lent his pupils, who literally read them to pieces." Adequate teachers were difficult to find, and those visionary New Englanders who came West to promote religion and education found low salaries (payment sometimes was made with produce or cloth) and suspicion. Eastern culture often clashed with western egalitarian pride. A story is told of a young New Englander who came to Fayette County to teach. On his first day, he was astonished that the children had no textbooks except their readers and spellers. They could spell words and read from books, but did not know the meaning of words. He asked if they owned dictionaries; they looked at him blankly, not knowing what dictionaries were. They had also never heard of geography or grammar. He asked them to tell their parents to buy these books for them, but he learned that he was the first person to make such a request. The parents told the children that if they learned their lessons from the speller and could write, they had learned enough. The children lost respect for the teacher and distressed him so that he resigned and left the county.[17]

James Hall's activism in education led him to found or guide several other educational organizations, as well as other kinds of societies. Shortly after moving to Vandalia, Hall became president of (and probably organized) the Antiquarian and Historical Society, the first of its kind in the state and only the eighth in the country. The society first met at the statehouse on December 8, 1827 and consisted mostly of politicians and members of the state judiciary—a few of them political enemies—who were interested in the state's antiquities and already in Vandalia on legal business. Hall asked members to collect all possible data about Illinois history, government, topography, population, and natural features. "All our exertion must at last center upon the one great object of rendering service and honor to our common country," he stated, "by fostering its infant literature, and developing its history, character, and resources."[18]

Hall was far ahead of his time in perceiving the necessity of developing a uniquely American culture and tradition. He saw more clearly than most that the frontier was an untapped reservoir of democracy and that a native literature and tradition from that region should be encouraged. Hall hoped to develop the West's culture through an active enthusiastic society. But when the society met again in December 1828, little progress had been made, although there were a few new members like John Mason Peck, William L. D. Ewing, Alexander F. Grant, James T. B. Stapp, and Peter Cartwright. In his speech, a tactful but enthusiastic pep talk for the fulfillment of the society's goals, Hall used the example of Vandalia to note the rapid advancement of population into the Illinois wilderness. Vandalia, a town for only eight years, had more than eight hundred persons, and other parts of the state were likewise becoming populated quickly. For such a state, "we should collect all the facts which tend to . . . desirable objects. . . . We should extend [Illinois'] population by holding up to our distant brethren a mirror which shall faithfully reflect the truth."[19]

The last time the *Intelligencer* mentioned the society was in the January 16, 1830 issue, which devoted three page-one columns to former governor Edward Coles's message on the state's capacity for navigation and commerce. One can find likely reasons for the death of the society. In spite of Hall's appeals, no one except Coles seems to have finished an assignment. If the society suffered from the lack of enthusiasm of its membership, it must have also suffered because of the members' political activities. There were already enemies within its ranks. Blackwell, Smith, Thomas Reynolds, McRoberts, Coles, and Brown had all been active and bitter participants on the convention crisis of 1823–24. The extraordinarily divisive 1830 gubernatorial race created new enemies among members like Hall, Grant, Sidney Breese, James M. Duncan, Alfred W. Cavarly, and others. Meetings of the Antiquarian and Historical Society beyond 1829 would have been strained to the breaking point if held at all.[20]

Additional evidence for the society's demise after 1829 are Hall's assumption of the society's goals via his *Illinois Monthly Magazine* and the almost identical club that was founded in December 1831. Josiah Holbrook of Boston, initiator of the American lyceum movement (an early form of adult education), stopped at Vandalia in November 1831 to give a lecture. Hall immediately began to promote the lyceum movement through the *Intelligencer*, and on December 8, 1831 several men met at Jacksonville to form the Illinois State Lyceum. Both Hall and John Russell, the teacher at the Vandalia High School, were among the founders, as well as Edward Beecher (who became president), Theron Baldwin, J. M. Sturtevant, Edward Coles, Henry Eddy, John Mason Peck, Sidney Breese, and Thomas Lippincott. To remain a member of the lyceum, one was required to execute assigned research and to encourage other lyceums in other communities. The lyceum's goals, otherwise, were essentially identical to the Antiquarian and Historical Society, but the lyceum was slightly more successful.[21] Three members presented papers at the August 1832 meeting. Thomas Lippincott presented a paper at the third meeting, held at Vandalia in December 1832. Hall published Lippincott's work in his Cincinnati journal, but the Vandalia newspapers did not report the meeting's proceedings. The next meeting, in August 1833, was cancelled due to the cholera epidemic at Jacksonville. By that time, interest in the lyceum had waned, and Hall, the guiding force in every organization to which he belonged, no longer lived in Illinois. At the last known meeting of the lyceum, nine members attended and only two had presentations ready. A similar organization was the Vandalia Lyceum, founded by Hall in February 1832. He delivered the first of a proposed series of weekly lectures, but thereafter the Vandalia Lyceum, too, disappeared from local news and presumably from existence.[22]

Three organizations founded at Vandalia were not educational but were addressed two contemporary social concerns: temperance and slavery. The Fayette County Temperance Society was the most durable of the organizations founded at Vandalia during this period. The society was founded in the autumn of 1831 and was followed a few months later by the new State Temperance Society. Both organizations reflected a growing national concern about widespread abuse of alcoholic beverages. Meeting alternately at the Presbyterian and Methodist churches, the Fayette County society consisted mostly of local churchmen like Hall (who was not a teetotaler), Moses Phillips, William H. Brown, and James Black. Temperance—in this era a stereotypically northern and whig concern—was not destined for widespread acceptance in this town of mostly southern-born democrats, however the society met sporadically throughout the 1830s.[23]

The Illinois Colonization Society reflected one aspect of the antislavery movement of the 1830s. Supporters of colonization sought to eradicate both slavery and a black American population through the transportation of free blacks to Africa; such a plan would also provide a long-term trading source with African nations. During the summer of 1830 the thirteen-year-old American Colonization Society appointed Cyrus Edwards as their agent for Illinois. Soon, with the blessing of the Yale Band, the Illinois Colonization Society was born. One of seven societies that Edwards orchestrated in Illinois, it continued for two or three years with members well known in the state.[24]

Was there a connection in Vandalia between the impetus for cultural or humanitarian organization and the social elite? "The early city fathers [of New York], confident of their position and proud of their city, had sought to encompass the whole community within their benevolent embrace and to improve in a variety of ways the quality of urban life without disrupting the social structure from which they benefited." Large urban areas saw greater disruption and distress as the century advanced, and benevolent organizations changed according to new requirements. But the quoted model of humanitarianism—well-to-do civic leaders equipped benevolent organizations in their spare time—follows the trends of Vandalia. The established and upper-class local leaders like McLaughlin, Hall, Prentice, Blackwell, Black, and Brown took the initiative in such community efforts, rather than representatives of the general population. Usually these people aimed at enhancing rather than criticizing the local social structures. (For example, there were no vocal abolitionists at Vandalia.) These efforts also reflected the assumption, prevalent in such organizations, that civilization's and Christianity's progress westward comprised a single movement. Consider the work of the Yale Band, the coincidence of benevolence and church membership on the part of Vandalia leaders, and the postwar patriotism exhibited by Hall that so often went hand in hand with educational or religious evangelism. This could also explain the failure of many Vandalia organizations because most local citizens did not participate in either church or civic efforts.[25]

The fact that religious leaders were also the organizers of voluntary societies does not necessarily mean that these leaders sought a kind of social control over the community. There is no evidence that local leaders, or the Yale Band, tried to use the organizations to gain social power except, conceivably, to improve their own social prestige through voluntarism. The voluntary organizations at Vandalia, rather, follow the pattern of historians who criticize the "social control" thesis. The promoters hoped to use democratic sentiment for useful social ends; they did not have disruptive, radical visions concerning those ends, but instead had naive, status quo ideas about cultural progress; they had difficulty enlisting and maintaining volunteers; and they exhibited sincerely benevolent motives.[26]

Was anyone at the capital actively opposed to these groups? Hardshell Baptists from the South, many of whom lived in Fayette County, theologically and emotionally distrusted northern religious liberalism, missionary efforts, and benevolent organizations. Little or no overt hostility seems to have taken place, however. Nonparticipation was a sufficient death blow during this era of tenuous voluntarism.[27]

Nonparticipation implies failed boosterism and the possibility of subsurface social discord. If local leaders hoped to secure moral and social control through these organizations, their efforts made little difference in Vandalia. Even the most crusading groups like temperance and the colonization failed to attract large followings or to achieve significant results. There is no evidence, as well, that these groups cooperated among themselves in any significant way. If a territorialness had been exhibited among members, their long-term effectiveness would have been impeded. The only extant example of attempted social control (and it failed) comes from the records of a Vandalia church. In the early 1830s, the leaders threatened a member, a Vandalia insurance representative, with expulsion—a common practice during the pioneer era—because of his frequent public drunkenness. The group did not revoke his membership until after urging his repentance several times, but the man expressed no such repentance.[28]

Certain individuals left cultural work which, to varying degrees, had lasting, historical impact. John Mason Peck and John Russell were frequent visitors to the capital, while James W. Berry, John A. Wakefield, and James Hall were local citizens. In addition to Hall's organization and civic work, he wrote twenty-five stories, many while he lived at Vandalia; these tales were important in the evolution of the short story genre. Through publications and organizational efforts he helped give the early West a voice and a cultural identity. Of persons figuring in

Vandalia's capital period, only Lincoln and Douglas have earned more biographic treatment than James Hall.[29]

After his move to Vandalia in 1827, Hall worked as state treasurer, newspaper editor, lawyer, organizer of educational organizations, and most importantly as a writer. His first book, *Letters from the West* (London, 1828), reproduced a series published earlier in the decade in the Shawneetown newspaper and the Philadelphia *Port Folio*. An entertaining and patriotic book, *Letters* contains anecdotes, legends, pioneer customs, stories about Daniel Boone and the cutthroat Harpe brothers, and lighthearted descriptions of the country via a boat trip from Pittsburgh to Shawneetown. Although Hall's style ranges from poetic to pedestrian, his essays display deep sensitivity to western characteristics and manners. Historians find the book an important source of description and comment, however most contemporary critics disregarded or dismissed *Letters*, and Hall subsequently abandoned thoughts of domestic publication.[30]

Hall's Philadelphia brothers pioneered giftbooks as outlets for writing talent. One of John Elihu Hall's giftbooks, *Winter Evenings* (Philadelphia, 1829), contained James's story "The Soldier's Bride."[31] James himself assembled a giftbook, *The Western Souvenir* (Cincinnati, 1828), which more than *Letters* earned him a reputation as a western chronicler. A collection of various authors' work, more than a third of the book was written by Hall himself. The *Souvenir* includes bold tales of whiskey-loving frontier characters: "The French Village," "The Indian Hater," "Pete Featherton," and "The Billiard Table." Although Hall was more skilled in characterization and description than in plot, in his *Souvenir* stories he innovatively used popular legend and regional verisimilitude. "The Indian Hater" is probably his most psychologically sophisticated and affecting story, and "Pete Featherton" is a humorous folk legend. Hall also wrote a number of poems for the *Souvenir*, most of them sentimental and forgettable.[32]

Besides his three-volume *History of the Indian Tribes of North America* of 1836–44 (Thomas L. McKenney shared disproportionate billing), Hall's most ambitious project was the *Illinois Monthly Magazine*, published in Vandalia and Cincinnati from 1830 to 1832. Only three other magazines had ever been attempted in the West, and this was the first in Illinois. Hall wrote about three-fifths of Volume 1 and half of Volume 2. Several of his better stories appeared in the journal: "A Legend of Carondelet," "The Intestate," "The Dentist," "The Very Useful Man," "The Silver Mine," and "Michel De Coucy." Hall also wrote biographical sketches on such western figures as Jedidiah Strong Smith, Daniel Boone, and Jo Daviess, as well as educational articles, a series on Illinois towns, and book reviews. In one review, he praised Nathaniel Hawthorne's work several years before Hawthorne was nationally known. Authors such as William Cullen Bryant, Arthur and John Howard Bryant, Morgan Neville, Salmon Portland Chase, Isaac Appleton Jewett, Edward Coles, John Russell, James Handasyd Perkins, Hugh Peters, Timothy Walker, and Frederick W. Thomas also contributed to the monthly.[33]

The journal was an impossible task. Hall edited and contributed to the monthly while performing his other professional and civic duties, while suffering a lawsuit filed by political enemies, and finally while grieving the August 1832 death of his wife. (Their newborn son also died shortly thereafter.) He lost money on the project; paper shortages and delayed mailings hampered publication. He was both lighthearted and distressed by the difficulties. He delighted in one letter from a semiliterate subscriber who complained of "tipogeographical errors," but he also wrote, "We think that we have done the state some service; and are sorry that we cannot, in the language of Othello, add, '*and they know it.*'"[34] Hall ceased publication in September 1832, after completing Volume 2.

Later that year Hall published a volume of tales called *Legends of the West* (Philadelphia, 1832), which reached an eighth edition by 1885 and from which stories were reprinted as late as 1929. This, and *The Soldier's Bride and Other Tales* (Philadelphia, 1833), collected many of Hall's best stories.[35] One other superior Hall story, "The Dark Maid of Illinois," was published in 1833 but not collected until Hall's *Tales of the Border* of 1835.[36] Hall also published his only novel in 1833, *The Harpe's Head: A Legend of Kentucky.* Although a frightening, true story of western lawlessness, the novel suffers from an insufficiently developed plot.

Although he continued to publish descriptive and historical texts after his 1833 move to Cincinnati, including another monthly, Hall's career as a fiction author coincides very closely to his six years in Vandalia. He died in Cincinnati in 1868 and is buried there beside his second wife. Like James Fenimore Cooper's, Hall's tales are more romantic than realistic. The stories often flawed by sentimentalism, romantic and one-dimensional characterization, and moralism. He rarely moves beyond current tastes to explore violent or tragic emotions and situations: "The Indian Hater" is an exception.[37] His use of colloquial speech and humor anticipated by forty years the works of Bret Harte and Mark Twain, but Hall, more interested in description, made far too little use of western language. From the standpoint of his own era, these writing flaws were not flaws but prevailing sensibility. Unfortunately, Hall will never be judged as more than a minor American writer because of his inability to transcend those tastes to any great degree. His work is variously applauded, mentioned in passing, and neglected by literary historians.

To find Hall's true legacy, then, is harder to pinpoint than one might suspect. The biographer Randolph Randall writes, "the publication of these twenty-five stories was an important milestone in the development of the American short story. Hall's use of native materials set a wholesome example when the craft was still young in this country. . . . Hall, by demonstrating that rich narrative veins could be exploited through careful observation and recording of distinctive regional characteristics, was, after Irving—who, indeed, had no competitors—the next most significant of the American short story writers who published a large number of tales between 1820 and 1832. . . . Among Western writers of short fiction of the period, he was supreme."[38] Randall points out that only Washington Irving had published extensively in the short narrative genre in 1832; Edgar Allan Poe and Hawthorne were just beginning their efforts in the genre. But Irving, although more prolific and beloved by contemporaries and posterity than Hall, by his own admission attempted nothing innovative. Even to put Hall's legacy sympathetically, as does Randall, unintentionally accords him faint praise, saying in effect: Hall was the second-best writer in America in a large field of poor, mediocre, or imitative writers, none of whom aspired to great heights or innovations.

True, Hall's deep sensitivity to and appreciation of regional mores and western distinctiveness sets him far above contemporaries like John Russell. Critics, literary historians, and western historians rightly emphasize the way Hall translated this appreciation into his tales. No other writer captured the flavor and minutiae of the early West like Hall did. No other writer fostered a cultural heritage for the West, spread interest in its lore, and took care to see and hear in such a manner as Hall. It is unfair to protest that his fiction should have been better, particularly in light of his tireless and selfless efforts to publish his and others' works, efforts carried on at no small personal and financial cost for the sake of western cultural identity. Had he concentrated upon innovativeness and quality in his prose, his important descriptive books, his groundbreaking western journals, his essays, and his speeches on western education and culture might have been lost. To gain Hall as a more important figure in the development of the short story genre might have lost him as the West's best and most active literary and cultural spokesman.

Hall was a complex individual. People noted his humor and light-heartedness, and his absolute fearlessness in the face of danger.[39] He enjoyed writing flowery poetry and bold stories of lawlessness. His contradictoriness, too, extends to his politics. One cannot compare Hall with his contemporaries George Bancroft and especially Walt Whitman, either in the quality of the works or in the Jacksonian convictions of these men. Yet like them he possessed faith in the democratic spirit to better the nation and to develop a uniquely American literature.[40] Hall's political conservatism—he was a whig—was kept strangely separate from his liberal vision, leading one historian to brand him as self-serving.[41] Repeatedly in his writings Hall justified his pursuits as attempts to foster appreciation of literature and education in the western country, regardless of political ideology. Although self-conscious about the farsightedness of his endeavor and of the risk of failure, he followed this self-appointed course with little or no thought of personal gain or recognition. If anything, he anticipated the contemporary failure of his efforts (and the lack of financial reward to him) if those efforts could be, at least, seminal. Although politically conservative, Hall was liberal in his faith (again, like Bancroft and Whitman) that American greatness lay in the improvement and witness of the common people.

Sadly, Hall's involvement in Illinois politics became detrimental to his liberal vision. His editorship of the *Illinois Intelligencer* embroiled him in the 1829–30 gubernatorial election, and his political enemies thereafter successfully ruined him financially. Hall's selfless dream for western betterment might have been shared by western Jacksonians who attacked him politically, men like Sidney Breese, John Reynolds, and the cultured Ninian Edwards. But the overtly factional, personal, and anti-intellectual qualities of Illinois Jacksonian politics in the late 1820s and early 1830s contributed to the failure of Hall's efforts in Vandalia, in spite of the changing cultural attitudes that made those efforts possible. Had Hall removed himself from political contention, the story might have been different, but this he would not do. For Hall, Jacksonian politics spelled disaster for Vandalia's potential as a center of learning. As in 1823–24, the distinction of being state capital hindered rather than assisted Vandalia's need for development.

Hall's place as a Vandalian is less complex than his character and legacy. He was an atypical booster; he enjoyed Vandalia so as to become a community-minded citizen, but his boosterism greatly transcended narrow local boundaries.[42] The gentility of his characterization of frontiersmen and the sentimentality of some of his stories places Hall unfortunately close to nineteenth-century Vandalia historiography, that is, the patriotic, moralistic, and sentimental parochialism discussed in chapter 3. Although his motives differed from those of the postbellum local historians, the results are curiously the same: both Hall's stories and the county histories romanticize frontier persons and glorify certain frontier mores. His nonfiction, descriptive volumes are better sources for history. Unfortunately for Hall's local legacy, the glorification of the man of action rather than the person of intellect, carried over into Vandalia's local memory. Forty years after the capital period the first Fayette County history gave more space to the exploits of a Jacksonian character like Tom Higgins than to the work of Higgins's local contemporaries, Hall (who receives almost no accurate attention in that history), and other writers. Later histories did not improve the situation; cultural activities did not inspire the same kind of symbolic meaning that ancestral life and folklore did for subsequent generations. (The artistic work of James William Berry is the exception, probably because Berry, unlike Hall, was known personally to writers of both county histories.) The author Mary Burtschi was the first to redress this imbalance in Vandalia historiography.[43]

One cannot know to what extent Hall drew upon personal Vandalia experiences for his stories. His interest in the French and the rivermen, and his disinclination to use experiences from the bench and bar, make it unlikely that he used many local incidents. Possibilities are intriguing. Hall provided Mary Ann Ernst with legal assistance in 1828; a few years later he wrote "The Emigrants," a story about an ill-starred foreign family whose head was the flute-playing Mr. Edgarton (Ferdinand Ernst had been a flutist). Perhaps after observing the charivary custom among the Illinois French or at Vandalia, he wrote the story "The French Village" wherein the custom is described. It is certain however, that Hall's years in Vandalia comprised the period in his life when his best work was written and published, a body of work upon which his importance rests. That Vandalia provided residence for such a man honors the town and its capital period.

Other writers were also associated with Vandalia. Edward Beecher, the first president of Illinois College and an associate of the Yale Band, wrote many religious articles and books, most notably a narrative on Elijah Lovejoy's murder.[44] John Howard Bryant, brother of William Cullen Bryant and a well-known Illinois whig, visited Vandalia during the Tenth General Assembly to lobby for internal improvements. Unlike Hall's, Bryant's many poems are still worth reading.[45] John Mason Peck took over as the state's best known author following Hall's departure in 1833.[46] Peck, an Alton minister, wrote *A Guide for Emigrants to the West*, *A Gazetteer of Illinois*, *A Traveller's Directory*, other descriptive and biographical books, and many articles. The *Gazetteer* is his best-known work. Stranded in Vandalia during the bad winter of 1837, Peck delivered two historical lectures at the statehouse. On the strength of the lectures, he was selected to head a committee to draft a history of Illinois. Peck did write six essays on Illinois and collected many books, but his history was never written.[47]

John Russell, a Bluffdale resident who was the local high school teacher, wrote many fiction and nonfiction pieces in his life, some published in antebellum Baptist periodicals and some in better-known magazines like Hall's *Illinois Monthly Magazine* and *Western Monthly Magazine*. Some of Russell's stories are "The Spectre Hunter: A Legend of the West," "The Emigrant," the longer story "The Mormoness," and a temperance piece "The Venomous Worm," published in McGuffey's Reader of 1848. His literary activity and published work was never equal to Hall's.[48]

One other Vandalia resident published a book. John A. Wakefield did not set out to write books or to promote education. A tavern keeper east of Vandalia and an active county politician (a political enemy of James Hall), Wakefield participated with a group of Fayette County men in the Black Hawk War. He later felt compelled to tell the war's story after he heard what he considered unjust criticisms of Governor Reynolds and the federal government. Wakefield's *A History of the War Between the United States and the Sac and Fox Nations of Indians* appeared in 1834. He hoped, in his preface, that "after the perusal of these letters and depositions, none will have the hardihood to say, that Governor Reynolds did wrong in the course he pursued to subdue those Indians." The book, both a documentary history and a contemporary account by a participant, is flawed by white racial distain for natives but has become an important contemporary source for the Indian–white conflicts of 1831 and 1832. The book achieved the status of a minor classic and has been republished as recently as 1975, 102 years after Wakefield's death in Kansas.[49]

James W. Berry was Vandalia's only resident artist. Self-taught portrait painters worked in Illinois during this period. Dr. Conrad Will may have had his portrait painted at Vandalia by an unknown itinerant artist in 1824. Berry, nineteen and the son of state auditor Elijah Berry and brother-in-law of William Ewing, was commended by the Fourth General Assembly when he gave two portraits to the government, perhaps a now-lost painting of Edward Coles and a known, unsigned painting of Shadrach Bond. A lifelong Vandalian and a thirty-year Fayette County circuit clerk, Berry painted many portraits during his life. Some were of state officials at Vandalia and some of family and friends, but few of Berry's works are known to exist. In 1838 the Eleventh General Assembly commissioned him to copy two paintings in the U.S. Capitol, of Washington and Lafayette. Berry told people that the doorkeeper of the U.S. House of Representatives could not distinguish the originals from his copies. The two large portraits, apparently the only ones he signed, now hang in Springfield's Old State Capitol. After acknowledging the artistic faults of Berry's known works—stiff poses and the absence of hard-to-paint hands—one is struck by the fine quality of the portraits. Prominent in a historic site, the copies are Berry's lasting gift to his state's history.[50]

Cultural and educational organizations and activity at the capital were neither self-generating nor alone indicative of the town; they sprung from the impulse of concerned citizens to improve the town's and the region's religious and intellectual life and from the vision of certain individuals. Because some of Vandalia's cultural events were sponsored by the state government and attended by legislative members, Vandalia was certainly the state's cultural center. Given human nature, Vandalia's early citizens probably sought greater social prestige through their voluntarism, but there are few extant examples of social control effected through these organizations. Frontier indifference to intellectual activities reflected in Vandalians' general lack of wide-spread support toward Hall's and the Yale Band's efforts, and Jacksonian politics' anti-intellectual impetus spelled failure for much of the cultural work done at Vandalia. However, the fact that the work was done, rather than its success, gave the capital period a cultural legacy unsurpassed by any other community of the time.

9

The End of the Era

As VANDALIA's capital period drew to a close during the 1830s, the
town's political and economic existence ironically gained greater
vitalization. Encouraged by a tide of economic optimism, the downtown
area grew with new businesses and increased trade. Although crowds
were still large, visitors could lodge at any one of at least thirteen downtown hotels, and visitors could enjoy the well-stocked bars and dining
rooms of some. The capital had a bookstore, jewelry stores, furniture
and retail businesses, clothing stores, and a brand-new statehouse.[1] En-
tertainment mingled with politics; the lower floors of the statehouse
were filled during late hours by the so-called "third house"—visitors,
legislators, and local people who gathered for fun and political discussion. One Vandalia lawyer believed that the debates in the third house
precipitated the internal improvements legislation of the Tenth General
Assembly. Powerful men like Stephen Douglas, William Ewing, and
Richard Young visited Vandalia and took turns addressing the happy
mob, supervised by James W. Whitney, nicknamed "Lord Coke," of
Pike County, who always traveled to the capital specifically to preside,
with mock gravity, over the lobby meetings.[2]

These were the best years for an important aspect of Vandalia's heritage; Illinoisans destined for future greatness served in the legislatures.
Men like Orville Hickman Browning, Stephen Douglas, John J. Hardin,
Edward D. Baker, James Shields, Abraham Lincoln, and others lodged
in Vandalia and walked its downtown sidewalks. Douglas and Lincoln
are Vandalia's most famous official visitors; their legacy overshadows
much of Vandalia's capital period in popular imagination. Douglas

moved to Illinois from New England in 1833, and made a stunning political speaking debut at a Jacksonville caucus. Befriended by fellow democrat John Wyatt, a member of the Eighth General Assembly, he and Wyatt began plotting the defeat of the powerful Morgan County whig John J. Hardin. Douglas first stepped from the stagecoach in Vandalia in December 1834, at the commencement of the Ninth General Assembly. A twenty-one-year-old bachelor who stood only five feet four inches, he had not yet acquired the pompadour hairstyle, immaculate dress, and unflattering portliness of the 1850s' photographs. In 1834 he was a tiny young man dressed in ordinary jeans, his longish dark-brown hair combed back. He found no hotel room in Vandalia, so he roomed with a fellow democrat, John Dement, who found Douglas better clothes and convinced him to get a haircut. Soon Douglas and his friends pushed through the legislature a bill he wrote authorizing state's attorneys to be elected by the general assembly rather than appointed by the governor. Thus Hardin, state's attorney for the First Judicial Circuit, was legislated out of a job. Soon Douglas was elected by the legislature to his first political office—the very same position Hardin had lost. This adroitly obtained office, however, was but a stepping stone; Douglas campaigned for and won the office of state representative from Morgan County in the Tenth General Assembly. His brilliant career in Illinois and national politics thus began—first at Jacksonville and then, decisively, at Vandalia.[3]

Nothing is known about Douglas's first encounter with Lincoln, except that it happened at Vandalia in December 1834. Lincoln was a tall, homely twenty-five-year-old representative from Sangamon County when he first came to Vandalia that month. The young New Salem resident stepped from the stage and located a place to lodge. Lincoln's four terms in the state legislature—three at Vandalia and one at Springfield—have been well-documented.[4] The facts that his political career began in Vandalia, that he made his first antislavery statement there, and that he was enrolled as a practicing attorney in the third statehouse makes Vandalia one of the Illinois towns especially associated with the sixteenth president. Lincoln's statement against slavery arose in response to legislative resolutions upholding the constitutional right of states to hold slaves and the right of the District of Columbia to retain slavery in spite of congressional efforts to the contrary. Lincoln was one of six of eighty-three representatives, in January 1837, to vote against the resolutions. Six weeks later his and representative Dan Stone's protest was entered into the house journal. Significantly, the men entered the protest after passage of important legislation, the internal improvements act and the selection of the permanent state capital. Considering the violent antiabolitionist attitudes of many people, Lincoln and Stone showed courage in stating their views. When Lincoln wrote an autobiographical sketch in 1860, he said of this first antislavery statement, "so far as it goes, it was then the same that it is now."[5]

Douglas and Lincoln served together in the Tenth General Assembly during the winter of 1836–37, when Vandalia's third statehouse was first occupied. As Paul Simon calculates, the two men voted alike on 75 recorded votes and differently on 119, differently 24 times for state officials and 12 times the same. Douglas voted for Jacksonville on all four ballots of the capital relocation vote in February 1837; Lincoln voted all four times for Springfield. Douglas favored the presidential administration, whereas Lincoln aligned with the newly forming whig party.[6] "We have adopted it as a part of our policy here," wrote Lincoln to a friend, "to never speak of Douglass at all. Is'nt that the best mode of treating so small a matter?"[7] (Douglas originally spelled his name with an additional *s*.) The potential division of Sangamon County, a bitter issue in both Sangamon and Morgan counties, caused the first recorded confrontation between the men. The debate was nothing more than a difference concerning which house committee should receive the bill, but given their fateful debates in 1858, this insignificant confrontation became portentous.[8]

It is a matter of conjecture where Lincoln lodged during the nearly ten months he served in Vandalia. Tradition indicates that he stayed at the Globe Hotel on Gallatin Street, and that he stayed at a small cottage on West Johnson Street near Sixth Street, a house razed in the 1960s.[9] Nothing exists to prove where he stayed except the oral traditions perhaps inspired by the later apotheosis of the martyred president.

There is an undying legend that Lincoln jumped from a window of the Vandalia statehouse to break a quorum when a vote was taken to keep the capital at Vandalia. This legend is certainly a confusion with the actual incident on December 5, 1840, when Lincoln made such a jump from the Springfield Second Presbyterian Church, the temporary location of the house of representatives. Whigs hoped, by preventing a quorum, to defeat a democratic scheme to cripple the state bank, but when a quorum existed, Lincoln and at least one other whig tried to leave. Discovering the doors blocked, the men leaped from a window, to the mocking delight of the state's democratic press. No evidence places a Lincoln jump at Vandalia, but by the turn of the century a Vandalia jump was locally accepted as fact. An ancestor of mine supposedly witnessed the event, as did Clara Greenup Ernst, the daughter of the town's surveyor and daughter-in-law of Ferdinand Ernst. The story is less known than the New Salem stories but as tenacious a legend as those and as illustrative of the symbolic power of Lincoln's career upon American consciousness.[10]

The end of Vandalia's twenty-year term finally drew near. Faced with the problem of a new capital, legislators of the Eighth General Assembly (1832–33) passed a bill that presented voters with a choice for the location of their state capital: Vandalia, Springfield, Jacksonville, Alton, Peoria, and the cartographically unspecified "geographic center of the state."[11]

County meetings throughout the state endorsed particular towns, but popular interest on relocation was disappointing; 24,449 men voted compared to 32,711 in the gubernatorial election held on the same day. The results were also close. Alton won by 33.4 percent, Vandalia received 31.6 percent (only 427 votes behind Alton), and Springfield received 28.7 percent of the votes. Other communities trailed. Predictably, the vote was sectional among Illinois counties, but the close results and voter disinterest made the referendum inconclusive.[12] Because the law could not take effect until Vandalia's capital period ended, the referendum was never enforced. In January 1837, during the Tenth General Assembly in the new capitol, Orville Hickman Browning introduced a bill in the senate mandating the legislature's selection of a site for the permanent seat of government. The bill was referred back and forth among committees, with state senator Robert McLaughlin pressing Vandalia's suitability. Finally the bill passed in early February, repealing the 1833 referendum law and setting February 28, 1837 as the date of the legislative election.[13] The two Vandalia papers during this time were more interested in the internal improvements bill than removal of the state capital. The *Register*, for instance, referred to the imminent "crisis" in one editorial, then went on to discuss the state banking bill.[14] On February 28, on the fourth ballot, Springfield received the necessary majority.[15] It would become permanent state capital following Vandalia's twenty-year term.

On May 6, William Walters finally mustered his formidable talent for biting commentary and wrote about the relocation bill:

> *How to populate a town!*—Let the roads be so bad . . . that, if a stranger succeeds in *getting in* . . . , he will abandon any notion of *getting out!*
> *Directions.*—In locating the town, select a large wet prairie or field, full of bogs and springs; so much so, that it will bear to be called Swamp-field, *Spring-field*, or the like.[16]

For the special session of July 1837 called by the governor in response to the national economic crisis, William L.D. Ewing took the place of William Hankins, who resigned, as representative from Fayette County.

The *Sangamo Journal* at Springfield noted: "Vandalia is wide awake, and she has her strong man, Gen. W. Lee D. Ewing [who] is a candidate for the legislature. She is calling through her newspapers for a repeal of the [relocation] law. All her energies are called into action."[17] Ewing immediately introduced a bill to repeal the relocation law. The bill was tabled for several days, and when taken up, the house eliminated the bill. McLaughlin in the senate attempted similar means to reconsider the 1837 law. Ewing and Lincoln exchanged sharp words during the debates. Almost a half-century later Usher Linder remembered that Ewing addressed Sangamon County delegation: "Gentlemen, have you no other champion than this coarse and vulgar fellow to bring into lists against me? Do you suppose that I will condescend to break a lance with your low and obscure colleague?" Although the exchange was recorded in this form some years after Lincoln's presidency and assassination, the two men did assault one another verbally; an observer feared the two could come to duel.[18] William Walters likened Ewing's confrontation with the Springfield delegates to Shakespeare's Macbeth facing the apparitions: "'Another, and yet another!'"[19]

The debate continued after adjournment, with the Vandalia papers and several others keeping the issue alive long after it otherwise would have died. At a July 7, 1838, Vandalia meeting chaired by William Linn, Montgomery County merchant C. B. Blockburger indicated Vandalia's benefits. Blockburger thought that a convention should choose the seat of government because the Sangmon County legislative delegation (the "Long Nine"), the Springfield land officers, and the president and directors of the state bank were "touching every interest and every cord that could secure a vote for their town." "[W]hen the question is decided by the people, as an isolated measure, standing alone upon its own merits, the citizens of Vandalia will submit to that decision without a murmur or complaint." Blockburger and Vandalia businessmen William Walters, William Hodge, W. L. D. Ewing, Nathaniel McCurdy, R. T. Edmonson, James Black, Thomas C. Kirkman, Thomas B. Hickman, William Linn, Harvey Lee, Henry Smith, and R. K. McLaughlin signed the document.[20]

This eleventh-hour attempt accomplished nothing. At the 1838–39 session, Ewing and William Hankins represented Fayette and Effingham counties in the house. The two men nearly succeeded in eliminating Lincoln's appropriations bill for the new Springfield statehouse, if not in securing a new relocation election in August 1840. At one point Ewing remarked that the relocation was unconstitutional and that it would be better to locate the seat on vacant land. Lincoln answered that although twenty years were specified for Vandalia's term, the people had the right to move it any time. He also pointed out, against Ewing's second remark, that Vandalia was evidence that the state could make no money by moving the capital to an uninhabited location.[21]

Pro-Vandalia efforts in the senate were less heated. Responding to a bill authorizing disposal of public property at Vandalia, Senator Robert Blackwell moved to refer the bill to the judiciary committee, with instructions that they clarify three points: when the location of the seat of government was made; whether the selection of a site, delineation of lots, or removal of public records constituted the location of the seat; and finally whether it was constitutional for the state supreme court to meet at Springfield before December 1840, the twentieth anniversary of the Second General Assembly at Vandalia. The committee's report stated that the language of the constitution implied that the initial establishment of the town comprised the beginning of the twenty-year period. Because the plat of Vandalia was dated July 1819, and because all that was authorized by the constitution concerning a seat of government had been done by July 1819, the twenty-year constitutional period ended in July 1839. The senate approved the committee's recommendation that Springfield be declared the seat of government and the supreme court as of July 4, 1839.[22]

Although July 4 was the official date, Vandalia's capital period essentially ended when the Eleventh General Assembly adjourned indefinitely in March 1839 and when the supreme court adjourned. (That general assembly reconvened in a second, special session in December 1839; since Springfield's new statehouse was not yet completed, the session met in rented facilities in Springfield.) The *Illinois State Register* made no mention of the date; it passed as another day in Vandalia. During the spring, state property was moved to Springfield. Sidney Breese had brought the state government's papers in one ox cart in 1820; in 1839 eleven men were paid to do a similar job. Benjamin Ward Thompson, L. Ginger, Benjamin F. Lee, R. Porter, H. Sydney, William Redmond, Daniel Snyder, Peter Smith, E. Davis, and J. Lutt were paid $533.33 for removing the public offices to Springfield. Thompson, the well-known early settler, received an additional $24 to move the office supplies of the clerk of the supreme court. William Walters of the local newspaper received $100 for hauling two loads of state paper to Springfield.[23]

A senate act passed in February gave all state-owned Vandalia lots and state property to Fayette County, including the capitol building itself, with stipulations as to its use. The Vandalia public square, on which the capitol stood, was reserved from public sale.[24] "Though 'Ilium Fuit' (Troy has existed but exists no longer) may not be appropriately inscribed on its ruins," wrote William Stuart of the *Chicago Daily American* about Vandalia in August 1839, "it nevertheless, on a small scale, has something of a melancholy appearance of departed greatness." The fence around the former capitol, he noted, was being unceremoniously taken down to be used as firewood. Stuart observed that most Vandalians felt considerable hostility to Springfield, the new state capital. He also noted that, even in July, the worst season of the year for diseases, Vandalia was extremely healthy, as citizens there always contended. "We took some pains to ascertain the fact, as we came there in a physical condition which prepared us quite readily to sympathize with the deseases of the climate, and were bound to remain two days for a stage to St. Louis."[25]

Friends of Vandalia unsuccessfully brought up the relocation issue at the 1839 special session and the 1840 session of the legislature, both at Springfield. At the 1840 session, Representative Bentley of Bond County offered a resolution for repeal of the relocation laws until the state debt was paid. In retrospect, this would have kept the seat of government at Vandalia until 1880.[26] After 1841, no other pro-Vandalia attempts were made.

A few capital-era merchants stayed in town—McLaughlin, Blackwell, Leidig, Remann, Black, Greenup, Flack, McCurdy, Elijah C. Berry, and others. Some like Ewing, Linn, and Walters went to Springfield. The several short-lived Vandalia newspapers published during the forties and early fifties shed little light upon the town's condition. Robert Ross, a county historian born in 1844, remembered that only three hundred persons lived in Vandalia in 1850, but "the building of the Illinois Central Railroad [in 1855] was one of the most important events in the history of the county [Fayette]. It brought new life to Vandalia and other towns and had the effect of bringing in many new settlers." Vandalia grew steadily thereafter, showing population increases at almost every census. The statehouse, made more impressive with the addition of columns and porticos, was used for county offices for nearly a hundred years; it is still referred to locally as the "old courthouse." In 1913 a group of Vandalia businessmen, including the historian Joseph C. Burtschi, saved the building from possible demolition by selling it to the state for $60,000. Ironically, the state government thus paid for the building twice. The old capitol is now a state historic site.[27]

With the coming of the railroads, Vandalia's early history came full circle. The settlers' desire for good land led to the town's establishment in 1818 and 1819; the population growth in the fertile central and northerly lands of Illinois led to the relocation twenty years later; finally, the same desire of settlers for land contributed to Vandalia's renaissance thirty-six years after its founding. Founded as state capital, Vandalia was, nevertheless, a small, homogeneous Southern Illinois town that during its capital period possessed characteristics both unique and typical. When Springfield became capital, Vandalia simply retained its typicalness as a downstate village. The coming of the railroads not only revitalized Vandalia, but it also freed the town to become that kind of growing village, unencumbered by post-relocation disappointment and by people's expectations for a capital city.

No "old settlers society" seems to have gathered in Vandalia during the antebellum years. When the *History of Fayette County* was compiled in 1878, most of the pioneer generation had died and second-generation Vandalians were middle-aged and older. But enough "old settlers" like Ward Thompson, John Enochs, James W. Berry, and Ferris Forman remained to assist community recollection. Along with biographies of local leaders in the 1870s (some of whom are ancestors of present-day leaders) and remarks about Fayette County's ambivalence toward the recent Union cause, that thin, poorly edited yet indispensible scrapbook of articles, reminiscences, and township and community histories provides a wide assortment of information about the capital era. Mixing historical reminiscence with small-town pride in progress, the text juxtaposes Vandalia's rude beginning with its postbellum prosperity.

This town was surveyed and laid out in July, 1819, by Wm. C. Greenup, Beal Greenup, and John McCullom, and was for about twenty years the seat of Government for the state. In the year 1820 the state capital removed here from Kaskaskia, and the village at once became a place of importance, and boasted a population of 2,000 people. In 1839 the capital was moved to Springfield, and Vandalia rapidly declined until its population numbered less than 500, at which figure it remained for many years.—However, on the building of the Ill. Central R.R. it began to grow in commercial and manufacturing importance, and bids fair to become an important and thriving city.

The location of the town is very beautiful, being upon rising ground surrounded by wooded hills. The court-house, formerly the state capitol, is a fine structure of brick, 60 × 100 feet, and stands in the centre of a handsome square. The Kaskaskia river flows along the east side of the town, and the main wagon road is spanned by a substantial iron bridge. The great National road from Washington has its western terminus here; the city now contains a population of upwards of 2,000, has several churches, an excellent graded school, three weekly newspapers and several well kept hotels, a number of manufacturing establishments, two banks and several fine stores. The town is adorned by a number of beautiful residences and substantial business houses.[28]

Grandson of capital-era furniture maker Moses Phillips, Robert Ross was a third-generation Vandalian. Ross's 1904 and 1910 local histories are as filled with civic pride as the 1878 text and are as indispensible for local history:

> When Vandalia was selected as the Capital of Illinois, it was thought that as long as the State itself enduring, the governing seat would be there located, yet within two decades another spot was chosen and the glory that had been Vandalia's departed. Fortunately, however, there were those left who realized that the real worth of the town was not changed, that its location was as beautiful, as desirable as ever. Some remained behind after the political exodus, perhaps a few because they could not afford to abandon what they had secured, but many because they had faith in Vandalia's future, and they had been very bountifully rewarded. Today Vandalia, one of the most beautiful of Illinois inland cities, is the center of a flourishing and steadily growing trade, and is the home of some of the most intellectual people of the State. It boasts handsome residences, substantial business houses, well paved streets, many civic improvements, a library, literary societies, several important newspapers, and the old capitol buildings [sic] that, set back among stately trees, shelter the county officials, and are landmarks for the whole State.
>
> Vandalia is historic; but it is more, it is modern and up-to-date, its thriving enterprises forming a pleasant setting for the traces of the old life. . . . Vandalia has always been in the fore in everything that lay in its power, and it is generally conceded that because of this its musical name was giving it. As it was in the van, or foreguard, and located in the midst of beautiful dales, it was appropriately named Vandalia.[29]

These two historical quotations reflect a civic spirit present in Vandalia since the town's beginning, but they also call attention to two things that sum up Vandalia's capital era. First, Vandalia's founding purpose was specifically to be the state's seat of government. The county historians already partially grasped the significance of that purpose; later generations were able to appreciate it more. As capital, Vandalia provided Illinois with a considerable historical heritage. State politics progressed from the petty disputes of the Illinois territory to a distinct if still evolving two-party system. Learned individuals in Vandalia laid the foundation for a cultural and literary heritage for the new state. State economic policy ran aground by 1839, but thereby lessons were learned that allowed Illinois to take a significant place among states of the Union. The presence of Lincoln and Douglas in Vandalia has captured the imagination of many, but if their careers were (to use the title of a well-known Lincoln history) "preparation for greatness," the Vandalia careers of other young men can be described in an identical manner. Edward Coles and, in a nonpolitical way, James Hall realized greatness at Vandalia. Settlers who lived at the capital contributed in their own way to this preparation.

The second point is that Vandalia's subsequent small-town progress is itself dependent upon Vandalia's founding purpose. Although Vandalia has few other buildings from the capital period, the old statehouse is a continual reminder that Vandalia exists at all because it was state capital.[30] Early local citizens hosted the state government and laid the groundwork for the future community. To paraphrase the first county history, there will always be an interest in this period of Vandalia, when the foundation for the town's social and material status was laid.[31] Many Vandalians trace ancestry to the capital; several Fayette County locations were established during this period; appellations of many county streams and landmarks date from the first part of the 1800s. Simply as pioneer heritage, Vandalia's first era of civic history would deserve preservation in local memory. A great deal of the pioneer period—the Ernst colony, various local challenges, and Vandalia's social character—cannot be distinguished from Vandalia's official status, however. It is pointless to speculate what Vandalia would have been like without the capital period, or whether it would have existed at all as a Kaskaskia River settlement. For the county historians, the continued progress and community spirit of an attractive, growing small town lay precisely in the greatness of Vandalia's capital era. That mooring in the capital era still holds.

The events of the town's first two decades—from the arrival of Sidney Breese's ox cart to the departure of the horse-drawn wagons of Ward Thompson and his associates—are singular for the community because, during those years, Vandalia's founding purpose was fulfilled. During those twenty years the community served its constitutional purpose, and thereby provided a priceless heritage for Vandalia and Illinois.

Notes

Abbreviations for frequently cited works:

DAG	*Deutsche-Amerikanische Geschichtsblätter*
FCCiC	Fayette County Circuit Clerk's office, Vandalia
FCCoC	Fayette County County Clerk's office, Vandalia
FF	*Fayette Facts* (Quarterly of the Fayette County Genealogical Society), 1974–present
Free Press	*Free Press and Illinois Whig* (Vandalia, 1837–42)
1878 History	*History of Fayette County, Illinois* (Philadelphia, 1878)
Ill. Adv.	*Illinois Advocate* (Edwardsville, 1831–32; Vandalia, 1833–36)
Ill. Int.	*Illinois Intelligencer* (Kaskaskia, 1818–20; Vandalia, 1820–32 [*Vandalia Whig and Illinois Intelligencer*, 1832–34?]
ISHL	Illinois State Historical Library, Springfield
ISR	*Illinois State Register* (Vandalia, 1836–39)
JISHS	*Journal of the Illinois State Historical Society*
JCB	Joseph Charles Burtschi, *Documentary History of Vandalia, Illinois* (Vandalia, 1954)
Laws of Illinois	*Laws of the State of Illinois Passed by the General Assembly*, published by authority of the secretary of state (followed by date of the legislature)

Senate or House Journal	Journal of the Senate [or House of Representatives] of the General Assembly of the State of Illinois, published by authority of the secretary of state (followed by the date of the legislature)
Ross 1904	Robert W. Ross, Historical Souvenir of Vandalia, Illinois (Effingham, 1904)
Ross 1910	Robert W. Ross and John J. Bullington, History of Fayette County, Illinois (included in Newton Bateman and Paul Shelby, Historical Encyclopedia of Illinois, Chicago, 1910)
TISHS	Transactions of the Illinois State Historical Society

INTRODUCTION

1. Alexis de Tocqueville, Democracy in America, trans. George Lawrence (Paris, 1835–40, New York, 1969), p. 62.

2. Edmund Flagg, The Far West: Or, A Trip Beyond the Mountains (New York, 1838), quoted in JCB, p. 95.

3. Northwestern Gazette and Galena Advertiser, July 9, 1837, quoted in Paul Simon, Lincoln's Preparation for Greatness (Norman, 1965), p. 72.

4. JCB, p. 96. Flagg's text after "We are told that. . . ." copies, nearly verbatim, part of James Hall's speech to the Antiquarian and Historical Society in December 1828. See Ill. Int., Jan. 3, 1829.

1. TO REEVE'S BLUFF

1. Edmund Flagg, The Far West: Or, A Trip Beyond the Mountains (New York, 1838), quoted in R. Carlyle Buley, The Old Northwest, Pioneer Period: 1815–1840 (Bloomington, Ind., 1950), 1: 42; Fred Gerhard, Illinois as It Is (Chicago, 1857), pp. 271ff.

2. James Hall, Letters from the West (London, 1828, repr. Gainesville, 1967), p. 172.

3. Thomas Ford, A History of Illinois from Its Commencement as a State in 1818 to 1847 (Chicago, 1854, repr. Ann Arbor, 1968), p. 38.

4. Solon J. Buck, Illinois in 1818, 2d ed. (Urbana, 1967), chapter 2; Theodore C. Pease, The Frontier State, 1818–1848 (Springfield, 1918, repr. Urbana, 1987), chapter 1.

5. Timothy Flint, Recollections of the Last Ten Years (Carbondale, 1968), p. 145; Michael Jones and Shadrach Bond to Edward Tiffin, Oct. 28, 1814, and Thomas Sloo to Josiah Meigs, March 11, 1815, both in Malcolm J. Rohrbough, The Land Office Business: The Settlement and Administration of American Public Lands, 1789–1837 (New York, 1968), pp. 60, 92–93.

6. Western Intelligencer, May 20, 1818; Ill. Int., May 27, June 3, Sept. 9, 1818; Buck, Illinois in 1818, pp. 288–90.

7. "Correspondent's Report, Jan. 20, 1817," in Samuel R. Brown, The Western Gazetteer, or Emigrant's Directory (Auburn, N.Y., 1817), p. 20.

8. Buck, *Illinois in 1818*, pp. 92, 289–90. Randall Parrish's *Historic Illinois* (Chicago, 1905), p. 310, and Irwin F. Mather's *The Making of Illinois* (Chicago, 1923), p. 158, both attribute to Thomas Ford the story that Reavis told the 1818 convention about the superiority of his bluff compared to Pope and Carlyle. The convention journal does not report who presented various petitions to the delegates; if the story is true, perhaps Reavis lobbied for his bluff at the 1819 senate session.

9. John F. Snyder, *Adam W. Snyder and His Period in Illinois History* (Virginia, Ill., 1906, repr. Ann Arbor, 1968), p. 40; Buck, *Illinois in 1818*, pp. 92, 288. Frankfort, Kentucky, Iowa City, Iowa, Columbus, Ohio, and Indianapolis, Indiana were, like Vandalia, founded as capital cities. Thomas Cox, who served in both the Iowa territorial and the Illinois legislatures, was instrumental in founding both Vandalia and Iowa City. See the biography of Cox in *Annals of Iowa*, January 1906, pp. 238ff.

10. This account of the constitution convention is from Buck, *Illinois in 1818*, chapter 10, and "Journal of the Convention," *JISHS* 6 (Oct. 1913): 355–424. The 1818 constitution's text is in Joseph Verlie, ed., *Illinois Constitutions* (Springfield, 1919), pp. 25–47; Section 13 of the "Schedule," concerning the state capital, is on pp. 45–46. Ironically, one of the six men at the convention who voted against the relocation clause, William McHenry, died and was buried at the new capital in 1835.

11. Buck, *Illinois in 1818*, p. 291.

12. Ibid., p. 309.

13. Ibid., pp. 292, 309–10.

14. See *Senate Journal, 1818–19*, for March 16.

15. Commissioners' report, JCB, pp. 10–11; *Ill. Int.*, April 13, 1819. Smith's failure to join the other four is surmised by the absence of his name on the official report (in JCB, p. 11).

16. W. Elmo Reavis, *The Reavis Family in America since 1700* (Los Angeles, 1949). Reavis died in Menard County, Illinois about 1836; his body was later moved to the family graveyard in Cass County. His son Isham Reavis lived near Vandalia for several years. Charles's daughter Nancy married Mr. Bowling Green of New Salem and was a close friend of Lincoln in the 1830s; her portrait appears in Stefan Lorant, *Lincoln: A Picture Story of His Life* (New York, 1975), p. 26.

17. The source of this name, that is, who mispronounced Reavis and why, has never been explained; John Moses, *Illinois Historical and Statistical* (Chicago, 1895), 1: 297. Various examples of contemporary spellings of *Okaw* are in *Ill. Int.*, Feb. 2, 1833 and *I.S.R.*, Aug. 12, 1839.

18. JCB, pp. 10f. The commissioners were not swayed from their decision to choose Reavis's idyllic bluff in spite of the fact that it was a sixteenth section of the federal township, reserved by law for school purposes. Congress granted the four sections for Vandalia, plus another section for Vandalia township to replace the sixteenth section. *Ill. Int.*, Dec. 23, 1820.

19. Ross 1904, p. 11. One of the commissioners told this story to a friend of Ross's, who related it to Ross.

20. The first mention of the problem of Vandalia's name is Hall's "Letters from the West" series of 1820. *Ill. Int.*, Aug. 10, 1822; Hall, *Letters from the West*, pp. 201–2. Hall provides the story that the name came from a Frenchman who once hunted in the area, but also reports the "Vandal tribe" story found in Thomas Ford. (Ross rejected this story because no such tribe ever existed.) Hall called the name "heathenish" in *Illinois Monthly Magazine* 2 (1832): 15; and "barbarous" in *Letters from the West*. Ross (1904, pp. 11, 167) gives the Van-Dalia story. Apart from its contrived nature, the story is suspect because many years lie between the event, Greenup's recounting to a friend, the friend's retelling of the story to Ross, and Ross's eventual publication of it. See also Mary Burtschi, *James Hall of Lincoln's Frontier World* (Vandalia, 1977), pp. 77–78, and Ford, *History of Illinois*, p. 35.

No contemporary writer made mention of the Vandalia Land Company as a possible derivation; no historian until Robert Ross in his 1910 history (p. 630) called attention to the name's previous existence. Other Vandalias in the United States seem to have been named for the one in Illinois; see Elnora Pope Hamel, *Vandalia Leader*, Oct. 2, 1969. On the abortive Vandalia Colony, see, for example, George Elmer Lewis, *The Indiana Company, 1763–1798* (Glendale, 1941).

21. Ross 1904, pp. 126–27; 1878 History, p. 30.

22. Ross 1910, p. 621; 1878 History, p. 26.

23. Town plat, July 1819, Book B (front of book), FCCoC

24. *Western Gazetteer*, p. 20. On Perryville, see folder "Perryville" in file box "Miscellaneous," FCCiC; *Laws of Illinois, 1823*, p. 156; Circuit Court Record Book A, 1821–32, pp. 119, 128ff, FCCiC; "Fayette's Lost Town," undated clipping in the papers of the Historic Vandalia Museum; and Paul E. Stroble, "Perryville, a Vanished Town," *Springhouse* 2 (March–April 1985): 23, 30, 36. Nothing is known of Independence, a town or town site near Perryville, except that it appears on a map in *Complete Historical Chronological and Geographical American Atlas* (Philadelphia, 1822), reproduced in JCB, p. 4. The area where these two towns and Pope's Bluff were located is now called Pope Township in Fayette County.

25. JCB, p. 27; *Edwardsville Spectator*, Aug. 29, 1819. If the tavern stood on the lot Reavis purchased in Vandalia in September 1819, this first known building in Vandalia stood on the southwest corner of Fifth and Johnson.

26. List of purchasers, September 1819, JCB, pp. 12–14.

27. 1878 History, p. 54.

28. Ross 1904, pp. 40, 149f; Ross's drawing is probably based on the photograph in the ISHL.

29. Ferdinand Ernst, *Bemerkungen auf einer Reise durch das Innere der Vereinigten Staaten von Nord Amerika im Jahre 1819* (Hildesheim, 1820), pp. 107–8; trans. E. P. Baker as "Travels in Illinois," *TISHS* 8 (1903) and reprinted in JCB, p. 24.

30. Ernst, *Bemerkungen*, p. 109, Baker's translation in JCB, p. 25.

31. List of purchasers, September 1819, in JCB, pp. 12–14. Lots 2, 4, 5, 6, and 8 in squares 17 through 46 were for sale, that is, 150 out of 496 Vandalia

lots, although numbers 4, 5, and 6 in square 52 were also sold; also JCB, pp. 26–27; Ernst, *Bemerkungen*, pp. 110–35.

32. Frederick Hollman's autobiography (1872), published by R. I. Dugdale, a descendent, in Platteville, Wisconsin and reproduced (through the account of Hollman's 1827 move from Vandalia) in JCB, pp. 25–35; also 1878 History, p. 26.

33. JCB, p. 28.

34. Ibid., p. 27.

35. Ibid., pp. 28–29; 1878 History, p. 26. In his autobiography Hollman stressed that only he and a servant named Franz were left in Vandalia by Ernst, but the 1820 census has four white males over twenty-one in Hollman's group. Margaret C. Norton, ed., *Illinois Census Returns, 1820* (Springfield, 1934), pp. 11–12.

36. Undated clipping, "Fayette's Lost Town," Historic Vandalia Museum.

37. Thomas Lippincott's recollections, *Alton Telegraph*, March 17, 1868.

38. N. Dwight Harris, *The History of Negro Servitude in Illinois and of the Slavery Agitation in That State, 1719–1864* (Chicago, 1904, repr. Ann Arbor, 1968), pp. 29–30.

39. *Ill. Int.*, Oct. 7, Dec. 14, 1820; 1878 History, p. 26; Mary Burtschi, *Vandalia: Wilderness Capital of Lincoln's Land* (Vandalia, 1963), p. 75.

40. Norton, *Illinois Census Returns, 1820*, pp. 11ff.

41. JCB, pp. 30, 29.

42. Ibid., p. 30; *Ill. Int.*, Dec. 14, 1820, Jan. 23, Feb. 13, 1821, Sept. 13, 1823.

43. Buck, *Illinois in 1818*, pp. 302f.

44. *Ill. Int.*, Dec. 15, 1820.

45. *Laws of Illinois, 1821*, p. 164.

46. Fayette County Commissioners' Record Book, FCCiC; two "Miscellaneous" files, FCCiC; Fayette County court records, Illinois Regional Depository, Sangamon State University (formerly at the Illinois State Archives). For material on county and villages officers and duties, see *Laws of Illinois, 1819*, pp. 5, 18, 21, 88, 162, 175, 186–95; *Laws of Illinois, 1821*, p. 62; *Laws of Illinois, 1823*, pp. 87, 132; *Laws of Illinois, 1825*, p. 70; Pease, *The Frontier State*, pp. 36ff.

47. *Laws of Illinois, 1821*, pp. 176–82, in JCB, pp. 17–20; *Ill. Int.*, March 6, 20, 27, 1821, Oct. 16, 1822; trustees ordinance in Fayette County court records, Illinois Regional Depository.

48. JCB, p. 30.

2. FERDINAND ERNST AND THE GERMAN COLONY

1. Paul E. Stroble, Jr., "Ferdinand Ernst and the German Colony at Vandalia," *Illinois Historical Journal* 80 (Summer 1987): 101–10. The primary sources are Ferdinand Ernst, *Bemerkungen auf einer Reise durch das Innere der Vereinigten Staaten von Nord Amerika im Jahre 1819* (Hildesheim, 1820) and Hollman's autobiography in JCB. Excellent German research, conducted early in this century, traces the colony's history and Ernst's biography: H. A.

Rattermann, "Wann kam Ferdinand Ernst zuerst nach Illinois?" *DAG* 3 (April 1903): 59–62; Emil Mannhardt, "Deutsche und deutsche Nachkommen in Illinois und den östlichen Nord-Central-Staaten: Fünfter Abschnitt, Das County St. Clair," *DAG* 7 (Oct. 1907): esp. 61–64; Emil Mannhardt, "Die ältesten deutschen Anstiedler in Illinois," *DAG* 3 (Oct. 1903): 50–59; Emil Mannhardt, "Die Nachkommen von Ferdinand Ernst und seiner Begleiter," *DAG* 3 (Jan. 1903): 9–11.

2. Mannhardt, "Die Nachkommen," p. 9; Heinrich Wilhelm Rotermund, *Das Gelehrte Hannover, oder Lexikon von Schriftstellern* (Bremen, 1823), 6pp. 82f. Ship's records for Ernst's arrival in Baltimore on October 2, 1820, list his age as thirty-six: Records of the Bureau of the Customs, Record Group 36, Microcopy 255; Passenger Lists of Vessels Arriving at Baltimore, 1820–91, National Archives; Ernst, *Bemerkungen*, p. iv.

3. JCB, pp. 25f; Mannhardt, "Die Nachkommen," p. 9.

4. Ludwig Gall, *Meine Auswanderung nach den Vereinigten-Staaten im Nord-Amerika* (Trier, 1822), 1: 19; Heinz Monz, *Ludwig Gall: Leben und Werk* (Trier, 1979); Rattermann, "Wann kam Ferdinand Ernst," pp. 61f; Stroble, "Ferdinand Ernst," p. 103, n7.

5. JCB, p. 26.

6. The account of Ernst's and Hollman's travels is based on *Bemerkungen*; also Baker's translation, pp. 150–53.

7. Ernst, *Bemerkungen*, p. 125.

8. JCB, p. 35; on the robbery, see note 6, chapter 4. It is impossible to identify all who accompanied Ernst to the United States; the only extant ship's record omits the names of many known colonists. See Paul Stroble, "The Ernst Colony," *FF* 6 (1977): 44–50.

9. Ernst, *Bemerkungen*, pp. 13f, 23.

10. 1878 History, p. 62; JCB, 30; *Niles Register*, Feb. 10, 1821, p. 400.

11. Stroble, "The Ernst Colony," pp. 47–50; *Ill. Int.*, June 8, 1822, Jan. 11, 1823.

12. 1878 History, pp. 26, 46, 48f; Ross 1904, pp. 18, 29; Mary Burtschi, *Vandalia: Wilderness Capital of Lincoln's Land* (Vandalia, 1963), p. 142; *Vandalia Union*, April 16, 1914.

13. Mannhardt, "Die Nachkommen," p. 62; 62; 1878 History, pp. 48f; Ross 1910, p. 683.

14. JCB, pp. 30–34; 1878 History, pp. 46, 54.

15. 1878 History, pp. 26, 48, 62; JCB, p. 33.

16. *Ill. Int.*, May 8, 1821.

17. Ernst Ludwig Brauns, *Amerika und die Moderne Völkerwanderung* (Potsdam, 1833), p. 280, quoted in Rattermann, "Wann kam Ferdinand Ernst," p. 60.

18. Circuit Court files 8, 29, 117, Record Book A, pp. 42f, FCCiC.

19. Circuit Court file 48, Record Book A, pp. 41, 45, 49, FCCiC.

20. *Edwardsville Spectator*, Aug. 31, 1823, quoted in "Ferdinand Ernst: Dokumentarische Feststellung seiner Niederlassung in Vandalia und seines

Todes," *DAG* 10 (1910): 187ff. Ernst's tombstone and Hollman's autobiography both incorrectly date Ernst's death as 1824.

21. *Ill. Int.*, Sept. 28, 1822; Probate File 251, FCCiC.

22. Circuit Court files 126, 178, 204, Record Book A, pp. 91, 92, 112, FCCiC. The court files that deal with Ernst's estate are: 14, 20, 107, 122, 158, 178, 179, 180, 181, 187, 204, 205, 206, 209, 219, 245, 248, 261, 285, 286, 290, 291, 319. References in Record Book A are pp. 31, 87, 88, 90, 91, 93, 100, 103, 106, 108, 109, 111, 112, 116, 117, 124, 135, 138, 145, 150, 165, 177, 197, 199, 207, 218, 228, 229, 248, 254, 265.

23. Circuit Court files 178, 179, 180, 181, Record Book A, pp. 87, 88, 113; *Laws of Illinois 1823*, pp. 177f, *Ernst v. President and Directors of the State Bank*, 1 Illinois 86–87.

24. Circuit Court files 209, 251, 319, Record Book A, pp. 108, 109, 111, 117, 124, 127, 199, 218, 229, 248, 254; *Ernst's Administrators v. Ernst*, 1 Illinois 316–20.

25. JCB, pp. 33f.

26. Gustav Körner, *Das Deutsche Element in den Vereinigten Staaten von Nordamerka, 1818–1848* (Cincinnati, 1880), p. 245; Probate file 171, Circuit Court file 902, FCCiC; 1878 History, p. 54; Mannhardt, "Die Nachkommen," p. 10. The Ernst family plot is at the center of the old graveyard. The older, vandalized monument at the Ernst family plot is no longer readable. Based on a 1974 examination, it probably marks the graves of Augusta Ernst and her husband, Dr. Robert Homer Peebles (d. 1835).

3. BY THEIR STRONG ARMS

1. 1878 History, p. 65

2. R. Carlyle Buley, *The Old Northwest, Pioneer Period: 1815–1840* (Bloomington, Ind., 1950), 1:138. Buley is exceptionally thorough on the topic of frontier life in the Old Northwest. See note 2, chapter 4 for other primary and secondary works on early Illinois life. Other sources include William V. Pooley, *The Settlement of Illinois from 1830 to 1850* (Madison, 1908, repr. Ann Arbor, 1968); Arthur C. Boggess, *The Settlement of Illinois, 1778–1830* (Chicago, 1908, repr. Ann Arbor, 1968); John Reynolds, *Pioneer History of Illinois* (Chicago, 1855, repr. Ann Arbor, 1968) and *My Own Times* (Belleville, 1857, repr. Ann Arbor, 1968); Dallas L. Jones, "Illinois in the 1830s," *JISHS* 47 (Autumn 1954): 252–63.

In 1978 and 1979 I made an appeal for primary material—illustrative anecdotes, letters, diaries, photographs, and other material on or by early settlers of the Vandalia area. This appeal was made in newspapers of Fayette, Bond, Montgomery, Effingham, and Marion counties, on radio, and in *FF*. Little came of this appeal; however I hope that this book will carry this still timely need to a wider audience.

3. 1878 History, pp. 25, 71f.

4. Guy Beck's tombstone in Bowling Green township (Township 8 North, Range 2 East) commemorates the tradition that he was the first white settler,

as do the county histories. *FF* 3 (Summer 1974): 38ff, states that Beck's father, Paul, blazed a trail to the present site of Vandalia during the same year, 1815.

5. For the earliest settlers of Fayette County, see *Fayette County Land Owners* (Vandalia: Fayette County Genealogical Society, n.d.); "Fayette County Tax Book, 1828–30," FCCiC; 1878 History, p. 25: township histories, passim; Ross 1910; and genealogical charts in *FF* since 1974. See also the list of purchasers of Vandalia lots, Sept. 1819, in JCB, pp. 12–14.

6. The existence of these maps was first reported in Mary Burtschi, *James Hall of Lincoln's Frontier World* (Vandalia, 1977), pp. 77–78. I have found no correspondence to Hill in Jefferson's collected works; Carl I. Wheat's *Mapping the Transmississippi, 1561–1861* (San Francisco, 1957) does not have comparable maps or appellations of the area. As indicated in this chapter, no Bond and Fayette County traditions support European settlement prior to 1815. However, the minutes of an early church in Bond County were owned by the same (now deceased) descendent who photocopied the maps for the Bond County Historical Society; see *FF* 12 (Sept. 1983): 54, 56. Isaac Hill is listed as a member of that church, and the minutes seem to be in the same handwriting as the maps. The authenticity of the maps would also depend upon whether Hill was the scribe of the church minutes as well as the artist of the maps.

7. James Hall, *Letters from the West* (London, 1828, repr. Gainesville, 1967), pp. 172f.

8. *FF* 4 (Sept. 1975): 61; 5 (March 1976): 3. On settlement patterns, cf. John Mack Faragher, *Sugar Creek: Life on the Illinois Prairie* (New Haven, 1986), pp. 56–59, 62–67. In a future study I hope to describe in detail these patterns and rates of persistence in Fayette County from 1820 to 1870.

9. Genealogical charts published in *FF* between vol. 3 (1974) and vol. 13 (1984) for immigrant heads of households coming to Fayette County before 1840 (and compared with later census records) show two family heads were born in New England states, twenty-four were from Pennsylvania, New York, Ohio, or Indiana, and eighty-four from southern states. See also Boggess, *The Settlement of Illinois, 1778–1830*, pp. 127, 145; and Pooley, *Settlement of Illinois from 1830 to 1850*, pp. 321, 323, 327.

10. 1878 History, p. 78.

11. *FF* 4 (June 1975): 4, 19, 41; 5 (Dec. 1976): 9; 7 (Sept. 1978): 15, 24.

12. On the German immigrants, see *FF* 6 (June 1977): 95–97; 8 (Dec. 1979): 31–32; 12 (Dec. 1983): 53. Literature on the self-made man includes Irvin Wyllie, *The Self-Made Man in America* (New York, 1954), especially on the glorification of the self-made man so common in early historiography, such as the 1878 History, pp. 48f, 58, 59, 60. See also Edward Pessen, *Riches, Class, and Power Before the Civil War* (Lexington, Mass., 1973), esp. chapter 5, for details on the issue, and Pessen, *Jacksonian America: Society, Personality, and Politics* (Urbana, 1985), esp. chapter 3.

13. *Ill. Adv.*, Nov. 12, Dec. 27, 1834; Jan. 10, 1835; *I.S.R.*, Aug. 26, 1836, June 1, 1838; *Senate Journal, 1838–39*, p. 86. Vandalia had developed sufficiently by the 1830s to support two editors (chapter 4). Vandalians' support

for the Polish immigrants indicates, too, that local society had apparently sufficiently coalesced to allow for civic helpfulness. Cf. Don Harrison Doyle, *Social Order of a Frontier Community: Jacksonville, Illinois, 1825–70* (Urbana, 1978), pp. 41–42.

14. Ross 1910, pp. 694–96. On prejudice toward Yankees, see also Buley, *The Old Northwest*, 1: 371; Thomas Ford, *A History of Illinois from Its Commencement as a State in 1818 to 1847* (Chicago, 1854, repr. Ann Arbor, 1968), pp. 280–81.

15. 1878 History, p. 49. On the effects of regionalism on community, see Doyle, *Social Order*, pp. 27f, 31f, 46–51, passim.

16. 1878 History, pp. 54, 60.

17. James Hall, *Seven Stories* (Vandalia, 1976), p. 50; on family groups in Fayette County, see, for example, FF 4 (Sept. 1975): 61; 5 (March 1976): 3; 14 (June 1985): 81; 1878 History, 25, 65, 67, passim; James A. Henretta, "Families and Farms: Mentalite in Pre-Industrial America," *William and Mary Quarterly* 35 (Jan. 1978): 3–32 (quote from 32). Thomas Bender, *Community and Social Change in America* (Baltimore, 1978), p. 96f, notes that persons who traveled westward in groups tended to remain in settings of mutuality, like political groups, churches, and voluntary organizations, once settled in a state. Churches in particular provided behavioral standards and models for participation.

It is unfortunately impossible to know the population and actual residents for the city of Vandalia for this period; therefore, pinpointing domiciles and neighborhood groupings is not possible until the 1860 census, which for the first time lists Vandalia's citizens separately from county (non-town) residents. The Nov. 11, 1835 *Ill. Adv.* reported that Fayette County had 8,000 persons, counted in the 1835 state census, compared with 3,500 in the 1830 census. The Feb. 17, 1836 issue reported 1,957 white males, 1,745 white females, and 32 blacks. Sangamon was the largest state county with 9,006, followed by Green and Cook counties.

18. Faragher, *Sugar Creek*, p. 139; 1878 History, p. 30. There was one major: John A. Wakefield. On Fayette County men in the Black Hawk War, see Ellen M. Whitney, ed., *The Black Hawk War, 1831–1832, Illinois Volunteers* (Springfield, 1970), pp. 206ff, 419–22, 543ff. On the war, see the introduction to Whitney; John A. Wakefield, *History of the Black Hawk War* (Jacksonville, 1834, repr. Chicago, 1975), Ford, *History of Illinois*, chapter 5; Reynolds, *My Own Times*, pp. 203–68; Theodore C. Pease, *The Frontier State, 1818–1848* (Springfield 1918, repr. Urbana, 1987), chapter 8; Buley, *The Old Northwest*, 2: 59–80.

19. Reynolds, *My Own Times*, p. 54; 1878 History, p. 83.

20. FF 8 (Sept. 1979): 36; *Illinois Monthly Magazine* 1 (1830): 126; 1878 History, pp. 61, 68, 85, 87; Ford, *History of Illinois*, pp. 107–8.

21. 1878 History, p. 84.

22. Among the many studies since the 1970s of frontier women's experiences, see Glenda Riley, "Images of the Frontierswoman: Iowa as a Case Study," *Western Historical Quarterly* 8 (April 1977): 189–202 (quote from

194); and Glenda Riley, *The Female Frontier: A Comparative View of Women on the Prairie and the Plains* (Lawrence, 1988); Sandra L. Myres, *Westerning Women and the Frontier Experience, 1800–1915* (Albuquerque, 1982); Arlene Scadron, ed., *On Their Own: Widows and Widowhood in the American Southwest, 1848–1939* (Urbana, 1988); Susan Armitage and Elizabeth Jameson, eds., *The Women's West* (Norman, 1987); and chapters 11 and 12 of Faragher, *Sugar Creek*; see also 1878 History, pp. 25 and 60.

23. 1878 History, p. 54; Ross 1904, pp. 56, 159, 160–62.

24. Paul E. Stroble, Jr., "Ferdinand Ernst and the German Colony at Vandalia," *Illinois Historical Journal* 80 (Summer 1987): 109f.

25. 1878 History, p. 61. On estates, see, for example, FF 9 (March 1980): 18; 9 (June 1980): 15, 25, 28–29.

26. On the duties and functions of the federal land program, see Malcolm Rohrbough, *The Land Office Business: The Settlement and Administration of American Public Lands, 1789–1837* (New York, 1968).

27. On daily life of frontier people, see Buley, *The Old Northwest*, 1: chapters 3–6.

28. FF 6 (Summer 1977): 106–8; 8 (June 1979): 5–12; 8 (Sept. 1979): 3–5; and *Fayette County Illinois Marriage Record, 1821–1877* (Vandalia, n.d.), contain records from FCCiC. The birth years of brides and grooms compared in the later census records and the genealogical charts in *FF* with the dates of marriages show that Vandalia people conformed to the average marital age of the era.

29. Mortality figures in Fayette County do not extend back to this era; a sampling of obituaries in Vandalia papers from 1819 to 1839 and the charts in *FF* indicate that the death of up to one-third of a family's offspring was not unknown.

30. 1878 History, pp. 48f, 60, 62.

31. Buley, *The Old Northwest*, 1: 240–47.

32. 1878 History, p. 67. On the cholera scare, see also *Ill. Adv.* May 25, July 20, 27, Aug. 3, 1833; 1878 History, p. 67; *FF* 10 (Dec. 1981): 27. See also Charles E. Rosenberg, *The Cholera Years* (Chicago, 1988); and Robert John Morris, *Cholera, 1832: The Social Response to an Epidemic* (New York, 1976), who points out that, depending on local health and sanitation, the disease could miss entire communities, as it did Vandalia.

33. Paul Angle, *Here I Have Lived: A History of Lincoln's Springfield* (Springfield, 1935), p. 32. Strangely, the George Ogle hanging in Vandalia on November 18, 1842 is skipped by the 1878 History. Ross 1904 (pp. 102–4) provides details of the only legal hanging in Fayette County. "The sentence was carried out at the appointed time, and that day has ever since been a memorable day, as being the coldest day ever known in Vandalia. Some old residents state that the thermometer registered 40 degrees below zero." The execution apparently took place at the present site of a funeral home, Fourth and Madison. See also Eleanor Atkinson, "The Year of the Deep Snow," *TISHS* 14 (1909): 49–55, reprinted in Robert P. Sutton, *The Prairie State: A Doc-*

umentary History of Illinois, Colonial Years to 1860 (Grand Rapids, 1976), 217–55. The Deep Snow did not make its way into Vandalia traditions.

34. *Ill. Int.*, March 29, 1823; chapter 6 herein.

35. William Oliver, *Eight Months in Illinois* (Newcastle upon Tyne, 1843, repr. Ann Arbor, 1968), p. 33; cf. Buley, *The Old Northwest*, 1: 319–321.

36. Zophar Case's letter book, Aug. 28, 1831, ISHL; James Hall, "The French Village," in *Seven Stories* (Vandalia, 1976), p. 30.

37. 1878 History, pp. 91, 80.

38. Buley, *The Old Northwest*, 1: 13, 37–38.

39. *FF* 5 (Spring 1976): 3; 7 (March 1978): 5–9; 8 (Sept. 1979): 31; 12 (Sept. 1983): 45–60; Oliver, *Eight Months in Illinois*, p. 101.

40. Township histories in 1878 History and Ross 1910; *FF* 12 (March 1983): 53.

41. 1878 History, p. 65f; *FF* 10 (Sept. 1981): 63.

42. Reynolds, *My Own Times*, p. 169; 1878 History, pp. 30f. For a rejection of the story of Higgins's 1814 encounter, see Reynolds, *Pioneer History*, p. 381. Reynolds remembered that Higgins died in 1829, rather than 1836; the county histories copied his error, and that is the date on the cenotaph on Vandalia Correctional Center property (Higgins's farm) north of Vandalia on U.S. 51. Higgins's obituary is in *I.S.R.*, April 15, 1836.

43. 1878 History, pp. 68, 72, 74, 78, 89, 91; *FF* 12 (March 1983): 53; 13 (June 1984): 53f; William Henry Perrin, ed., *History of Bond and Montgomery Counties, Ill.* (Chicago, 1882), p. 32; cf. William Lynwood Montell, *Killings: Folk Justice in the Upper South* (Lexington, Ky., 1986).

44. *FF* 7 (March 1978): 5–9; 1878 History, p. 62; JCB, p. 79; Mary Burtschi, *Vandalia: Wilderness Capital of Lincoln's Land* (Vandalia, 1963), p. 85.

45. 1878 History, pp. 78f; Paul E. Stroble, "The Big Jump: An 'Unknown' Lincoln Legend from Southern Illinois," *Springhouse* 5 (Feb. 1988): 6f; *FF* 16 (March 1987): 53. The Lincoln jump is not what Dorson calls "Fakelore," that is, erroneous folklore used for profit; see Richard M. Dorson, *American Folklore* (Chicago, 1959). Although the legend is demonstrably false, it is a tenacious bit of genuine folklore, largely overlooked by Lincoln scholars and not exploited for Vandalia tourism.

46. 1878 History, p. 54.

47. Doyle, *Social Order*, p. 255.

48. Ibid., chapter 8; see also Bender, *Community and Social Change in America*, pp. 94f, 107f. Bender cites Stuart M. Blumin's study of Kingston, New York (*The Urban Threshold: Growth and Change in a Nineteenth-Century American Community*, Chicago, 1976), to note that feelings of community intensified by 1860, more than had been the case in 1820; local identity and concomitant feelings of community intensified as the antebellum period progressed. As Doyle points out, the impulse to connect historical reinterpretation with small-town and urban identity increased during this period.

4. HIGH ON THE OKAW'S WESTERN BANK

1. JCB, pp. 76f contains some of the earliest photographs Vandalia buildings. The earliest known photograph of the third statehouse is a photograph

dating from the 1860s or 1870s, presently displayed in the Historic Vandalia Museum and reproduced courtesy of Sandra Leidner.

2. The major histories of Vandalia are, in chronological order: *History of Fayette County* (Philadelphia, 1878); Robert W. Ross, *Historical Souvenir of Vandalia, Illinois* (Effingham, 1904); Robert W. Ross and John J. Bullington, *History of Fayette County* (Chicago, 1910); William Baringer, *Lincoln's Vandalia* (New Brunswick, 1949); Joseph C. Burtschi, *Documentary History of Vandalia, Illinois* (Vandalia, 1954); Mary Burtschi, *Vandalia: Wilderness Capital of Lincoln's Land* (Vandalia, 1963); the continuing issues of the *Fayette Facts* (Vandalia: 1974 to present); and Mary Burtschi, *James Hall of Lincoln's Frontier World* (Vandalia, 1977). Mary Burtschi's 1963 work is a selection of material concerning Vandalia's capital era and overall heritage; her 1977 book considers James Hall's role in Vandalia's early history. Joseph Burtschi's book collects primary sources and documents about the capital era. Baringer's book considers Lincoln's legislative career at Vandalia. Although written and compiled long after the pioneer era, the 1878 history and Ross's works contain sufficient traditional and primary information to be considered, like Joseph Burtschi's book, primary sources for Vandalia's capital period.

Besides those mentioned elsewhere in these notes, books of observation and travel from this period include: C. O. Barbaroux, *L'Historie des Etats-Unis d'Amerique* (Philadelphia, 1839); Morris Birkbeck, *Letters from Illinois* and *Notes on a Journey in America* (both London, 1818, repr. Ann Arbor, 1968); Paul Wilhelm, Duke of Wuerttemberg, *Travels in North America in 1822–4* (Norman, 1973); Basil Hall, *Travels in North America in the Years 1827 and 1828* (Edinburgh, 1829); Abner Jones, *Illinois and the West* (Philadelphia, 1838); Samuel Augustus Mitchell, ed., *Illinois in 1837* (Philadelphia, 1837); Henry R. Schoolcraft, *Travels in the Central Portions of the Mississippi Valley* (New York, 1825); and J. Calvin Smith, *The Western Tourist* (New York, 1836).

Among books on early Illinois besides those often mentioned in these notes (Ford, Pease, Reynolds, and Buley on the Old Northwest) are: John W. Allen, *Legends and Lore of Southern Illinois* (Carbondale, 1963) and *It Happened in Southern Illinois* (Carbondale, 1968); Newton Bateman and Paul Shelby, *Historical Encyclopedia of Illinois* (Chicago, 1910); Alexander Davidson and Bernard Stuvé, *A Complete History of Illinois from 1673 to 1884* (Springfield, 1884); Edward Dunne, *Illinois, the Heart of the Nation*, 5 vols. (Chicago, 1933); Ninian Wirt Edwards, *History of Illinois from 1773 to 1833, and Life and Times of Ninian Edwards* (Springfield, 1870); Robert Howard, *Illinois: A History of the Prairie State* (Grand Rapids, 1972); Irwin Mather, *The Making of Illinois* (Chicago, 1923); John Moses, *Illinois Historical and Statistical* 2 vols. (Chicago, 1889, 1895); Theodore C. Pease, *The Story of Illinois* (Chicago, 1925, 1949, 1965); and Randall Parrish, *Historic Illinois* (Chicago, 1905).

3. In the Fayette County records, Illinois Regional Depository, there is an undated order, probably from the mid-1830s, for a plank sidewalk through downtown Vandalia. On the possible paving of the streets in the 1830s and

1840s, see City Book of Records, p. 58, Vandalia City Hall; Fayette County Commissioners Court Records, 1844–49, p. 157, FCCiC.

4. Paul E. Stroble, "Vandalia Businesses and Establishments, 1819–1839," *FF* 15 (June 1986): 43–64, provides names and possible locations of all the known businesses and professional offices in capital-era Vandalia. Before 1822, more Vandalia businesses operated on Main Street (north of the public square) than on Gallatin Street (south of the public square). The third statehouse was constructed in 1836 to face Gallatin Street.

5. *Ill. Adv.*, July 19, 1834, and *Beardstown Chronicle*, Dec. 6, 1834, both in Baringer, *Lincoln's Vandalia*, pp. 31–31, 35.

6. On McCullom's hotel, see 1878 History, p. 26; *Ill. Int.*, July 23, 1825, Dec. 18, 1830. McCullom's widow, Sarah, then John Charter, ran the hotel after 1823. It was located on lot 5, block 42, or on the southeast corner of Fifth and Gallatin. In his autobiography, Hollman stops just short of naming McCullom as a participant in the 1823 Vandalia bank robbery and as an accomplice behind the 1820 looting of the Ernst's chests. Hollman cited the discovery of the cash in the unnamed man's hotel stables (some cash was in fact found in McCullom's stables), his Madison County origins, and the fact that the man died shortly after the robbery. (A few weeks after the robbery, McCullom died on April 17, 1823.) This suggests that McCullom was the man of whom Hollman was thinking, but the robbers were never discovered and no one was brought to trial.

7. On Vandalia hotels during the capital period, see Stroble, "Vandalia Businesses and Establishments"; 1878 History, p. 26; *Edwardsville Spectator*, July 31, Aug. 29, 1819; *Ill. Int.*, Oct. 7, Dec. 14, 1820, March 6, Sept. 3, 1821, April 20, Aug. 10, 1822, May 17, Nov. 16, 1823, June 11, Oct. 22, 1824, April 14, July 23, 1825, June 15, 1826, Dec. 18, 1830, April 16, 1831; *Ill. Adv.*, April 6, Dec. 27, 1833, Jan. 11, Feb. 1, 1834, April 1, Nov. 18, Dec. 2, 1835; *I.S.R.*, April 22, 1836, Dec. 15, 1836, June 3, 1837, May 17, 1839; and *Free Press*, Oct. 14, 1837, Feb. 10, 1838.

8. On McLaughlin's hotel, see *Ill. Int.*, May 8, July 10, 1821, Nov. 1, 1828, Sept. 30, 1831; *Ill. Adv.*, Feb. 1, 1834; *Vandalia Whig*, April 17, 1834. This seems to have been a building near Gallatin. Newspaper references call McLaughlin's establishment "the brick house" as if it were something unique in Vandalia.

9. Burtschi, *Vandalia: Wilderness Capital*, pp. 42–43; Stroble, "Vandalia Businesses and Establishments."

10. Among the governors only Shadrach Bond, who lived with his relatives the McLaughlins, is known to have had a house in which to stay at Vandalia.

11. *Ill. Int.*, July 26, Nov. 16, 1823, June 14, Nov. 1, 1828; *I.S.R.*, April 22, 1836, June 3, 1837; *Free Press*, Dec. 27, 1838.

12. Fayette County Commissioners' Record Book, April 16, 1821, and Circuit Court Record Book B, 1832–39, p. 6, both in FCCiC.

13. On frontier taverns and hotels, see R. Carlyle Buley, *The Old Northwest, Pioneer Period: 1815–1840* (Bloomington, 1950), 1: 481–87; and John Mack Faragher, *Sugar Creek: Life on an Illinois Prairie* (New Haven, 1986),

pp. 153f. The poem is from James Hall, "Parody" (1818), quoted in Burtschi, *James Hall*, p. 16.

14. Edmund Flagg, *The Far West: Or, A Trip Beyond the Mountains* (New York, 1838), quoted in JCB, p. 94.

15. Benjamin Godfrey to Theron Baldwin, Jan. 5, 1837, letters of John F. Brooks, Manuscript Division, ISHL, quoted in Paul Simon, *Lincoln's Preparation for Greatness* (Norman, 1965), p. 55.

16. On attorneys at Vandalia, see *Edwardsville Spectator*, Nov. 7, 1819; *Ill. Int.*, Oct. 7, 1820, Jan. 16, 1821, Oct. 11, March 8, Dec. 28, 1822, March 8, 15, May 3, Nov. 16, 1823, Feb. 13, 1824, July 8, Sept. 9, 1825, Dec. 23, 1826, March 3, Aug. 18, 1827, Sept. 30, 1831; *Ill. Adv.*, April 27, May 19, June 1, 22, 1833; *I.S.R.*, May 11, Dec. 15, 1836, June 3, 1837; *Free Press*, Oct. 14, 1837; Stroble, "Vandalia Businesses and Establishments."

On physicians in Vandalia, see Stroble, "Vandalia Businesses and Establishments"; 1878 History, p. 26; *Ill. Int.*, Jan. 9, 16, 1821, Nov. 16, 1822, May 8, June 15, July 10, 1822, Feb. 22, 1823, March 16, April 29, Dec. 2, 1836, June 3, 1837.

17. On blacksmiths, see Buley, *The Old Northwest*, 1: 227; Stroble, "Vandalia Businesses and Establishments"; *Ill. Int.*, Jan. 16, Dec. 18, 1821, June 15, 1822, May 17, 1823, March 6, 1824; *Vandalia Union*, April 16, 1914.

18. On the Duncan family, see Burtschi, *James Hall*, pp. 87–91, 166–67, 174–75; Elizabeth Duncan Putnam, "The Life and Services of Joseph Duncan," *TISHS* 25 (1919). On James M. Duncan's troubles in his position as cashier of the state bank, see *Ill. Int.*, July 3, 17, 1830; and George Dowrie, *The Development of Banking in Illinois, 1817–1863* (Urbana, 1913), pp. 52–53. Matthew Duncan's obituary appears in *Illinois Sentinel* (Vandalia), Jan. 24, 1844.

19. Lewis Atherton, *The Frontier Merchant in Mid-America* (Columbia, 1971), pp. 13–14.

20. On Prentice's estate, see Probate Record, 1821–47, B, 399–424, FCCiC; see also *Free Press*, Nov. 25, 1837.

21. On frontier stores, see, for example, Buley, *The Old Northwest*, 1: 234–36, 554–58, and Atherton, *The Frontier Merchant*. On Vandalia stores, see 1878 History, p. 46; Stroble, "Vandalia Businesses and Establishments"; *Ill. Int.*, July 16, 1821, June 21, 1823, July 8, 1825, June 17, July 8, 1826, Sept. 8, 1827, Aug. 21, 28, Oct. 23, Dec. 11, 1830; *I.S.R.*, March 16, April 8, 15, 22, Nov. 4, Dec. 15, 1836, Dec. 20, 27, 1838; and *Free Press*, Oct. 14, 1837, Feb. 10, 1838, Oct. 12, 1839.

22. *Ill. Int.*, March 20, 1821, Jan. 1, July 20, Aug. 31, Oct. 26, 1822; *Sangamo Journal*, Aug. 3, 1833; Buley, *The Old Northwest*, 1: 552f.

23. On Ernst colonists' businesses, see *Ill. Int.*, April 20, 1822, Feb. 22, May 17, 1823, June 11, 1824, April 14, 1825, Nov. 22, 1828, April 18, 1829, Dec. 11, 1830; *Ill. Adv.*, April 6, 1833; JCB, p. 31; Stroble, "Vandalia Businesses and Establishments"; Record for the ship the *Virgin*, Baltimore, Oct. 2, 1820, Records of the Bureau of the Customs, Record Group 36, Microcopy

255, National Archives, in Paul E. Stroble, "The Ernst Colony," *FF* 6 (Summer 1977): 41.

24. On local mills, see 1878 History, p. 46; JCB, pp. 29, 83; *Ill. Int.*, March 20, May 1, July 4, 1821, Feb. 4, 1825; Probate File 251, FCCiC.

25. Buley, *The Old Northwest*, 1: 558–561.

26. *Ill. Int.*, May 17, 1823, Feb. 7, April 18, 1829; *Free Press*, Oct. 14, 1837; Burtschi, *Vandalia: Wilderness Capital*, p. 151.

27. *Ill. Int.*, April 18, 1825, Dec. 11, 1830.

28. 1878 History, p. 57; Ross 1904, pp. 11, 28, 129, passim.

29. On the history of the Vandalia statehouses, see Joseph C. Burtschi and Lester O. Shriver, *Lincoln and Vandalia* (Vandalia, 1946); and Illinois Department of Conservation notes on the three Vandalia statehouses, files of the Vandalia Statehouse. See also chapter 7.

30. Hall, *Letters from the West*, p. 227.

31. William Oliver, *Eight Months in Illinois* (Newcastle upon Tyne, 1843, repr. Ann Arbor, 1968), p. 76.

32. Oliver, *Eight Months in Illinois* p. 67. See also Robert V. Hine, *Community on the American Frontier* (Norman, 1980), pp. 136–37. Thomas Bender, *Community and Social Change in America* (Baltimore, 1978): "It is clear that a sense of human connection coincided with the geographic boundaries of a town. . . . Unfortunately, existing studies are not very precise in delineating the character of social relationships. In arguing for the importance of localized social orientations, scholars have failed to specify different kinds and qualities of interactions that may have characterized these relationships. . . . A claim that residents of mid- nineteenth-century towns were intimately involved with or even knew everyone in the town is hardly credible" (pp. 98–99). Due to the lack of relevant primary material, this study cannot redress Bender's complaint. Obviously not everyone at Vandalia knew each other; but Vandalia's "human connections" were surely of both an intracommunity nature and a town–county character.

33. No permanent structure existed on Vandalia's public square until the third statehouse of 1836.

34. On speech, see, for example, Buley, *The Old Northwest*, 1: 350–58; and Burtschi, *James Hall*, pp. 58–59.

35. *Sangamo Journal*, Dec. 12, 1835.

36. Thomas Ford, *A History of Illinois from Its Commencement as a State in 1818 to 1847* (Chicago, 1854, repr. Ann Arbor, 1968), p. 65.

37. Abraham Lincoln to Mary S. Owen, Dec. 13, 1836, in *The Collected Works of Abraham Lincoln*, ed. Roy P. Basler et al., 9 vols. (New Brunswick, 1953–55), 1: 54.

38. Ford, *History of Illinois*, p. 65.

39. JCB, p. 33.

40. L. C. Beck, *Gazetteer of the States of Illinois and Missouri* (Albany, 1828, repr. New York, 1975), pp. 161–63.

41. JCB, p. 80 [Dec. 11, 1830 advertisement in *Ill. Int.*]; Probate File 117, Pack 3, FCCiC; *FF* 9 (June 1980): 28–29; *Ill. Adv.*, March 2, June 15, 29,

1833, May 31, July 19, Sept. 3, 1834, Jan. 27, 1835; Stroble, "Vandalia Businesses." On the agriculture of this period, see, for example, Allan G. Bogue, *From Prairie to Corn Belt* (Chicago, 1963); James W. Whitaker, ed., *Farming in the Midwest, 1840–1900* (Washington, 1974); John T. Schlebecker, *Whereby We Thrive: A History of American Farming, 1607–1972* (Ames, 1975); Earle D. Ross, *Iowa Agriculture: An Historical Survey* (Iowa City, 1951); Richard Bardolph, *Agricultural Literature and the Early Illinois Farmer* (Urbana, 1948); Paul Gates, *The Farmer's Age: Agriculture, 1815–1860* (New York, 1960); Richard Bardolph, "Illinois Agriculture in Transition, 1820–1870," *JISHS* 42 (Sept., Dec. 1948): 244–64, 415–37. See also Bender, *Community and Social Change*, pp. 113f. Because larger, translocal markets challenged the familiar and communal patterns of social order and of social interaction, Vandalia's small-town and small-county mentality would not have been challenged by the small local economy. See also Bender on localized social relationships: the family and close friends were the innermost core of community (pp. 99f).

42. Malcolm Rohrbough, *The Land Office Business: The Settlement and Administration of American Public Lands, 1789–1837* (New York, 1968), esp. chapters 7 and 8; Murray N. Rothbard, *The Panic of 1819* (New York, 1962). Land sales (in acres) at the Vandalia land office between 1821 and 1839 were: 1821: 9,227; 1822: 2,205; 1823: 640; 1824: 614; 1825: 895; 1826: 1,472; 1827: 1,743; 1828: 3,591; 1829: 19,405; 1830: 35,362; 1831: 43,174; 1832: 8,021; 1833: 21,615; 1834: 20,207; 1835: 29,165; 1836: 127,345; 1837: 183,891; 1838: 109,516; and 1839: 178,239. During the mid 1820s, the Vandalia office had the lowest numbers of acres sold of all Illinois land offices. During the 1830s the office had the slowest rate of increase. See Theodore C. Pease, *The Frontier State, 1818–1848* (Springfield, 1918, repr. Urbana, 1987), pp. 176–77. For specific Fayette County acres sold, see *Fayette County Illinois Land Records* (Vandalia: Fayette County Genealogical Society, n.d.).

43. On the first state bank, see Dowrie, *The Development of Banking in Illinois*, chapter 3; also Pease, *The Frontier State*, pp. 68–69 and chapter 3; Bray Hammond, "Banking in the Early West: Monopoly, Prohibition and Laissez Faire," *Journal of Economic History* 8 (May 1948); and Rohrbough, *The Land Office Business*, esp. chapters 5–8. See also File 178, FCCiC. Cases in the Second Circuit Court at Vandalia, in which the state bank sued various individuals for debts and defaulted loans, are in the following files in the FCCiC: 189, 196, 197, 216, 224, 225, 237, 239, 240, 242, 243, 255, 257, 288, 310, 365, 366, 367, 592, 594, 609, 624, 704, 718, 740, 743, 780, 781, 782, 783, 784, 790, and 800.

44. Probate Court Record, B-1, 1829–38, pp. 399–424 (Prentice), FCCiC; Probate Files 187, Pack 8 and 188, Pack 1 (the McLaughlins); Probate File 566, (McCurdy); cf. Atherton, *Frontier Merchant in Mid-America*, pp. 14, 47, 163, passim.

45. Probate Court Record, B-1, pp. 136–43 (Peebles); pp. 192–214 (John Y. Sawyer); pp. 215–16 (Higgins); pp. 306–14 (Jeremiah Evans); Probate Court Files 167, Pack 15 (James Kelley); 169, Pack 8 (John Hull); 187, Pack 15

(McCullom); 189, Box 1 (Peebles); 107, Pack 5 (John N. Johnson); 117, Pack 3 (John Taylor); 116, Pack 1 (John Y. Sawyer); 110, Pack 7 (Allen McPhail); 172, Pack 1 (James Black); 241, Pack 5 (John Roy); 251, Pack 8 (Jeremiah Evans); 258, Pack 15 (William Berry).

46. City deed records for this period are found, interspersed with county records, in Deed Books A, B, and C, FCCoC. Deed Book A is copied in *FF* 11 (March 1982): 41–48; 11 (June 1982): 47–56; and 11 (Sept. 1982): 37–49. Deed Book B is in *FF* 12 (June 1983): 43–52, and 13 (June 1984): 41–53. Deed Book C is in *FF* 13 (Sept. 1984): 41–50; 13 (Dec. 1984): 49–54; and 14 (March 1985): 37–48. Many deeds were not recorded. See also *Fayette County Land Patents to 1847*. On the problem of neighborhood configuration and persistence, see note 17, chapter 3.

47. Tax Record Book, 1828–30, FCCiC.

48. Beck, *Gazetteer of the State of Illinois and Missouri*, pp. 161–63; Chester A. Loomis, *The Notes of a Journey to the Great West in 1825* (Ontario County, N.Y., 1825), quoted in JCB, p. 93; Edmund Flagg, *The Far West: Or, A Tour Beyond the Mountains* (New York, 1838), quoted in JCB, pp. 94–96 and in the Introduction; Frederick Gustorf, "Frontier Perils Told by an Early Illinois Visitor," *JISHS* 55 (Summer 1962): 152–54; John J. Hardin to Sarah Hardin, Dec. 14, 1836, quoted in Robert W. Johannsen, "History on the Illinois Frontier: Early Efforts to Preserve the State's Past," *JISHS* 68 (April 1975): 123.

49. William Wilson to Mary Wilson [Dec.] 29, 1836, quoted in Johannsen, "History on the Illinois Frontier," p. 123; Abraham Lincoln to Mary S. Owen, Dec. 13, 1836, quoted in *The Collected Works*, ed. Basler et al., 1:54–55.

50. *Ill. Adv.*, Oct. 29, 1834. In *Ill. Adv.*, Dec. 24, 1834, Sawyer reported that Vandalia had fifteen wholesale and retail stores. Local prices were: cornmeal, 50 cents a pound; potatoes, 50 cents a pound; flour, $2 to $2.50 a pound; corn, 31 to 38 cents a pound; apples, $4 a pound; cranberries, 37.5 cents a quart; cheese, 18¾ to 20 cents a pound; oranges, 12 to 18¼ cents; turkeys, 12.5 to 25 cents; pork and beef, $2 to $2.50 a pound; venison hams, 25 to 50 cents a pair.

51. [James Hall], *Illinois Monthly Magazine* 2 (1832): 172–76, quoted in JCB, pp. 43–46.

52. J. M. Peck, *A Gazetteer of Illinois* (Jacksonville, 1834), p. 346.

53. J. M. Peck, *A Traveller's Directory* (New York, 1839), pp. 153–54.

54. On the founding of Vandalia's newspapers, see JCB, pp. 67–68, the uncredited source of which is Franklin William Scott, *Newspapers and Periodicals of Illinois, 1814–1879* (Springfield, 1910). On Blackwell, see Ross 1904, pp. 40, 149–50. Although the death year is broken from his tombstone, William Berry's obituary is in *Ill. Int.*, Feb. 2, 1828.

55. The *Intelligencer* became the *Vandalia Whig and Illinois Intelligencer* after Blackwell and Hall sold the paper. For its decline and demise, see A. F. Grant to John Reynolds, Feb. 6, 1834, Reynolds to Grant, Feb. 10, 17, 1834, R. W. Clarke to Grant, Feb. 20, 1834, Clarke to Grant, April 6, 1834, Henry Eddy Papers, Manuscripts Division, ISHL.

56. Gustorf, "Frontier Perils Told by an Early Illinois Visitor," pp. 154. In his *Reminiscences of the Bench and Bar of Illinois* (Chicago, 1879), Usher F. Linder remembered that Sawyer was ill-tempered and that he weighed more than four hundred pounds. See also, John F. Snyder, *Adam W. Snyder and His Period in Illinois History* (Virginia, Ill., 1906, repr. Ann Arbor, 1968), pp. 194–97. The *Illinois Advocate* was a forerunner of the present *State Journal-Register* in Springfield; see Andy Van Meter, *Always My Good Friend: A History of the State Journal-Register and Springfield* (Springfield, 1981). The *Advocate* was preceded by a paper called *Crisis*, probably supported by Theophilus W. Smith, in 1831.

57. *Free Press*, Nov. 15, 1838; *I.S.R.*, March 25, 1837. Hodge died December 13, 1844 and is interred at the east side of Vandalia's old city cemetery, near the grave of the merchant James Black and his wife. On Walters's last years, see Pease, *The Frontier State*, pp. 289–300. It is an indication of a more well-developed community that by the 1830s Vandalia had, for the first time, competing editors.

58. On the second state bank and internal improvements, see Dowrie, *Development of Banking in Illinois*; Pease, *The Frontier State*; John H. Krenkel, *Illinois Internal Improvements, 1818–1848* (Cedar Rapids, 1958); W. G. Shade, *Banks or No Banks: The Money Issue in Western Politics, 1832–1865* (Detroit, 1972); F. M. Huston, *Financing an Empire: A History of Banking in Illinois,* 4 vols. (Chicago, 1926); Bray Hammond, *Banks and Politics in America from the Revolution to the Civil War* (Princeton, 1957); and Fred B. Marchkoff, "Currency and Banking in Illinois before 1865," *JISHS* 52 (Autumn 1959): 365–418.

59. *I.S.R.*, March 4, 1837.

60. On increased businesses, see Stroble, "Vandalia Businesses and Establishments," 55–64; *I.S.R.*, April 24, Nov. 4, Dec. 15, 1836, April 22, 1837; *Free Press*, Oct. 14, 1837, Feb. 10, 1838.

61. *I.S.R.*, March 16, April 24, Nov. 4, Dec. 15, 1836, April 22, 1837

62. *Ill. Adv.*, Feb. 15, 1835; *I.S.R.*, Oct. 14, Nov. 18, 1836, Jan. 2, 1837, Feb. 2, 1838, March 22, 1839; *Free Press*, Oct. 14, 1836, Feb. 10, 1838, March 4, 1839, July 17, 1840.

63. Cases in the Second Circuit Court at Vandalia, in which the state bank brought debt suits against individuals, are in the following files in the FCCiC: 795, 796, 798, 813, 848, 851, 852, 853, 867, 881, 882, 883, 884, 885, 886, 887, 888, 977, 978, 979, 980, 981, 982, 983, 984, 985, 986, 987, 999, 1027, 1029, 1030, 1031, 1032, 1033, 1034, 1035, 1036, and 1037.

64. Pease, *The Frontier State*, chapter 11.

65. *Free Press*, Oct. 21, 1837, Feb. 10, 1838.

66. Ross 1904, p. 23; the entire description (pp. 23–30) is of interest.

67. Ross 1910, pp. 626–27. See also Paul Wallance Gates, *The Illinois Central Railroad and Its Colonization Work* (Cambridge, 1934), esp. chapters 1 and 2.

5. "BOOSTING" THE STATE CAPITAL

1. Stanley Elkins and Eric McKitrick, "A Meaning for Turner's Frontier, Part 1: Democracy in the Old Northwest," *Political Science Quarterly* 69 (Sept. 1954): 321–53. Problems of frontier community have been considered in variety of studies. Don Harrison Doyle, *The Social Order of a Frontier Community: Jacksonville, Illinois, 1825–1870* (Urbana, 1978); John Mack Faragher, *Sugar Creek: Life on the Illinois Prairie* (New Haven, 1986); Robert R. Dykstra, *The Cattle Towns* (New York, 1968); Richard C. Wade, *The Urban Frontier* (Chicago, 1959, 1971); Thomas Bender, *Community and Social Change in America* (Baltimore, 1978); Edward M. Cook, Jr., *The Fathers of the Towns* (Baltimore, 1976); Randolph B. Campbell, *A Southern Community in Crisis: Harrison County, Texas, 1850–1880* (Austin, 1983); Stephan Thernstrom, *Poverty and Progress: Social Mobility in a Nineteenth-Century City* (Cambridge, 1964); Page Smith, *As a City upon a Hill: The Town in American History* (New York, 1966); Herman R. Lantz, *A Community in Search of Itself: A Case History of Cairo, Illinois* (Carbondale, 1972), Stuart M. Blumin, *The Urban Threshold: Growth and Change in a Nineteenth-Century American Community* (Chicago, 1976); Merle Curti et al., *The Making of an American Community: A Case Study of Democracy in a Frontier County* (Stanford, 1959); Lewis Atherton, *Main Street on the Middle Border* (Bloomington, Ind., 1954); Don Martindale and R. Galen Hanson, *Small Town and the Nation* (Westport, 1969); and Robert V. Hine, *Community on the American Frontier* (Norman, 1980).

2. The birth years of Vandalia's capital-era leaders and professionals are: Matthew Branch, 1777; Robert K. McLaughlin, 1779; Elijah C. Berry, 1781; John Frederick Yerker, 1781; Ferdinand Ernst, ca. 1784; Mariane Ernst, ca. 1785; William Greenup, 1785; John York Sawyer, 1789; Matthew Duncan, 1790; James M. Duncan, probably 1790s; William Berry, 1790; Isabella Bond McLaughlin, 1791; Frederick Hollman, 1791; William Hodge, 1791; Abner Flack, 1792; William L. D. Ewing, ca. 1795; Robert Blackwell, 1796; William H. Brown, 1796; Ebenezer Capps, 1798; Charles Prentice, 1800; William Walters, 1802; John Dement, 1804; James William Berry, 1805; Frederick Remann, 1807; Ferris Forman, 1811; and George Leidig, unknown (died 1849).

3. Elkins and McKitrick, "A Meaning for Turner's Frontier," esp. 333ff. See chapters 6 and 7 herein on politics and local participation. Observations concerning local participation of Vandalia are based on the published proceedings of meetings from 1819 to 1839, whenever lists of members and/or participants are included, which is not always the case. Bender, *Community and Social Change*, pp. 102f, notes that only by the 1830s and 1840s did men place local political parties on a higher level than social unity.

On local improvements, see ibid., pp. 105f: "To the extent that the state government intruded into local affairs, it delegated responsibility to local communities to undertake some general purpose within the framework of local life." Such an observation pertains to Vandalia; local responsibility for the town, and the need for cooperation, extended beyond simple town improvement because legislative foot-dragging concerning the town's betterment extended even to the construction of adequate public buildings.

4. Dykstra, *The Cattle Towns*, pp. 355–78.

5. Doyle, *Social Order*, Introduction; see also chapter 6 herein.

6. Ronald L. F. Davis, "Community and Conflict in Pioneer St. Louis, Missouri," *Western Historical Quarterly* 10 (July 1979): 337–55, esp. 337, 341, 343ff.

7. Lewis A. Coser, *Continuities in the Study of Social Conflict* (New York, 1967), p. 20: "Conflict within and between groups in a society can prevent accommodations and habitual relations from progressively impoverishing creativity. The clash of values and interests, the tension between what is and what some groups feel ought to be, the conflict between vested interests and new strata and groups demanding their share of power, wealth, and status, have been productive of vitality." Similarly, "if, within any social structure, there exists an excess of claimants over opportunities for adequate reward, there arises strain and conflict" (pp. 26ff). In Vandalia's case, the local social structure apparently was such that the number of claimants was in close proportion to opportunities, so that such vital and creative conflict did not arise to a sufficiently significant degree.

8. Cf. Dykstra, *The Cattle Towns*, pp. 374ff. Vandalia was not a closed society (Dykstra's criticism of the Elkins-McKitrick model); yet outside influences, such as state politics or temperance, seem not to have upset internal social mechanisms to appreciable degrees.

9. Although tardy, strident local protests about relocation of the state capital certainly indicate an active town leadership and community spirit. As I suggest in the Introduction, Vandalia's problems were in a way greater than the relocation issue; the fact that most community leaders stayed in town after 1839 suggests a greater desire for community betterment than capital-era examples provide. Too, one Vandalia booster, William Hodge, consistently pressed for larger solutions as internal improvements and the completion of the National Road for Vandalia's benefit, and continued to do so after the relocation bill passed in February 1837. It might be hypothesized that Hodge was not the exception to local community spirit at all, but simply the most obvious example due to his editorial work.

10. James Hall, *Letters from the West* (London, 1828, repr. Gainesville, 1967), pp. 73f.

11. John F. Snyder, "Forgotten Statesmen of Illinois: Conrad Will," *TISHS* 11 (1905): 351–77; John T. Flanagan, "John Russell of Bluffdale," *JISHS* 42 (Sept. 1949): 272–91; Paul Angle, *Here I Have Lived: A History of Lincoln's Springfield* (Springfield, 1935), pp. 7ff. Hall breaks the pattern of Bender in that his solutions went beyond the local.

12. His portrait in Davidson and Stuvé is reproduced in JCB, p. 62; the portrait at the Illinois Capitol at Springfield is the artist Lloyd Ostendorf's conception. See also John F. Snyder, *Adam W. Snyder and His Period in Illinois History* (Virginia, Ill. 1906, repr. Ann Arbor, 1968), p. 173; and Mary

Burtschi, *James Hall of Lincoln's Frontier World* (Vandalia, 1977), pp. 45, 51.

13. Local histories' glossing-over of Ewing's character is a good example of Doyle's and Dykstra's point; portrayals of frontier situations are often sweetened by boosteristic writers of local history. On Ewing's criminal history, see, for example, 1878 History, p. 15; Record Book A, pp. 140, 182, FCCiC; Zophar Case's letter book, June 11, July 28, Nov. 13, 1831, July 2, 31, 1833, Manuscripts Division, ISHL; "Letter from the Treasury Department Transmitting Information in Relation to a Robbery of the Land Office at Vandalia in the State of Illinois," Washington, 1824, copy at Evans Public Library, Vandalia.

14. Robert P. Howard, *Mostly Good and Competent Men* (Springfield, 1988), pp. 56–59, 341–42.

15. See Bender, *Community and Social Change*, pp. 117ff: "Communal patterns of behavior, with their emphasis on face-to-face relationships, affective bonds, and diffuseness of obligation, remained appropriate and functional, but people painfully learned that these communal ways did not work in the larger society where their public activities were undertaken."

6. ON THE TRACK AT VANDALIA

1. A thorough analysis of early Illinois politics within the confines of a local history is precluded by the large number of execllent studies on the Jacksonian period and the concomitant necessity to do justice to the era's politics and economics. A highly selective list of secondary sources, in addition to those cited elsewhere in these notes, include Lee Benson, *The Concept of Jacksonian Democracy* (Princeton, 1961); Shaw Livermore, Jr., *The Twilight of Federalism* (Princeton, 1962); Marvin Meyers, *The Jacksonian Persuasion: Politics and Belief* (Stanford, 1960); Edward Pessen, *Jacksonian America: Society, Personality, and Politics* (Urbana, 1985); G. S. Borit, *Lincoln and the Economics of the American Dream* (Memphis, 1978); Robert W. Johannsen, *Stephen A. Douglas* (Oxford, 1973); D. W. Lusk, *Eighty Years of Illinois Politics and Politicians* (Springfield, 1889); Arthur M. Schlesinger, Jr., *The Age of Jackson* (Boston, 1946); William Gerald Slade, *Banks or No Banks: The Money Issue in Western Politics, 1832–1865* (Detroit, 1972); Charles W. Thompson, *The Illinois Whigs Before 1846* (Urbana, 1915); Thomas Brown, *Politics and Statesmanship: Essays on the American Whig Party* (New York, 1985); Robert V. Remini, *Andrew Jackson and the Course of American Democracy, 1833–1845* (New York, 1984); Donald B. Coles, *Martin Van Buren and the American Political System* (Princeton, 1984); Mary W. M. Hargreaves, *The Presidency of John Quincy Adams* (Lawrence, 1985); Richard P. McCormick, *The Second American Party System: Party Formation in the Jacksonian Era* (Chapel Hill, 1966); Richard L. McCormick, *The Party Period and Public Policy: American Politics from the Age of Jackson to the Progressive Era* (New York, 1986); Ronald P. Formisano, *The Birth of Mass Politics: Michigan, 1827–1861* (Princeton, 1971); Herbert Ershkowitz and William G. Shade, "Consensus or Conflict? Political Behavior in the State Legislatures during the Jacksonian Period," *Journal of American History* 58 (Dec.

1971): 591–621; Ronald P. Formisano, "Toward a Reorientation of Jacksonian Politics," *Journal of American History* 69 (June 1976): 42–65; Daniel Elazar, "Gubernatorial Power and the Illinois and Michigan Canal, A Study of Political Development in the Nineteenth Century," *JISHS* 58 (Winter 1965): 396–423; Mason McCloud Fishback, "Illinois Legislation on Slavery and Free Negroes, 1818–1865," *TISHS* 9 (1904): 414–32; Lynn L. Marshall, "The Strange Still-birth of the Whig Party," *American Historical Review* 72 (1967): 445–68; Jacob W. Myers, "History of the Gallatin County Salines," *JISHS* 14 (Oct. 1921–Jan. 1922): 337–50; Arnold Shankman, "Partisan Conflicts, 1839–41, and the Illinois Constitution," *JISHS* 63 (Winter 1970): 336–67; Robert M. Sutton, "1837, Illinois' Year of Decision," *JISHS* 58 (Spring 1965): 34–52; Andrew R. L. Cayton, "The Contours of Power in a Frontier Town: Marietta, Ohio, 1788–1803," *Journal of the Early Republic* 6 (Summer 1986): 103–27; John Michael Rozett, "The Social Bases of Party Conflict in the Age of Jackson: Individual Voting Behavior in Green County, Illinois, 1838–1848," Ph.D. diss., University of Michigan, 1974.

Collections of letters and speeches include Roy P. Basler et al., eds., *The Collected Works of Abraham Lincoln*, 9 vols. (New Brunswick, 1953–55), esp. vol. 1; E. B. Greene and C. W. Alvord, eds., *The Governors' Letter-Books, 1818–1834* (Springfield, 1909); Elihu B. Washburne, *The Edwards Papers* (Chicago, 1884); Robert W. Johannsen, *The Letters of Stephen Douglas* (Urbana, 1961); Henry Eddy Papers, Manuscripts Division, ISHL; the papers of Sidney Breese and Elias Kent Kane, Illinois Historical Survey, Urbana.

Thomas Ford's 1854 history remains a classic of political interpretation. Theodore C. Pease's *The Frontier State, 1818–1848* (Springfield, 1918, repr. Urbana, 1987) is this century's most thorough treatment of the era's politics. Rodney O. Davis's Ph. D. dissertation, "Illinois Legislators and Jacksonian Democracy," University of Iowa, 1966, is the best treatment of the Jacksonian period, improving in important ways on Pease. My unpublished study for the Illinois Department of Conservation, "The Legislatures of the Vandalia State-house: An Analysis of the Tenth and the First Session of the Eleventh General Assemblies of Illinois," analyzes the political makeup of these legislative sessions and describes the legislative procedures used during the 1830s.

2. Joseph E. Suppinger, "Amity to Enmity: Ninian Edwards and Jesse B. Thomas," *JISHS* 67 (April 1974): 170–86; see also C. W. Alvord, *The Illinois Country, 1673–1818* (Springfield, 1918); Ninian Wirt Edwards, *History of Illinois from 1778 to 1833, and Life and Times of Ninian Edwards* (Springfield, 1870); and John F. Snyder, "Forgotten Statesmen of Illinois: Hon. Jesse Burgess Thomas," *TISHS* 9 (1904): 514–25.

3. Edwards, *History of Illinois*, chapter 13; Pease, *The Frontier State*, chapter 5; Josephine E. Burns, "Daniel Pope Cook," *JISHS* 6 (Oct 1913): 425–44; H. B. Chamberlin, "Elias Kent Kane," *TISHS* 13 (1908): 162–70.

4. John F. Snyder, "Forgotten Statesmen of Illinois: Conrad Will," *TISHS* 11 (1905): 351–77; author interviews with Will's descendents Kurt Jensen and Jesse Graff Jensen, Murphysboro, Illinois, 1979; Paul M. Angle, "Nathaniel Pope, 1784–1850: A Memoir," *TISHS* 43 (1936): 111–81; "Colonel Thomas

Cox," *Annals of Iowa* 7 (Jan. 1906): 240–69; B. D. Monroe, "The Life and Services of William Wilson," *JISHS* 11 (Oct. 1918): 391–400; Frank E. Stevens, "Alexander Pope Field," *JISHS* 4 (April 1911): 7–37; *Ill. Adv.*, March 2, 1833.

5. *Ill. Int.*, July 22, 1820, July 27, Aug. 10, 1822, July 6, Aug. 3, 1826; *Edwardsville Spectator*, July 27, 1820; Pease, *The Frontier State*, pp. 103–4; Edwards, *History of Illinois*, pp. 225–29, 230–31, 429. On the full Hall–Cook exchange, see *Illinois Gazette*, June 29, July 6, 27, Aug. 3, 1822. On the evolution of these and related issues, see Davis, "Illinois Legislators," pp. 54–96.

6. *Ill. Int.*, Nov. 30, 1822, Feb. 1, 1823, Aug. 13, 1824, March 25, 1825, July 6, 1826, and July 19, 1828.

7. *Ill. Int.*, March. 17, 1828; July 26, Aug. 9, Sept. 13, 1823, March 25, 1825, March 24, Aug. 4, Oct. 12, 1827, Jan. 5, March 1, 29, May 10, and June 21, 1828; see also July 6, 1822, June 21, July 5, 1823, and July 8, 1825.

8. *Ill. Int.*, July 8, 1825.

9. Thomas Ford, *A History of Illinois from Its Commencment as a State in 1818 to 1847* (Chicago, 1854, repr. Ann Arbor, 1968), pp. 55–56; Theodore C. Pease, *Illinois Election Returns, 1818–1848* (Springfield, 1923), pp. xviii–xix; E. Patchett to James Hall, Sept. 4, 1823, Henry Eddy Papers, Manuscripts Division, ISHL.

10. *Ill. Int.*, July 22, 1820; Pease, *The Frontier State*, chapter 5.

11. *Ill. Int.*, June 22, June 29, July 6, 20, 27, Aug. 3, 1826; Pease, *The Frontier State*, pp. 107–13; *Edwardsville Spectator*, May 27, June 30, July 7, 28, Aug. 4, 1826; Washburne, *The Edwards Papers*, pp. 237ff, 254ff.

12. Fayette County returns are (from Pease, *Illinois Election Returns*): 1822: 75 percent (175 in 234 voting) for Daniel Pope Cook (18th Cong.), 45 percent (104 in 232 voting) for Edward Coles (governor); 1824: 64 percent (158 in 247 voting) for Daniel Pope Cook (19th Cong.), 51 percent (125 in 246 voting) for the constitutional convention, 57 percent (65 in 115 voting) for "Jackson or Clay" presidential elector; 1826: 67 percent (242 in 361 voting) for Joseph Duncan (20th Cong.), 61 percent (222 in 361 voting) for Thomas Sloo, governor; 1828: 69 percent (144 in 209 voting) for Joseph Duncan (21st Cong.), 74 percent (200 in 274 voting) for Andrew Jackson; 1830: 58 percent (244 in 422 voting) for William Kinney, governor; 1831: 78 percent (405 in 518 voting) for Joseph Duncan (22d Cong.); 1832: 80 percent (374 in 465 voting) for Zadoc Casey (23d Cong.), 85 percent (468 in 553 voting) for Andrew Jackson; 1834: 76 percent (480 in 632 voting) for Zadoc Casey (24th Cong.), 81 percent (540 in 665 voting) for Robert K. McLaughlin, governor; 1836: 76 percent (448 in 591 voting) for Zadoc Casey (25th Cong.), 77 percent (268 to 348 voting) for Martin Van Buren; 1838: 100 percent (405 voting) for Zadoc Casey (26th Cong.), 59 percent (450 in 760 voting) for Thomas Carlin, governor; 1840: 59 percent (645 in 1087 voting) for Martin Van Buren.

See the conclusion of this chapter for further consideration of local politics. Extant Fayette County poll books found on Reels 30–153, 30–154, Illinois State Archives; thus far in *FF*: 10 (March 1981): 31–38; 10 (June 1981): 31–36; 10 (Sept. 1981): 31–36; 11 (March 1982): 57–60; 11 (June 1982): 57–60;

12 (March 1983): 37–44; 13 (Sept. 1984): 33–39; 13 (Dec. 1984): 37–48; 14 (March 1985): 67–70; 14 (June 1985): 63–66; 15 (March 1986): 37–40.

13. R. O. Davis, "The People in Miniature: The Illinois General Assembly, 1818–1848," *Illinois Historical Journal* 81 (Summer 1988): 95–108; and Davis, "Illinois Legislators," p. 101.

14. Solon Buck, *Illinois in 1818*, 2d ed. (Urbana, 1967), pp. 218f, 242–49, 255ff, 277–82, 296ff. On the background of the controversy and the campaign itself, see the material in C. W. Alvord, ed., *Governor Edward Coles* (Springfield, 1919); N. Dwight Harris, *History of Negro Servitude in Illinois* (Chicago, 1904, repr. Ann Arbor, 1968), chapters 3 and 4; Pease, *The Frontier State*, chapter 4. On Eddy's resolution, see Pease, *The Frontier State*, pp. 73–74; *House Journal, 1820–21*, pp. 259–61.

15. On the plot, see *Ill. Int.*, July 24, 1820; *Edwardsville Spectator*, July 11, 25, 1820. On the campaign, see *Ill. Int.*, July 31, Aug. 21, 1821, Feb. 26, Sept. 7, 1822, Dec. 7, 1822; *Edwardsville Spectator*, April 9, 1822. According to Warren, Coles was one who criticized his revelation of the 1820 plot; when a man subsequently attacked Warren for making the revelation, Coles made bail for the attacker and found his legal counsel. See Alvord, ed., *Governor Edward Coles*, p. 339. Coles, a complex individual and one of the greatest Illinois governors, remains one of the state's most intriguing biographical subjects and deserves further consideration. See Robert M. Sutton, "Edward Coles and the Constitutional Crisis in Illinois, 1822–1824," *Illinois Historical Journal* 82 (Spring 1989): 33–46; Kurt Edwin Leichtle, "Edward Coles: An Agrarian on the Frontier," Ph.D. diss., University of Illinois-Chicago; Kurt Edwin Leichtle, "The Rise of Jacksonian Politics in Illinois," *Illinois Historical Journal* 82 (Summer 1989): 93–107; Robert P. Howard, *Mostly Good and Competent Men* (Springfield, 1988), pp. 21–30.

16. Harris, *History of Negro Servitude*, pp. 34–39; Alvord, ed., *Governor Edward Coles*, pp. 64–67.

17. *Ill. Int.*, Feb. 15, 1823; *Edwardsville Spectator*, Feb. 15, 22, April 12, 19, 1823; Harris, *History of Negro Servitude*, pp. 37–38. Hooper Warren called the legislative proceedings "Vandalism" and the February 12 mob a "Vandal convention." Even Governor Coles used the term: see Alvord, ed., *Governor Edward Coles*, p. 150.

18. *Ill. Int.*, Feb. 15, 1823; Harris, *History of Negro Servitude*, p. 38.

19. *Ill. Int.*, Feb. 22, May 29, June 21, July 5, 1823, Feb. 13, 1824.

20. Ibid., July 9, 23, 1823, Jan. 30, Feb. 13, 1824.

21. Alvord, *Governor Edward Coles*, pp. 117–34, 139–60, 148–49, 364–76; Harris, *History of Negro Servitude*, pp. 42–47.

22. *Ill. Int.*, Dec. 13, 1823, in JCB, pp. 23–24; *Edwardsville Spectator*, Dec. 11, 1823; Harris, *History of Negro Servitude*, p. 46. Harris combined the two events of December 9, but the statehouse conflagration happened very early that morning and the mob very late the following evening.

23. *Ill. Int.*, Dec. 13, 1823; *Edwardsville Spectator*, Dec. 11, 1823; Harris, *History of Negro Servitude*, p. 46; issues of *Ill. Int.* after May 24, 1824, esp. June 4, July 9, and Aug. 13, 1824; see also, Pease, *Illinois Election Returns*,

pp. 27–29; and Alvord, ed., *Governor Edward Coles*, pp. 149–50, 158–61, 162–69, 205–21.

24. Hamilton County legislator James Hall's observation is from *TISHS* 16 (1911): 41–42. On Blackwell's alarm at the Jacksonian enthusiasm, see *Ill. Int.*, Nov. 4, 1826, Aug. 4, 11, Sept. 8, 15, Oct. 13, 20, Nov. 17, Dec. 1, 1827, Jan. 4, March 1, April 3, May 10, 24, July 5, 12, 26, Nov. 8, 1828; see also, Pease, *The Frontier State*, pp. 123–28.

25. On the 1829–30 gubernatorial campaign, see John Reynolds, *My Own Times* (Belleville, 1857, repr. Ann Arbor, 1968), pp. 187–89; John F. Snyder, *Adam W. Snyder and His Period in Illinois History* (Virginia, Ill., 1906, repr. Ann Arbor, 1968), pp. 87, 91–99; John Reynolds to A. F. Grant, Feb. 7, 1829, S. H. Kimmel to Henry Eddy, Feb. 11, 1827, both in Henry Eddy Papers, Manuscripts Division, ISHL; *Ill. Int.*, Jan. 9, Feb. 20, April 3, 10, 17, June 12, July 10, 24, 1830.

26. Washburne, *The Edwards Papers*, pp. 419ff, also 463ff.

27. On Hall's involvement and previous controversies, see *Ill. Int.*, Nov. 8, 1828, June 13, July 4, 1829; George Forquer to A. F. Grant, June 11, 1829, and George Churchill to A. F. Grant, June 29, 1829, Henry Eddy Papers, Manuscripts Division, ISHL.

28. *Ill. Int.*, June 12, July 3, 10, 17, 24, 31, 1830; *Illinois Gazette*, Sept. 19, 1829, July 22, 31, 1830; Randolph Randall, *James Hall: Spokesman for the New West* (Columbus, 1964), pp. 163f; Washburne, *The Edwards Papers*, p. 440.

29. Pease, *The Frontier State*, pp. 143–47.

30. Ibid.; *Ill. Int.*, Feb. 18, 1832.

31. *Ill. Int.*, Dec. 4, 1830, May 21, July 16, Sept. 24, 1831, Feb. 18, 1832; *Vandalia Whig and Illinois Intelligencer*, April 13, 1834.

32. On the campaign, see Pease, *The Frontier State*, pp. 144–46; *Ill. Adv.*, Feb. 2, 1833, March 15, April 19, May 24, July 26, 1834; *Vandalia Whig*, April 3, 1834; *Sangamo Journal*, Feb. 1, April 19, Aug. 30, Oct. 4, 18, Dec. 6, 1834; *Chicago Democrat*, March 4, May 21, July 2, 23, Aug. 27, Sept. 17, Nov. 12, 1834; A. F. Grant to John M. Robinson, Jan. 14, 29, 1834; John Reynolds to A. F. Grant, Feb. 10, 17, 1834; John M. Robinson to A. F. Grant, Feb. 21, May 13, 1834; John Reynolds to Henry Eddy and R. W. Clarke, July 6, 1834; and A. F. Grant to H. L. Webb, Nov. 8, 1834, all in Henry Eddy Papers, Manuscripts Division, ISHL.

33. *Ill. Adv.*, Dec. 13, 1834; Snyder, *Adam W. Snyder*, pp. 170ff; Howard, *Mostly Good and Competent Men*, pp. 56–59.

34. Paul Simon, *Lincoln's Preparation for Greatness* (Norman, 1965), p. 49.

35. The five men's deteriorated original tombstones were replaced in 1859 by a tall obelisk; the obelisk was subsequently moved to Vandalia's South Hill Cemetery, when the men's remains may have been reinterred.

36. On issues of 1835–36, see, for example, *Ill. Adv.*, Jan. 31, April 22, 29, May 6, 27, June 3, Sept. 30, Oct. 14, 28, Dec. 16, 1835, Feb. 17, 1836; *I.S.R.*, June 3, Sept. 2, 1836; *House Journal, 1834–35*, pp. 213–17, 258–63,

355–59; *Senate Journal, 1835* (Special Session), pp. 76–78, 254–58; *House Journal, 1835* (Special Session), pp. 62–63, 211–13, 234–40.

37. On the second state bank and concomitant politics, see Davis, "Illinois Legislators," pp. 83–96, 101–91, 329–80; George Dowrie, *The Development of Banking in Illinois, 1817–1863* (Urbana, 1913), chapter 3; Reginald Charles McGrane, *The Panic of 1837* (Chicago, 1965); and Pease, *The Frontier State,* chapters 10 and 11.

38. *Ill. Adv.,* Jan. 31, 1835.

39. On issues of public and private enterprise and internal improvements, see Davis, "Illinois Legislators," pp. 192–246, 381–430; see also *I.S.R,* July 29, Dec. 8, 1836; 1878 History, p. 19; Snyder, *Adam W. Snyder,* p. 215; and Simon, *Lincoln's Preparation for Greatness,* pp. 54–56. On the path of the internal improvements bill through the legislature, see *Senate Journal 1836–37,* pp. 45, 87, 89, 127, 445–52, 464–66, 469–75, 487, 490, and 531; *House Journal 1836–37,* pp. 36, 69, 97–102, 363–70, 375, 413, 430, 441, 443, 668–83, 720–24, 735, and 739. See also John H. Krenkel, *Illinois Internal Improvements, 1818–1848* (Cedar Rapids, 1958), chapters 1, 2, and 3.

40. McGrane, *The Panic of 1837,* chapters 4 and 5.

41. *Senate Journal, 1837* (Special Session), pp. 67, 70–71; *House Journal, 1837* (Special Session), pp. 63, 74; *I.S.R.,* July 28, Aug. 4, 1837.

42. *I.S.R.,* May 20, June 2, July 15, April 4, 25, Sept. 1, 1837; David M. Gahey to E. K. Kane, Feb. 16, 1832, Kane Letters, Illinois State Historical Survey, Urbana; Pease, *The Frontier State,* pp. 245–50. On democratic debates, see *I.S.R.,* Aug. 4, Oct. 20, Nov. 10, Dec. 9, 1837, Feb. 9, June 1, July 13, 27, and Aug. 3, 31, 1838. On the whig observations, see *Sangamo Journal,* April 22, July 8, 15, Aug. 5, Oct. 14, 28, Nov. 5, Dec. 2, 9, 1837, and Jan. 20, 1838.

43. *Free Press,* Nov. 11, 18, 1837; *I.S.R.,* Jan. 19, 1838. Hodge gleefully wrote that fifteen people, most of whom were Vandalians, had attended the recent "statewide" democratic convention. Others, he said, were National Road workers brought in to fill the meeting.

44. On the convention system, see Pease, *The Frontier State,* chapter 13. See also James Staton Chase, "Jacksonian Democracy and the Rise of the Nominating Convention," *Mid-America* 45 (Oct. 1963): 229–49.

45. *I.S.R.,* Jan. 5, Feb. 19, 1838. The best study of the whig party in the 1830s is Davis, "Illinois Legislators"; see also Thompson, *Illinois Whigs;* Pease, *The Frontier State,* chapter 13; and Lynn L. Marshall, "The Strange Stillbirth of the Whig Party," *American Historical Review* 72 (Jan. 1972): 445–68.

46. 1878 History, pp. 31f.

47. *I.S.R.,* Jan. 5, 19, Feb. 9, May 11, June 8, July 13, 1838.

48. For a more comprehensive picture of the whigs and democrats, see Davis, "Illinois Legislators," pp. 318–27, passim.

49. On democratic views on the bank, see *I.S.R,* July 28, 1837, June 14, 1839; *Free Press,* June 7, 1839. On the whig view, see *Sangamo Journal,* May 17, 24, June 14, 28, and July 19, 26, 1839. A Jacksonville paper in 1838

computed the improvements debt as $15,146,444, or $378.66 per taxpayer; see Simon, *Lincoln's Preparation for Greatness*, pp. 153–54. On the 1838 guberatorial campaign, see *I.S.R.*, May 11, June 8, 1838; Howard, *Mostly Good and Competent Men*, pp. 70–76; and Pease, *The Frontier State*, pp. 249–50.

50. On the Whig party in 1839 and 1840, see Martha McNeil Davidson, "Southern Illinois and Neighboring States at the Whig Convention of 1840," *TISHS* 20 (1914): 150–59; Arnold Shankland, "Partisan Politics, 1839–41, and the Illinois Constitution," *JISHS* 63 (Winter 1970): 336–67; 2 Illinois, 122ff; Circuit Court Record Book B, 1833–41, p. 340, FCCiC; transcript by Sidney Breese in File "Miscellaneous," FCCiC.

51. Pease, *The Frontier State*, pp. 326 and 194: "The internal improvements scheme of 1837 is not only the opening of a new era in the state's history; it is also the climax of the former one."

52. *I.S.R.*, May 6, 1836.

53. Davis points out the problem of methodology for any time period before the 1850s: "Illinois Legislators," pp. 101–4.

54. The framentary poll book records, the difficulty for this period of separating town voters from county voters, the sketchy biographical information available on the voters themselves, as well as the possibility of devoting a book-length study on local voting behaviors alone (as with Rozett's dissertation "The Social Bases of Party Conflict") make it necessary to confine these remarks on voting behavior to Vandalia's leaders ("leaders" defined here as men known to have operated businesses in downtown Vandalia). In the 1822 gubernatorial election, two men voted for Phillips, all the German-born businessmen for Coles, and non-German businessmen for Browne (excepting Robert H. Peebles, who voted for Coles). In the 1830 gubernatorial election, all leaders voted for Reynolds except Prentice, R. Blackwell, McLaughlin, and James Hall, who voted for Kinney. In the 1831 congressional race, eleven voted for Joseph Duncan, two for Sidney Breese (Lemuel Lee and William Hodge), and two for Coles (J. T. B. Stapp and R. H. Peebles). In the 1832 congressional race, seventeen voted for Casey, twelve for Ewing, four for McLaughlin (including his relatives Matthew Duncan and William Linn), and two for Archer (William Hodge and William H. Brown). Comparing voter behavior with the 1828–30 Tax Book and with probate records of those voters who died before 1840 yields little basis for saying that the rich voted conservatively and the less wealthy voted for democrats. Vandalia's wealthiest men, like Prentice, McLaughlin, and McCurdy, were apparently strong and orthodox democrats not whigs. See also Donald J. Ratcliffe, "Voter Turnout in Early Ohio," *Journal of the Early Republic* 7 (Fall 1987): 223–51.

55. Thomas Bender, *Community and Social Change in America* (Baltimore, 1978), p. 98.

56. Robert V. Hine, *Community on the American Frontier* (Norman, 1980), pp. 142–43.

57. *Edwardsville Spectator*, Feb. 22, April 12, 19, 1823.

58. Davis, "Illinois Legislators," p. 101.

7. DISCORD AND CONCORD

1. The bank and Robert McLaughlin's house may have been the only brick structures in Vandalia during the early 1820s.

2. *Ill. Int.*, Feb. 1, 1823, quoted in JCB, pp. 22f.

3. On the robbery, homicide, and trial, see Record Book A, pp. 90, 97–98, and File 144, FCCiC; Gershom Flagg to Artemias Flagg, July 20, 1823, *TISHS* 15 (1910): 173; *Ill. Int.*, March 29, July 12, Aug. 9, 1823. The 1878 History, p. 27, erroneously states that the money was found in the stables twelve years after the robbery.

4. John Reynolds, *My Own Times* (Belleville, 1857, repr. Ann Arbor, 1968), p. 142.

5. *Ill. Int.*, Aug. 16, 1823; "Letter from the Treasury Department Transmitting Information in Relation to a Robbery of the Land Office at Vandalia in the State of Illinois," copy at Evans Public Library, Vandalia (my thanks to Candy M. Zeman for obtaining this source); Record Book A, pp. 140, 182, FCCiC.

6. Leonard L. Richards, "Gentlemen of Property and Standing," in *Anti-Abolition Mobs in Jacksonian America* (Oxford, 1973), p. 155.

7. "Ames" in the *Kaskaskia Republican*, copied in *Illinois Republican*, July 21, 1824.

8. On frontier crime, see David J. Bodenhamer, "Law and Disorder on the Early Frontier: Marion County, Indiana, 1823–1859," *Western Historical Quarterly* 10 (July 1979): 323–36, a helpful study, considering the contemporaneity and common purpose of the two capitals, Indianapolis and early Vandalia. See also Malcolm J. Rohrbrough, *The Trans-Appalachian Frontier: People, Societies, and Institutions, 1775–1850* (New York, 1978); Stephen Thernstrom and Richard Sennett, eds., *Nineteenth-Century Cities* (New Haven, 1969); Michael Feldberg, *The Turbulent Era: Riot and Disorder in Jacksonian America* (New York, 1980); Roger D. McGrath, *Gunfighters, Highwaymen, and Vigilantes* (Berkeley, 1984); Patrick B. Nolan, *Vigilantes on the Middle Border* (New York, 1987); Robert M. Utley, *High Noon in Lincoln: Violence on the Western Frontier* (Albuquerque, 1987); Carl E. Prince, "The Great 'Riot Year': Jacksonian Democracy and Patterns of Violence in 1834," *Journal of the Early Republic* 5 (Spring 1985): 1–20; James A. Rose, "The Regulators and Flatheads in Southern Illinois," *TISHS* 11 (1906); R. Carlyle Buley, *The Old Northwest, Pioneer Period: 1815–1840* (Bloomington, 1850), 1: 318–19.

9. On legal system and legal punishments, see Theodore C. Pease, *The Frontier State, 1818–1848* (Springfield, 1918, repr. Urbana, 1987), pp. 44–45; Rohrbrough, *The Trans-Appalachian Frontier*, pp. 116, 126; *House Journal, 1825–26*, p. 58; *House Journal, 1828*, p. 7; Record A, 1821–32, p. 248, and County Commissioners Order Book, p. 347, FCCiC.

10. Cases recorded in the Second Circuit Court, 1821–39, in Record A, 1821–32, and Record B, 1833–39, FCCiC, included at least ten affray cases, five for riot, five for larceny, four for "keeping a gaming room," one for highway obstruction, and several adultery or fornication charges. Bodenham-

mer discusses the problem of obtaining a whole picture of a town's crime in "Law and Disorder," pp. 324, 326. The interpretive problems here are the facts that the second circuit covered a larger area than Vandalia and thus many cases were not local, grand juries handed down indictments that were either never pressed or never subsequently recorded, and outcomes of cases are frequently missing.

11. For cases, see Record Book A, pp. 3, 9f, 11, 30, 49, 58, 62. 66f, 73, 90, 130ff, 148f, 151, 155ff, 161ff, 166, 173, 178, 180ff, 185, 187, 190, 191, 192, 194, 201, 203, 204ff, 207, 211, 221ff, 279, passim; Record B, pp. 82, 95, 236, passim, FCCiC.

12. Richards, "Gentlemen of Property and Standing," pp. 155, passim; Bodenhamer, "Law and Disorder," pp. 327, 334–36, on public perception versus reality.

13. On Parks, who lived in Montgomery County, see Record Book A, p. 248, FCCiC. William Carr and Martin Means were also ordered to be given lashes in 1828 larceny cases: pp. 235, 247. See also Record A, pp. 155, 160, 295; Record B, pp. 6f, 235, 335, FCCiC.

14. 1878 History, p. 31; *Ill. Int.*, July 11, 1829; Zophar Case's letter book, June 11, July 28, Nov. 13, 1831, Manuscripts Division, ISHL; Usher F. Linder, *Reminiscences of the Bench and Bar of Illinois* (Chicago, 1879), pp. 221ff.

15. T. C. Browne to Henry Eddy, Feb. 11, 1827, S. H. Kimmel to Eddy, Feb. 7, 11, 1827, Henry Eddy Papers, Manuscripts Division, ISHL; Thomas Ford, *A History of Illinois from Its Commencement as a State in 1818 to 1847* (Chicago, 1854, repr. Ann Arbor, 1968), pp. 81–83.

16. *I.S.R.*, Dec. 22, 1837, Jan. 19, March 2, 1838; *Free Press*, Feb. 17, 1838.

17. *Busy Body*, Feb. 18, 1838. The premier issue is the only one extant.

18. Linder, *Reminiscences of the Bench and Bar*, concerning Thomas C. Browne (pp. 43–45).

19. *Ill. Int.*, Oct. 12, 1820.

20. Ibid., July 20, 1822; Ross 1904, p. 171; Ross 1910, p. 696; Harris, *History of Negro Servitude*, pp. 10, 24; Alvord, ed., *Governor Edward Coles*, p. 332.

21. E. B. Greene and C. W. Alvord, eds., *The Governors' Letter-Books, 1818–1834* (Springfield, 1909), p. 51.

22. 1 Illinois, 131–23, 242ff, 247–51, 268ff; 2 Illinois, 258–61, 317. On Fanny, see also File 362, FCCiC.

23. *Free Press*, Nov. 18, 1837. On attitudes of southerners on slavery, see Don Harrison Doyle, *The Social Order of a Frontier Community: Jacksonville, Illinois, 1825–70* (Urbana, 1978), p. 51; Eugene H. Berwanger, *Frontier Against Slavery: Western Anti-Negro Prejudice and the Slavery Extention Controversy* (Urbana, 1967); and C. Robert Haywood, "'No Less a Man': Blacks in Cow Town Dodge City, 1876–1886," *Western Historical Quarterly* 19 (May 1988): 161–82.

24. On Ward, see *Ill. Int.*, Nov. 16, 1822, cited in Burtschi, *Vandalia: Wilderness Capital*, p. 52; *Ill. Int.*, Sept. 23, 1820, May 21, 1824; Record

Book A, 1821–32, pp. 136, 187–88, 225, FCCiC; File "1835–77 Transcripts and Executions" and File "Miscellaneous," FCCiC. Ward is buried on the south side of the old Vandalia graveyard.

25. *Ill. Adv.*, July 6, 1833; see also Burtschi, *Vandalia: Wilderness Capital,* p. 50.

26. 1878 history, p. 10.

27. Robert P. Howard, *Illinois: A History of the Prairie State* (Grand Rapids, 1972), p. 204n; Pease, *The Frontier State*, pp. 176–77.

28. Ferdinand Ernst (d. Aug. 1822) is the earliest known burial at that cemetery, although the lot presumably was used before that time. Nearly all the stones from the 1820s and 1830s are now illegibile.

29. Book A, pp. 145, 279, 331; Book B, pp. 57, 215–16, FCCoC; *Ill. Int.,* July 18, Aug. 1, 1829; JCB, pp. 50–51.

30. *Ill. Int.*, March 1, 1823; Buley, *The Old Northwest*, 1: 455.

31. Philip D. Jordan, *The National Road* (Indianapolis, 1948), p. 136, quoted in Burtschi, *Vandalia: Wilderness Capital*, p. 146; Buley, *The Old Northwest*, 1: 444–64.

32. *Ill. Adv.*, Dec. 13, 1834; Thomas L. Hardin, "The National Road in Illinois," *JISHS* 60 (Spring 1967): 5–22. One of twelve Madonna of the Trail statues was placed at Vandalia by the Daughters of the American Revolution in October 1928. Vandalia's statue commemorates both Lincoln and the National Road. The unveiling and pageant parade also celebrated the centennial of the road's survey to Vandalia. Burtschi, *Vandalia: Wilderness Capital*, pp. 141–42.

33. *Ill. Int.*, Dec. 9, 1819, May 8, 1821; JCB, p. 57; Thelma Eaton, *The Covered Bridges in Illinois* (Ann Arbor, 1968), pp. 16, 143; George Flower, *A History of the English Settlement* (Chicago, 1882, repr. Ann Arbor, 1968), pp. 294ff; "Fayette's Lost Town," clipping in the papers of the Historic Vandalia Museum archives.

34. JCB, pp. 85f; 1878 History, pp. 25, 66f. On the river's navigability, see *Ill. Int.*, Feb. 3, 10, 1819; *Edwardsville Spectator*, Dec. 11, 1819; JCB, pp. 44–45; George W. May, *Down Illinois Rivers* (Metropolis, 1981).

35. Buley, *The Old Northwest*, 1: 471–74; E. B. Washburne, ed., *The Edwards Papers* (Chicago, 1884), p. 213; Will C. Carson, *Historical Souvenir of Greenville, Ill.* (Effingham, 1905), p. 20; *Ill. Int.*, Nov. 16, 1822, May 1, 1824; *Star of the West*, Nov. 30, 1822; *Free Press*, Oct. 14, 1837. Flint is quoted in Buley, *The Old Northwest*, 1: 475.

36. Hall is quoted in Buley, *The Old Northwest*, 1: 489.

37. Ibid., 1: 465–71; JCB, p. 79.

38. Ibid., 1: 469; *Ill. Int.*, Dec. 9, 1820.

39. On the first and second statehouses, see research notes on the three Vandalia statehouses by the Illinois Department of Conservation, Vandalia Statehouse State Historic Site; JCB, p. 70; *Ill. Int.*, Feb. 13, Dec. 3, 1824, Feb. 4, 1825; Joseph Charles Burtschi and Lester O. Shriver, *Lincoln and Vandalia* (Vandalia, 1946).

40. Illinois Department of Conservation research, Vandalia statehouse.

41. *I.S.R.*, Aug. 12, 1836.

42. Illinois Department of Conservation research, Vandalia statehouse.

43. Burtschi and Shriver, *Lincoln and Vandalia*, pp. 20ff; JCB, p. 68.

44. Illinois Department of Conservation research, Vandalia statehouse.

45. *Laws of Illinois, 1839*, pp. 306ff.

46. *Age of Steam and Fire* (Vandalia), Aug. 23, 1855.

47. In 1954 in the Hotel Evans John Matthew Heller painted a mural of downtown Vandalia as it may have looked in 1836; Joseph C. Burtschi was the historian who assisted him. The mural was destroyed in 1969 when the hotel burned. Burtschi, *Vandalia: Wilderness Capital*, pp. 150ff.

48. *Peoria Register*, Dec. 29, 1838. The statehouse has been extensively researched and restored. See Joseph Booten and George Nelved, *Record of the Restoration of the Third Statehouse, Vandalia, Illinois, 1930–1945* (n.p.) and MacDonald and Mack Partnership, *Structural Inventory: Third Vandalia Statehouse, Fayette County, Vandalia, Illinois* (n.p., June 1979).

49. Ross 1904 (p. 13) states that the third statehouse was built to forestall the issue of capital relocation. Letters to Governor Duncan as well as William Walters's editorial comments indicate that the new statehouse was constructed simply because the old one was uninhabitable. Such letters and editorials, of course, would not reflect underlying motives.

8. LIKE OXFORD OR CAMBRIDGE

1. James Stuart, *Three Years in North America* (New York, 1833), 2: 227, quoted in JCB, pp. 93–94.

2. Thomas Ford, *A History of Illinois from Its Commencement as a State in 1818 to 1847* (Chicago, 1854, repr. Ann Arbor, 1968), pp. 94ff; see also Donald F. Tingley, "Anti-Intellectualism on the Illinois Frontier," in *Essays in Illinois History: In Honor of Glenn Huron Seymour* (Carbondale, 1968), pp. 3–17.

3. *Ill. Int.*, Dec. 14, 1820, Dec. 13, 1823.

4. Ibid., April 10, 1821; on the Masons, see Ross 1904, p. 116; John C. Reynolds, *History of the M. W. Grand Lodge of Illinois* (Springfield, 1869), pp. 55, 104, 125–26; Sydney E. Ahlstrom, *A Religious History of the American People* (New Haven, 1971), pp. 557–58; Robert V. Hine, *Community on the American Frontier* (Norman, 1980), pp. 138–40; Don Harrison Doyle, *The Social Order of a Frontier Community. 1825–70* (Urbana, 1978), pp. 156–57.

5. *Ill. Int.*, July 6, 1822, July 5, 1823; *I.S.R.*, Dec. 24, 1837, Dec. 13, 1838, Jan. 4, 1839; *Free Press*, Dec. 2, 1837; Mary Burtschi, *Vandalia: Wilderness Capital of Lincoln's Land* (Vandalia, 1963), pp. 37ff, 42f, 47; Claude G. Bowers, *The Party Battles of the Jackson Period* (Boston, 1922), pp. 26ff; William Baringer, *Lincoln's Vandalia* (New Brunswick, 1949), pp. 32, 35f; Hine, *Community on the American Frontier*, p. 133f. On Lafayette's visit to Illinois, see *Ill. Int.*, Feb. 13, March 5, 1824, April 22, 29, May 13, 17, June 10, July 5, 1825; C. W. Alvord, ed., *Governor Edward Coles* (Springfield, 1920), pp. 188–91; John Reynolds, *My Own Times* (Belleville, 1857, repr.

Ann Arbor, 1968), p. 164. Reynolds erroneously remembered that Lafayette visited Vandalia; the 1878 History, which frequently cites Reynolds, repeats his error (p. 16).

6. Quoted in Paul Simon, *Lincoln's Preparation for Greatness* (Norman, 1965), p. 161.

7. Quoted in John F. Brooks to Jane E. Bradley, Feb. 28 and April 2, 1830, letters of John F. Brooks, Manuscripts Division, ISHL; Zophar Case's letter book, Aug. 28, 1831, Manuscripts Division, ISHL.

8. *History of Fayette County* (1878), pp. 37f; E. Duane Elbert, "The Roots of German Lutheranism in Illinois," *Illinois Historical Journal* 78 (Summer 1985): 97–112; Ross 1910, 701–2; the uncredited article by Mary Burtschi in *Vandalia Union*, March 23, 1965; Ross 1904, pp. 83–84; and township histories in the 1878 and 1910 county histories. Norma Bauer of Altamont, Illinois, provided the information about her ancestors, the Shaffers and Hocketts.

9. 1878 History, p. 39; Record Book of the Vandalia Presbyterian Church, 1828–66 (my thanks to Rev. John Nipper and the church council for allowing use of this source); JCB, p. 48; C. L. Conkling, "The Church Bell at Vandalia," *JISHS* 8 (Oct. 1915): 466f. Illinois Riggs Graf was born 1827 and died in 1911.

10. 1878 History, p. 36.

11. Ahlstrom, *Religious History of the American People*, pp. 419–20, 436–41; Theodore C. Pease, *The Frontier State, 1818–1848* (Springfield, 1918, repr. Urbana, 1987), pp. 414–15; T. Scott Miyakawa, *Protestants and Pioneers: Individualism and Conformity on the American Frontier* (Chicago, 1964). Nathaniel and Olivia McCurdy are buried beneath the present church.

12. *Ill. Adv.* Sept. 7, 1833; *150 Years of Methodism in Vandalia, Illinois* (n.p., 1981).

13. *Ill. Int.*, Dec. 20, 1828, Nov. 4, 1829, June 12, Dec. 11, 1830, Jan. 8, 1831.

14. J. M. Sturtevant, *An Autobiography* (New York, 1896); Charles Henry Rammelkamp, *Illinois College: A Centennial History, 1829–1929* (New Haven, 1928), which also contains portraits of the Yale Band.

15. *Ill. Int.*, Oct. 23, 1830. Public high schools such as those today did not exist until the 1890s; see J. M. Gwynn, *Curriculum Principles and Social Trends* (New York, 1960), pp. 14–16.

16. *Ill. Int.*, March 29, 1828; *Free Press*, Oct. 14, 1837; *House Journal, 1837* (Special Session), pp. 43–45; 1878 History, pp. 18, 32–33; Ross 1910, pp. 694–97. On educational laws in Illinois, see Pease, *The Frontier State*, pp. 429–33.

17. Ross 1910, pp. 694–96.

18. On the society, see Robert W. Johannsen, "History on the Illinois Frontier: Early Efforts to Preserve the State's Past," *JISHS* 68 (April 1975): 124–35.

19. *Ill. Int.*, Jan. 3, 1829.

20. Among the members who were also embroiled in the 1830 gubernatorial campaign were A. F. Grant, Sidney Breese, George Forquer, Timothy Gard, A. W. Cavarly, and James M. Duncan (chapter 6).

21. On the lyceum, see *Ill. Int.*, Dec. 10, 1831, Feb. 18, Nov. 14, 1832; "Records of the Illinois State Lyceum," Manuscripts Division, ISHL.

22. *Ill. Int.*, Feb. 18, 1832.

23. Ibid., Oct. 29, Nov. 12, Dec. 17, 1831; *Ill. Adv.*, April 13, 1832; *I.S.R.*, Feb. 11, 1836; *Free Press*, April 19, 26, 1839; Doyle, *Social Order of a Frontier Community*, p. 213.

24. On the society, see *Ill. Int.*, March 19, 1831; *Ill. Adv.*, Jan. 19, 1833; Merton Lynn Dillon, "Antislavery Movement in Illinois, 1824–1835," *JISHS* 47 (Summer 1954): 160–66. At the January 10, 1833 meeting of the society, the following men were appointed managers: John Reynolds, Zadoc Casey, Joseph Duncan, Peter Cartwright, William H. Brown, Alfred Cowles, Elijah Iles, Benjamin Mills, Sidney Breese, James Hall, William K. Steward, George Forquer, John Dement, Henry Eddy, W. P. McKee, Moses Leman, Ninian Edwards, Samuel McRoberts, Henry I. Mills, John M. Robinson, Elias Kent Kane, Charles Slade, Milton K. Alexander, John M. Peck, Newton Cloud, Asa Turner, and Nathaniel M. McCurdy.

25. M. J. Heale, "From City Fathers to Social Critics: Humanitarianism and Government in New York, 1790–1860," *Journal of American History* 63 (June 1976): 21–41 (quote from p. 41); Doyle, *Social Order of a Frontier Community*, pp. 192ff, 212ff, 223ff.

26. Among the several sources on this issue, see, for example, Clifford S. Griffin, "Religious Benevolence as Social Control, 1815–1860," *Mississippi Valley Historical Review* 44 (Dec. 1957): 423–44; Lois W. Banner, "Religious Benevolence as Social Control: A Critique of an Interpretation," *Journal of American History* 60 (June 1973): 23–41; Ann W. Boylan, *Sunday School: The Formation of an American Institution, 1790–1880* (New Haven, 1988), p. 39; Doyle, *Social Order*, chapter 7; Bertram Wyatt-Brown, "The Antimission Movement in the Jacksonian South: A Study in Religion Folk Culture," *Journal of Southern History*, 36 (Nov. 1970): 501–29; Lawrence Frederick Kohl, "The Concept of Social Control and the History of Jacksonian America," *Journal of the Early Republic* 5 (Spring 1985): 21–34; Edward Pessen, *Riches, Class, and Power Before the Civil War* (Lexington, 1973), chapter 12, and pp. 276ff; and Heale, "From City Fathers to Social Critics," pp. 26, 28, 31.

27. Wyatt-Brown, "The Antimission Movement," p. 503.

28. Record Book of the Vandalia Presbyterian Church, 1828–66; this action reflects the policy during the 1830s, not contemporary policy in the Presbyterian church.

29. There are three book-length biographies of James Hall. Randolph Randall's *James Hall: Spokesman of the New West* (Columbus, 1964) is a comprehensive study of his life and work and contains his complete bibliography. Mary Burtschi's *James Hall of Lincoln's Frontier World* (Vandalia, 1977) is a study of Hall's life, particularly in Shawneetown and Vandalia, concentrating on how Hall's experience in Illinois informed his best writing. John T. Flanagan's *James Hall: Literary Pioneer of the Ohio Valley* (Minneapolis, 1941), approaches Hall from a literary critic's and literary historian's viewpoint. See

also Flanagan, "James Hall: Pioneer Editor and Publicist," *JISHS* 23 (Summer 1955): 19–36; Esther Schultz, "James Hall in Vandalia," *JISHS* 32 (April 1930): 92–112, an unsympathetic article; Mary Burtschi, "Portfolio for James Hall," a commemorative booklet published at the centennial of Hall's death; and [William Anderson Hall?] "Sketch of James Hall," Cincinnati Historical Society. Twentieth-century editions of Hall's writings are *Seven Stories by James Hall* (Vandalia, 1976) and *Letters from the West* (Gainesville, 1967), a reprint edition of the 1828 volume.

30. Randall, *James Hall*, pp. 138–45. The book was supposed to have been published pseudonymously but appeared with the name "Hon. Judge Hall"; the judicial title contrasted to the book's lighthearted and rather Anglophobic tone helped damn the book's reception in Britain.

31. Ibid., pp. 146, 300. Flanagan's 1941 biography (p. 88) attributes the entire book to James Hall.

32. Randall, *James Hall*, pp. 147–54. Hall's poems "bear the mark of hasty composition, as if they were the product of an hour's leisure seized during a lull in courtroom proceedings or during a shower that kept visitors from his office" (ibid., p. 148). See also John E. Hallwas, ed., *Illinois Literature: The Nineteenth Century* (Macomb, 1986), p. 46.

33. Randall, *James Hall*, chapter 11.

34. *Illinois Monthly Magazine* 2: 15, 104.

35. Randall, *James Hall*, pp. 187ff.

36. Hallwas, *Illinois Literature*, p. 46.

37. Ibid.

38. Randall, *James Hall*, p. 190.

39. Ibid., p. 178.

40. Cf. Arthur M. Schlesinger Jr., *The Age of Jackson* (Boston, 1946), chapter 29.

41. Schultz, "James Hall in Vandalia," 111f.

42. On Hall's community involvement in Vandalia, see *Ill. Int.*, July 26, 1828, Jan. 30, May 10, Aug. 1, Dec. 5, 12, 1829, Feb. 6, Aug. 28, Nov. 6, 1830, Dec. 17, 1831, Jan. 28, 1832; Record Book of the Vandalia Presbyterian Church, 1828–66, Dec. 5, 1829.

43. See the incorrect (and sole) information on Hall in 1878 History, pp. 33 (a Hall quote attributed to Robert Blackwell) and 40. Mary Burtschi, "James Hall: The Foremost Literary Figure of the Early West, in Illinois," in JCB, pp. 36–40, is the first publication (1954) by a Vandalian to express appreciation and insight (and to provide accurate information) concerning Hall's work.

44. Hallwas, *Illinois Literature*, pp. 76ff.

45. Burtschi, *Vandalia: Wilderness Capital*, pp. 79–81

46. Hallwas, *Illinois Literature*, p. 40.

47. Johannsen, "History on the Illinois Frontier," pp. 140–41

48. John T. Flanagan, "John Russell of Bluffdale," *JISHS* 42 (Sept. 1949): 272–91; the papers of John Russell, Manuscripts Division, ISHL; John Moses, *Illinois Historical and Statistical* (Chicago, 1895), 1: 392.

49. *Ill. Adv.*, April 19, 1834; letters in the papers of the Wakefield family, Manuscripts Division, ISHL.

50. Snyder, "Forgotten Statesmen of Illinois: Conrad Will," 353; Mary Burtschi, "James William Berry," *JISHS* 67 (Nov. 1974): 519–29; Ross 1910, p. 715; Betty Madden, *Arts, Crafts and Architecture in Early Illinois* (Urbana, 1974), pp. 90, 152–54.

9. THE END OF THE ERA

1. William Baringer, *Lincoln's Vandalia* (New Brunswick, 1949), p. 32; Claude G. Bowers, *The Party Battles of the Jackson Period* (Boston, 1922), pp. 26ff.

2. Jesse M. Thompson, *Pike County History* (Pike County, 1968), pp. 36ff; 1878 History, pp. 19f.

3. Robert W. Johannsen, *Stephen A. Douglas* (Oxford, 1973); "Autobiography of Stephen A. Douglas," *JISHS* 5 (Oct. 1912): 323–426.

4. Lincoln's biographies and biographic treatments include thousands of books, monographs, and articles. The best treatment of Lincoln's career in the Illinois legislature is Paul Simon, *Lincoln's Preparation for Greatness* (Norman, 1965).

5. *House Journal, 1836–37*, pp. 243f, 817ff; Roy P. Basler et al., eds. *Collected Works of Abraham Lincoln*, 9 vols. (New Brunswick, 1953–55), 1: 74f, 4: 65.

6. Simon, *Lincoln's Preparation*, chapter 5.

7. Basler, *Collected Works*, 1: 226.

8. Simon, *Lincoln's Preparation*, p. 115.

9. JCB, p. 79; Mary Burtschi, *Vandalia: Wilderness Capital of Lincoln's Land* (Vandalia, 1963), pp. 48ff.

10. Paul E. Stroble, "The Big Jump: An 'Unknown' Lincoln Legend from Southern Illinois," *Springhouse* 5 (Feb. 1988); Harry Pratt, "Lincoln's Jump from the Window," *JISHS* 48 (Winter 1955): 456–61; David Donald, "The Folklore Lincoln," *JISHS* 40 (Dec. 1947): 377–96; Burtschi, *Vandalia: Wilderness Capital*, p. 62; Simon, *Lincoln's Preparation*, chapter 11.

11. *Ill. Adv.*, Jan. 12, 1833; John F. Snyder, *Adam W. Snyder and His Period in Illinois History* (Virginia, Ill., 1906, repr. Ann Arbor, 1968), pp. 153ff; Theodore C. Pease, *The Frontier State, 1818–1848* (Springfield, 1918, repr. Urbana, 1987), p. 202. The earliest call for a new state capital was from "Ames" in a summer 1824 *Kaskaskia Republican*, who complained that Vandalia was inconveniently located, "frequent and severe calamities and homicide, suicide, robbery and conflagrations are common occurrences there" (referring to the events of 1823), and that the remains of the burned statehouse had not yet been cleared. He suggested moving the capital to a town near St. Louis in order to establish a commercial rival for that city. The letter was copied in the *Illinois Republican*, July 21, 1824.

12. Theodore C. Pease, *Illinois Election Returns* (Springfield, 1923), pp. 94–97. An extreme example of voter apathy was Putnam County, which gave 383 votes to the 1834 gubernatorial race and only 4 votes to the relocation

issue. Returns do not include LaSalle, Jo Daviess, Mercer, Henry, and Peoria counties. Counties east of the Third Principal Meridian and below Sangamon County's southern boundary went for Vandalia, except for Pope County, which went for Alton. Counties west of the meridian and below Sangmon County were for Alton, except for Bond, Perry, and Montgomery, which went for Vandalia. North of that horizontal line, all the counties were for Springfield save Tazewell, Putnam, and Cook, which went for Peoria; Rock Island, which favored Alton; and Macon County, which went for the "geographic center of the state."

13. On the bill in the legislature, see *Senate Journal, 1836–37*, pp. 285, 301, 336–37, 341ff; *House Journal, 1836–37*, pp. 701ff; Simon, *Lincoln's Preparation*, pp. 57–60, 102.

14. On editors' seeming lack of interest, see *I.S.R.*, Feb. 10, 1837; see also March 6, 1837.

15. *Senate Journal, 1836–37*, pp. 341ff; *House Journal, 1836–37*, pp. 701ff.

16. Quoted in Baringer, *Lincoln's Vandalia*, p. 109.

17. *Sangamo Journal*, July 1, 1837.

18. Usher F. Linder, *Reminiscences of the Bench and Bar of Illinois* (Chicago, 1879), pp. 62–63. On the special session, see *House Journal, 1837*, pp. 21, 48, 104–5, 119, 140; *Senate Journal, 1837*, pp. 128, 139, 143.

19. *I.S.R.*, July 28, 1837.

20. Ibid., July 20, Aug. 10, 1838; see also Simon, *Lincoln's Preparation*, p. 59. Simon demolishes the long-held myth that Lincoln and his eight colleagues from Sangamon County, the "Long Nine," traded votes with internal improvements advocates to obtain a majority for Springfield on the relocation bill. In *A History of Illinois from Its Commencement as a State in 1818 to 1847* (Chicago, 1854, repr. Ann Arbor, 1968), pp. 186–88, Thomas Ford first published the story, which seems to have begun in the late 1830s by opponents of the Springfield move.

21. *House Journal, 1838–39*, pp. 127, 182–83, 185–89, 199, 434; *Free Press*, Jan. 10, 1839; Basler et al., eds., *Collected Works*, 1: 126–27, 143.

22. *Senate Journal, 1838–39*, pp. 200, 211–12.

23. *Laws of Illinois, 1839*, p. 134.

24. Ibid.

25. *Chicago Daily American*, Aug. 7, 1839.

26. *House Journal, 1839–40*, pp. 233f, 324; *House Journal, 1840* (Special Session), p. 38; Basler et al., eds., *Collected Works*, 1:230f.

27. Ross 1904, p. 23; Ross 1910, p. 627. On the use and restoration of the statehouse in the 1850s, see Fayette County Commissioners' Record Book A, pp. 293, 344, 390f, 452f, 474, 476, 540, 546, and 569; Record Book B, pp. 2, 3, 17, 19, 20, 51, 60, 70, 74, 80, 83, 115, 117, 144f, 152, 156, 160, 167, 173, 196, 199, 232, 237, 243, and 245; both books in FCCiC. Attorney Fountain S. Crump (buried near W. C. Greenup) advertised in the August 30, 1853 *Age of Steam and Fire* that his office was in the statehouse. A daguerreotypist advertised in the August 23, 1853 issue that his operation had been set up in the statehouse. See also Burtschi, *Vandalia: Wilderness Capital*, pp.

60ff, and Mary Burtschi, *Biographical Sketch of Joseph Charles Burtschi* (Vandalia, 1962).

28. 1878 History, p. 46

29. Ross 1910, p. 630.

30. In 1985 many of Vandalia's six thousand citizens assembled on Gallatin Street for a promotional photograph as a plan to encourage new industry through national and international news coverage. The statehouse towered over the proceedings. *USA Today*, Aug. 19, 1985.

31. 1878 History, p. 54.

Index

Abbot, Jeremiah, 110
Abolitionism, 98, 124–25
Adams, James, 82
Adams, John Quincy, vi, 58, 65, 73, 79–80, 82, 86
Agriculture, 3, 34–36, 54. *See also* Fayette County
Alexander, Milton K., 165
Alexander, William, 12–13
Alton, Ill., vi, 7, 8, 11–12, 49, 126
American Colonization Society, 114
American Home Missionary Association, 110
Anti-intellectualism, frontier, 3, 89, 106, 115, 119, 121
Antiquarian and Historical Society, vi, 2, 112–13

Baker, Edward D., 83, 123
Baldwin, Rev. Theron, 107–10, 113
Baltimore, Maryland, 20, 24
Banking: as a political issue, 74–75, 81–82, 84–89; Bank of the United States, 82, 84–85; first state bank, v, 3, 55, 59, 84; robbery of Vandalia branch, 91–93, 145; second state bank, vi, 59, 60, 84–85, 87–88; Vandalia banks, 52, 61, 62, 91–93, 102–3, 105, 126
Bärensbach, Julius, 25
Bates, Edward, 93
Bathrick, Daniel, 17, 20, 48

Baugh, John, 41
Bear Grove township, 30, 37, 42–43, 97. *See also* Fayette County
Beck, Guy, 14, 30
Beck, Lewis Caleb, 54
Beck, Paul, 14, 19, 31, 37, 43, 56, 140
Beecher, Edward, 110, 120
Bemerkungen auf einer Reise (Ernst), 24–25
Benson, Rev. J. P., 108
Berry, Arthur, 25
Berry, Claibourne B., 51
Berry, Elijah Conway, 15, 21, 31, 55, 62, 64, 68, 78, 97, 107, 121, 129, 151
Berry, James William, 2, 21, 31, 62, 115, 120, 121, 130, 151
Berry, Mildred Stapp (Mrs. Elijah C.), 15, 21, 31, 62, 68
Berry, William, 13, 15, 18, 21, 31, 33, 58, 62, 72–74, 76, 78–79, 88–89, 102, 151
Black, Emily (Mrs. James), 150
Black, James, 33, 51–52, 55–56, 61, 62, 64, 88, 100, 104, 108, 110, 114, 127, 129
Black Hawk War, vi, 2, 25, 34, 44, 81, 98–99, 121
Blacks: in Vandalia, 33, 91, 97–98; laws concerning, 97–98. *See also* Slavery
Blackwell, David, 78–79, 95
Backwell, Robert, 39, 41, 105, 106, 112, 151; civic leader, 33, 55, 61, 62, 64,

100, 104, 111, 114, 127–29; early
Vandalia settler, 15, 21, 31; local
editor, 33, 58; political views of, 72–
74, 79, 88–89
Blankenship family, 31
Blockburger, Christian B., 127
Bluffdale, Ill., 68, 110, 121
Bond County, Ill., 9, 19
Bond, Shadrach, v, 2, 3, 18–19, 24, 37,
71, 76, 121, 145
Bone family, 31
Boone, Daniel, 116
Boosterism: in local writings, 44–46, 65,
130–32; local, 4, 63–69, 119–20;
theory of, 4, 63–69. *See also*
Community; Vandalia, social climate,
social dynamics
Botsford, Moss, 51, 92, 107
Botsford, Russell, 92–93, 94
Bowling Green (town), 42
Branch, Matthew, 93, 151
Brazel family, 31, 43
Breese, Sidney, 18, 80, 113, 119, 132,
165
Brooks, Rev. John F., 107–8, 110
Browenski, Nicholai, 32
Brown, William Hubbard, 27, 58, 64,
76–77, 79, 99, 100, 108, 110, 112,
114, 151, 165
Browne, Thomas C., 71, 97
Browning family, 31
Browning, Orville Hickman, 83, 123,
126
Brownsville, Ill., 68
Bryant, Arthur, 117
Bryant, John Howard, 117, 120
Bryant, William Cullen, 117, 120
Burtschi, Joseph C., 129
Burtschi, Mary, 120
Busy Body, 96–97
Butterfield, Justin, 89

Calhoun, John C., 58
Canal, John B. Emanuel, 62, 83–84
Capital relocation: as a political issue,
10–11, 126–27; in 1818–19, v, 2, 9–
11; in 1837–39, vi, 60–61, 87–88,
89, 105, 126–29, 168
Capitols. *See* Statehouses

Capps, Ebenezer, 32, 52, 54, 56, 62, 65,
85, 104–5, 151
Carlin, Thomas, vi, 72, 87
Carlyle, Ill., 7, 8, 12, 17, 70. *See also*
Hill's Ferry
Carroll family, 31
Carson family, 31
Cartwright, Peter, 72, 112, 165
Case, Zophar, 68, 95, 108
Casey, Zadoc, 32, 72, 86, 89, 165
Cavarly, Alfred, 113, 165
"Charivary," 41, 108
Charter, John, 48, 55, 62, 103, 105
Chase, Salmon Portland, 117
Chicago, 99
Chicago Daily American, 129
Cholera, 3, 70, 113
Cincinnati, 117
Clark, Benjamin, A., 62, 83–84
Clay, Henry, 58, 65, 73–76, 79–80, 82,
86, 88–89
Clopitski, Baron Louis, 32
Cloud, Newton, 83, 165
Coles, Edward, v, 2, 76–79, 89, 97, 103,
112–13, 117, 121, 131, 156
Community: and conflict, 32–33, 41–42,
65–68; and cooperation, 32–33, 63–
64, 65–68; and individualism, 33, 63;
examples of, 22, 30–34, 63–64, 89;
Gemeinschaft, 41, 65; theory of, 63–
64, 65–67. *See also* Fayette County;
Vandalia
Constitution of Illinois (1818), v, 10–11,
77–78
Constitutional Convention, in 1818, v,
4–5, 10–11, 77; proposed in 1823, v,
41, 65, 76–79, 89, 93, 119
Cook, Daniel Pope, 32, 71–76, 80, 89,
107
Cooper, J. F., 117
Corydon, Ind., 4
Courts: circuit, 27–28, 94; federal, 71;
supreme, 27–28, 97–98, 128
Covington, Ill., 10, 70
Cowles, Alfred, 72, 165
Cox, Thomas, 12–13, 20, 48, 71, 135
Crawford, William H., 65, 73, 76, 79
Crimes, 36, 44, 91–96; dueling, 44, 95;
punishments for, 36, 94–95. *See also*
Vandalia

Crump, Fountain S., 169
Cumberland Road. *See* National Road
Curlee, Jesse W., 60, 109

Daniels, Robert, 17
Daviess, Jo, 116
Davis, E., 128
Davis, Levi, 83, 103, 15, 111
Dement, John, 34, 81, 104, 124, 151, 165
Depew family, 31
Dickerson, John, 97
Dieckmann family, 32, 33
Dixon, George, 97
Douglas, Stephen A., 45, 83, 89, 115, 123–25, 131; "donkey legend" and, 44
DuBois, Jesse K., 83
Duncan, James M., 20, 41, 50, 55, 61, 75, 80, 95, 97, 107, 113, 151, 165
Duncan, Joseph, vi, 32, 50, 61, 72, 75, 81–82, 85, 89, 103–4, 165
Duncan, Matthew, 50, 97, 106, 151
Duncan, Polly. *See* Linn
Duncan family, 31
Dyer and Myer, tailors, 51

Eccles, Joseph T., 35, 60, 108, 111
Eddy, Henry, 76, 84, 101, 113, 165
Edmondson, Dr. R. T., 127
Edwards, Ninian, vi, 14, 70–72, 75–76, 109, 119, 165
Edwards, Ninian Wirt, 70
Edwardsville, Ill., 7, 8, 24, 25, 93
Edwardsville Spectator, 76, 79
Effingham County, Ill., 42, 127
Elam family, 31
Ellis, J. M., 110
Enoch family, 31
Enochs, John, 31, 36, 130
Ernst, Augusta. *See* Peebles
Ernst, Clara Greenup (Mrs. Hermann), 125
Ernst colony, v, 15–16, 20–21, 23–28, 33, 37, 38–39, 51, 63–64, 88–89, 108
Ernst, Ferdinand, v, 2, 15–16, 18–21, 22–29, 35–37, 43, 48, 51, 62, 105, 120, 125, 151
Ernst, Hermann, 23, 28

Ernst, Mary Ann (Mrs. Ferdinand), 23, 28, 37, 43, 46, 108, 120, 151
Ernst, Rudolf, 23, 28
Evans, Akin, 31, 43, 61
Evans, Charles A., 43
Evans, Jeremiah, 31, 37, 43
Ewing, Caroline Berry (Mrs. William L. D), 68
Ewing, William Lee Davidson, 42, 61, 62, 93, 94, 97, 129, 151; Illinois governor, vi, 82; local leader, 20, 31, 33, 34, 64, 66, 68–69, 88–89, 100, 107, 112, 121; politician, 68–69, 81, 86, 123, 126–28
Ewington, Ill., 42

Fayette County, Ill.: character of people, 9, 14, 32–42, 53; everyday life in, 35–37, 37–42; folklore of, 43–46; government of, 19, 97; homogeneity of, 32–34, 40–41, 66–67; hospitableness of, 32–34; lands in, 7, 29–30; organization of, 19–20; origin of name, 19; settlement of, 30–32, 42–43; society and culture of, 34–42; sources for, 29–30; southern influence in, 31–34; 140; waterways of, 29, 43; "Yankees" in, 32–33
Fayette County Manual Labor Seminary, 111
Fayette County Temperance Society, 113–14
Ficklin, Orlando B., 83
Field, Abner, 95
Field, Alexander Pope, 62, 64, 71f, 81, 81, 87, 95, 100, 104, 105, 107
Flack, Abner, 48, 60, 62, 105, 107, 129, 151
Flack, Edmund, 5, 49
Fletcher, C. B., 50–51
Flint, Timothy, 9, 101
Ford, Thomas, 7, 8, 53, 83, 87–88
Forquer, George, 75, 83, 165
Forman, Ferris, 83, 86, 30, 151
Four Mile Prairie, 43, 98
Free Press and Illinois Whig, 59, 86, 95
French, Augustus, 83
Frogtown. *See* Wilberton

Gall, Ludwig, 23

Gallatin Co., Ill., 10, 71
Gard, Seth, 10f
Gard, Timothy, 165
Gatewood family, 31
Gatewood, Thomas A., 38
Gatewood, Thomas R., 31, 43
General Assemblies of Illinois; First
 (1818–19), v, 10–12, 70, 71, 97;
 Second (1820–21), v, 1, 18–20, 102,
 128; Third (1822–23), v, 27, 72, 77–
 79, 99, 102; Fourth (1824–26), v,
 121; Fifth (1826–27), vi; Sixth (1828–
 29), vi; Seventh (1830–31), vi; Eighth
 (1832–33), vi, 126; Ninth (1834–36),
 vi, 59, 71, 82, 84; Tenth (1836–37),
 vi, 59, 83, 85, 126–27; Eleventh
 (1838–40), vi, 1, 61, 87, 107, 121,
 126–29; Twelfth (1840–41), 129
Golconda, Ill., 8
Gorin, J. D., 110
Grant, Alexander F., 62, 80, 83–84, 112–
 13, 165
Greathouse, John S., 83
Greenup, Beal, 14, 130
Greenup, William, 13–14, 15, 17, 21, 23,
 31, 55, 61, 62, 86, 104, 129, 130,
 151
Greenville, Ill., 19
Griffith, Ezra, 38
Grosvenor, Mason, 110

Hall, James (author): attorney, 28, 115,
 120; critical evaluations of, 117–20;
 cultural leader, 2–3, 68, 106–10,
 112–22; newspaper editor, 58, 72–73,
 80–81, 110, 119; literary figure, vi,
 2–3, 115–22; local leader, 64, 99,
 107, 108, 109–10, 112–14, 119–20;
 politician, 72–73, 80–81, 89, 115,
 119; quoted, 7, 13–14, 30, 33, 35,
 49, 52, 57, 101–2; works written by:
 22, 116–17. See also Illinois
 Intelligencer, Illinois Monthly
 Magazine
Hall, James (Hamilton County legislator),
 79
Hall, John Elihu, 116
Hall, Joseph, 61
Hall, Mary Louisa, 117
Hall, Mary Posey, 62, 108

Hamilton, Alexander, 72
Hamilton, William S., 72
Hankins, William S., 126, 127
Hansen, Nicholas, 77–78, 93
Hardin, John J., 83, 107, 123–24
Hardin, Sarah (Mrs. John J.), 2, 107
Hardy, Rev. Solomon, 108
Harrison, William Henry, 83
Harte, Bret, 117
Hawthorne, Nathaniel, 2, 117, 118
Heller, John Matthew, 105, 163
Hickerson family, 31
Hickman, Thomas B., 104, 127
Higgins, Thomas, 40, 43, 45, 56, 94,
 120, 143
Hill, Isaac, 30, 140
"Hill's Ferry" (Carlyle, Ill.), 10
History of the War Between the United
 States and the Sac and Fox Indians
 (Wakefield), 2, 121
Hockett, John W., 108
Hodge, William, 31, 50, 59, 61, 62, 64,
 82, 86–87, 95–96, 98, 104, 108, 127,
 150, 151, 152
Hogan, John, 83
Holbrook, Josiah, 113
Hollman, Frederick, v, 15–18, 20, 23–28,
 29, 37, 48, 50, 54, 55, 65, 66, 105,
 145, 151
Hollman, Martha Thompson (Mrs.
 Frederick), 37
House of Public Worship, 3, 99, 105,
 109
Houston, Samuel, 34
Houston family, 31
Hubbard, Adolphus Frederick, 14
Hull, John, 102, 104
Hurricane Creek, 29–30, 42

Iles, Elijah, 68, 165
Illinois: Central, 5, 7, 29–30, 57, 65–66,
 70; conditions in 1818, 8–10;
 population growth in, 4–6, 7–9;
 Southern, 5, 7, 31, 34, 50, 65–66;
 statehood of, v, 9–11; Territory, 8–10,
 70–72
Illinois and Michigan Canal, 73, 85, 88
Illinois Advocate, 58, 82, 83, 84
Illinois Central Railroad, 62, 129–30
Illinois College, 3, 110

Illinois Colonization Society, 112
Illinois Gazette, 80–81
Illinois Intelligencer, 13, 18, 26–27, 58, 72–81, 98, 99, 102, 110, 112, 119
Illinois Monthly Magazine, v, 2, 113, 116–17
Illinois State Register, 59, 84–87, 95–96, 102, 126–28
Illinois State Temperance Society, 113
Illinois Sunday School Union, 109–10
Independence, Ill., 14, 42
Indianapolis, 4, 42, 94, 135
Indians in Fayette County, 91, 98–99
Internal improvements, vi, 59, 60–61, 73–75, 83–85, 87–89, 101, 124; legislation concerning, vi, 59, 85
Iowa City, 135
Irving, Washington, 2, 118

Jackson, Andrew, vi, 50, 58–59, 65, 73–76, 79–82, 84–86, 89
Jacksonville, Ill., 3, 4, 45, 65–66, 103, 123, 126
Jefferson, Thomas, 30, 76
Jenner, Elisah, 110
Jewett, Isaac Appleton, 117
Johnson, Abner, 60
Johnson, Andrew, 83
Johnson, John N., 48
Johnson, Richard M., 14, 81
Johnson, William, 19
Johnson and Graves, 104
Jones Precinct, 42

Kane, Elias Kent, 11, 18, 71, 74, 82, 165
Kaskaskia, Ill., v, 5, 8, 10–14, 24, 26, 29–30, 70, 85, 93, 95, 130
Kaskaskia River ("Okaw"), 7–8, 12–14, 17, 20, 43, 100–101, 132; danger of, 100–101; navigation on, 61, 101; origin of nickname, 12
Kellogg, John, 48
Kelly, James, 56, 92–93
Kinney, William: state official, 79–82, 89; Vandalia merchant, 17, 50
Kirby, William, 110
Kirkman, Thomas C., 127
Kirkman, William, 52
Kitchell, Joseph, 10

Lafayette, Marquis de (Gilbert Montier), 2, 19, 45–46, 76, 121; and Vandalia, 44, 164
Land: as a political issue, 72–73, 75; districts, 8–9, 14, 38, 99; federal officers, 8–9, 93; sales in 1818–19, 3, 8–9, 55; sales in 1835–39, 56–57, 99; speculation, 9–11
Lee, Abisha, 43
Lee, Asahel, 103–4
Lee, Benjamin F., 43, 128
Lee, Harvey, 43, 61, 104, 111, 127
Lee, Lemuel, 43, 44, 51, 61, 64
Lee, William H., 21, 43, 101
Lee family, 43
Leidig, George, 21, 25, 26, 28, 39, 51, 55, 57, 88–89, 103, 105, 129, 151
Leidig, George Jr., 25
Leidig, Olivia. *See* Whiteman
Leidig, Sophia Remann (Mrs. George Sr.), 21, 25, 29
Lemen, Moses, 165
Lincoln, Abraham, 53, 69, 70, 83, 93, 103, 115, 123–29, 131; attributed lodging places of, 44, 125; "jump legend," 45, 125–26, 143; local lore about, 43–46, 48, 89–90, 125–26
Lincoln, Thomas (Tad), 25
Linder, Usher F., 83, 97, 127
Linn, Polly Duncan (Mrs. William), 50
Linn, William, 35, 50–51, 55, 60, 65, 100, 104, 111, 127, 129
Lippincott, Thomas, 64, 109–10, 113
Lockwood, Samuel Drake, 71, 101, 109–10
Logan, John (father), 83
Logan, John A. (son), 83
"Long Nine," 127, 168
Loogootee, Ill., 42, 44
Lovejoy, Elijah P., 98, 120
Loveless family, 31
Luther, William G., 60
Lutt, J., 128
Lynch, Michael, 61

Mabry family, 31
McClernand, John, 83
McClintoc, Sam, 16
McCullom, John, 14, 17, 20, 48, 56, 130, 145

McCullom, Sarah (Mrs. John), 14
McCullom, Vandalia, 14
McCurdy, Nathaniel Masters, 56, 64, 101, 108–9, 111, 127, 129, 164, 165
McCurdy, Olivia (Mrs. Nathaniel), 108, 164
McHenry, William, 62, 83–84, 135
McKee, W. P., 165
McKendree College, 107
McLaughlin, Isabella Bond (Mrs. Robert K.), 15, 18, 21, 37, 61–62, 151
McLaughlin, Robert K., 18, 61–62, 84, 104–5, 151; described, 15; hotel owner, 48, 53, 55; local leader, 19, 20, 21, 33, 37, 55–56, 64, 77, 88–89, 107, 109, 126–27, 129; politician, 75, 81–82, 126–27; store owner, 37, 50, 51, 55
McLean, John (Gallatin County politician), 71
McLean, John (U.S. Supreme Court justice), 107
McPhail, Allen, 60
McRoberts, Samuel, 72, 81, 112, 165
Maddox, Waterman & Co., 104
Madison, James, 76
Madison County, Ill., 12, 14
Madonna of the Trail statue, 36, 100
Mahon, Benjamin, 41
Mahon family, 31
Mail: routes, 17; service, 102
Marshall, William S., 60
Mather, Thomas, 72
Mentalité, 33–34
Messinger, John, 9
Mezynski, Konstantly, 32
Militia, state, 34–35
Mills, Benjamin, 165
Mills, Henry I., 165
Monroe, James, v, 12, 76
Morgan County, Ill., 124–25

National Road, vi, 7, 31, 36, 42, 61, 64, 72, 87, 89, 100, 130
"New Haven theology," 109
New Salem, Ill., 124, 125

Ogle, Goerge, 39, 40, 142
Ohio River, 1, 7–8, 24, 29
Okaw. See Kaskaskia River

Oliver, William, 42
Otego township, 43. See also Fayette County

Palestine, Ill., 8
Panic of 1819, v, 3, 55–56
Panic of 1837, vi, 60–61, 85–86
Parks, Wilson, 94
Peck, John Mason, 57, 64, 109, 111–13, 120, 165
Peebles, Augusta Ernst (Mrs. Robert H.), 23, 28, 105, 139
Peebles, Dr. Robert Homer, 23, 55–56, 64–65, 100, 110, 139
Pendergrass, John, 52, 54
Peoria, Ill., 126
Perkins, James Handasyd, 116
Perryville, Ill., 14, 17, 19, 30, 42
Peters, Hugh, 117
Phelps, E. S., 60
Phillips, Joseph, 76
Phillips, Moses, 60, 108, 111, 114, 131
Pike County, Ill., 77, 89
Pilcher, Winslow, 31, 104, 125
Pilcher family, 31
Polern, Upeski, 32
Polish immigrants, at Vandalia, 32, 46
Politics: campaigns, 53–54, 75, 76–82, 87; convention system, 86; democratic and whig, 32–33, 50, 81–89; factionalism, 1, 10, 70–76; Jacksonian, 58, 71, 75–76, 79–87, 119; local, 88–89; Locofocoism, 59, 86
Pope, Nathaniel, 9, 71
Pope's Bluff, Ill., 9–10, 14, 17, 42–43, 70
Porter, R., 128
Prentice, Charles, 17, 21, 34, 50–52, 55–57, 61, 62, 64, 86–87, 88–89, 100, 104, 111, 114, 151

Randolph, John, 14
Reavis, Charles, 9–10, 12–13, 14, 16, 135
Reavis, Isham, 135
Reavis, Nancy (Mrs. Bowling Green), 135
Redmond, Thomas, 48, 51, 65, 128
Redmond, William, 48
"Reeve's Bluff," 9–10, 14–16, 31, 63, 135

Remann, Frederick, 25, 26, 39
Remann, Frederick, Jr., 21, 25–26, 28, 32–33, 29, 61, 94, 98, 104, 129, 151
Remann, Frederick, III, 26
Remann, Frederick, IV, 26
Remann, Henry C., 108
Revolutionary War, 31, 34
Reynolds, Catherine (Mrs. John), 89
Reynolds, John, vi, 14, 27, 35, 71, 79–81, 89, 93, 95, 98, 119, 121, 165
Reynolds, Thomas, 95, 112
Richardson, William A., 83
Riggs, Illinois (Mrs. Graff), 108
Riggs, Romulus, 108
Ripley, Ill., 9
Roads, 37, 94–96; Carlyle Road, 17; condition of, 8, 100; to and from Vandalia, 17, 19, 99–102; Vincennes Road, 19. See also National Road
Robb, John, 94
Robbins, W. H., 60
Robinson, John M., 165
Rosemeyer, August, 25
Ross, Robert W., 60, 61, 69, 111, 131
Roy, John, 97
Russell, John, 2, 68, 95, 110, 115, 117–18, 121

St. Clair, Arthur, 14
St. Elmo, Ill., 42
St. Louis, 1, 16, 64, 66
Sangamo Journal, 127
Sangamon County, Ill., 19, 125, 127
Sangamon River Valley, 6, 24
Sawyer, John York, 47, 56, 57, 82, 84, 100, 151
Scantland, J. M. S., 48
Scantland, Mrs. J. M. S., 36
Semple, James, 83
Sharon township, 42. See also Fayette County
Shawneetown, Ill., 8, 81–82, 84, 99
Shields, James, 83, 85, 123
Shobonier, Ill., 42–43
Sidwell, Abraham, 35
Slade, Charles, 165
Slavery: as a political issue, 76–79; in Illinois, 76. See also Blacks, Constitutional Convention
Smith, Rev. G., 26

Smith, Guy, 12
Smith, Jedediah Strong, 116
Smith, John, 17
Smith, Peter, 128
Smith, Robert (congressman), 83
Smith, Robert "Cupid" (ferryman), 97
Smith, Theophilus W., 14, 72, 92, 112
Snyder, Ann Eliza (Mrs. Emanuel), 25
Snyder, Augustus, 36, 39, 44
Snyder, Daniel, 128
Snyder, Emanuel, 25, 26, 39
Snyder, Henry, 25, 35
Snyder, Dr. John F., 10
Social control, 114–15. See also Vandalia, Organizations
Sonnemann family, 32, 33
Spillman, Rev. Thomas A., 108
Springfield, Ill., vi, 5, 6, 53, 68, 69, 125–30
Stage coach travel, 101–2
Stapp family, 31
Stapp, James T. B., 31, 64, 95, 100, 112
Starnes, Abraham, 41
Statehouses: first in Vandalia, v, 17, 52, 62, 78, 93, 102; in Springfield, 121–22, 127–28; second in Vandalia, vi, 47, 52, 62, 64, 102–4; third in Vandalia, vi, 47, 52, 62, 64, 103–5, 126, 128–32
Steinhauer family, 32, 33
Stewart, William K., 165
Stolle, Frederick, 60
Stone, Dan, 124
Stout & Johnson, 60
Stuart, James, 106
Stuart, John T., 83
Stuart, William, 129
Sturtevant, J. M., 110, 113
Szczuroski, Boneventura, 32

Taylor, John & Co., 104
Taylor, Nathaniel W., 109
"Third House," 123
Third Principal Meridian, 11, 12
Thomas, Fredcrick W., 117
Thomas, Jesse B., 12, 70–71, 79
Thompson, Benjamin Ward, 37, 39–40, 128, 130, 132
Thompson, Harrison, 61
Thompson, John (settler), 35, 83–84

Thompson, John (state official), 62, 83–84
Thompson, Paddy, 35
Thompson, Susanna (Mrs. Benjamin Ward), 39
Tindal, George S., 48
Townsend, E. M., 25
Tunstall, Edmund, 17, 48
Turner, Asa, 110, 165
Turner, Jonathan Baldwin, 110
Turney, James, 80
Twiss, Moss, 25, 51

Van Buren, Martin, vi, 50, 53, 81, 84, 85–86, 88
Van Vleck, Dr. John H., 107
Vandalia: after 1839, 61–62, 129–32; anamnesis, 29–30, 45–46, 62; appearance of, 3, 48, 52–54, 61–62; area surrounding, 1, 29–46; bank robbery in, 92; businesses in, 3, 17–18, 47–52, 57–62, 97, 123; cemetery in, 21, 39, 62, 99; churches in, 57, 60, 64, 107–10, 113, 115; community improvement, 20, 99–102; crime in, 91–97; cultural center, 1–3, 64, 91, 106–22; earlier French settlement, 30, 46, 140; economy of, 54–57, 59–62, 149; education in, 57–58, 64, 110–13; effect of politics on, 4, 53–55, 89; established by state government, 9–21; government of, 20; healthiness of, 99, 129; hotels in, 17–19, 20, 25, 47–49; jail in, 19, 109; land sales in, 5, 56–57; law enforcement, 94–95; local leadership of, 12, 55–57; 62–68, 87–89; lots in, v, 3, 56–57; organizations in, 1–2, 107–9, 112–15; origin of name, 13–15, 131, 136; population of, 5, 18, 47, 62, 141; problem of domicile patterns for capital era, 141; reputation of, 1–6, 48–49, 95–97; social climate of, 52–55, 91–98, 106–22, 123–24; social dynamics in, 52–54, 63–69; state government relocated from, 60–62, 67, 69, 126–29; visitors' impressions of, 3, 5–6, 48, 49, 52, 95–96, 106. See also Community, Fayette County

Vandalia Academy and Free School, 111
Vandalia Historical Society, 62
Vandalia Lyceum, 113
Vandalia Union, 26
Vandalia Whig, 81
Vienna, Ill., 8
Vincennes, Ind., 17

Wabash River, 7–8, 29
Wageman, Henry, 25, 41
Wakefield, John A., 2, 15, 19, 31, 43, 88–89, 98, 103, 113, 121
Walker, Timothy, 117
Walters, William, 58–59, 84–87, 95–96, 103–5, 111, 127–29, 151
War of 1812, 12, 34, 43
Ward, Jonathan, 98
Warnock, John, 107
Warren, Hooper, 4, 87, 95
Washburn family, 31
Washington, D. C., 1, 4, 11–12, 23–24, 58, 124
Washington, George, 2, 19, 121
Waterman, David B. & Co., 104
Western Monthly Magazine, 121
Westervelt, Evert, 60
White, Hugh L., 53, 84
White, Leonard, 10
Whiteman, Olivia Leidig, 25
Whiteside, Gen. John D., 60, 101
Whiteside, Samuel, 12–13
Whitlock, James, 51
Whitney, James W. ("Lord Coke"), 89, 123
Wilberton ("Frogtown"), 42–43
Will, Conrad, 68, 71, 83, 121
Wilson, William, 58–60, 71, 101
Wolff, Fritz, 26, 101
Workman, Isaac, 31
Wright, Tilghman, 51
Wyatt, John, 124

"Yale Band," 3, 110, 114–15, 120, 122
Yale Theological Seminary, 3, 107, 109, 110
Yerker, Henry, 26, 27
Yerker, John Frederick, 21, 27, 28, 151
Young, Richard M., 83, 123

A Note on the Author

PAUL E. STROBLE, JR., is a United Methodist minister who teaches university courses in religious studies in Louisville, Kentucky. He holds a Ph.D. in theology from the University of Virginia. A Vandalia native, he is a descendent of early Fayette County settlers, one of whom assisted in the construction of the Vandalia statehouse in 1836.